'Dean Fink and colleagues have demystified t of significant scope. From Australia to Lithu innovative perspectives and a unified body of research linking trust, accountability, school success, economics, and history. Recognizing that both trust and verification are keys to school improvement, the authors ask: what is the delicate balance between the two? The answers are contextually calibrated and multifaceted. *Trust and Verify* is a treasure trove of deep insights and clear action for school leaders and policy makers.'

Linda Lambert, consultant and Professor Emeritus, California State University, East Bay

'*Trust and Verify* is a timely reminder of the humanity of all who work in education. Of course we must trust teachers more. But trust alone is not enough, and so we also need rigorous reflective practices too. I particularly like the breadth of opinion in this set of essays. Its message is its medium, with the editor trusting his contributors and being richly rewarded with their insights as a consequence. This book should be read by politicians, policy makers, headteachers, teachers, and researchers as a salutary reminder of our over-reliance on apparently important external data when, at least as often, we need to look more closely at what is going on under our own noses.'

Bill Lucas, Professor of Learning, University of Winchester

'This book extends the research on trust in schools beyond the school house to explore the dynamics of trust and distrust in the policy environment at the national level. Using a common research method across seven countries, Dean Fink and his colleagues have compared the perceptions of teachers and principals across these diverse contexts to reveal both commonalities and places of divergence. Although the findings reaffirm the role that trust plays in the implementation of policy, it also reveals disturbing trends resulting from the movement toward a production model of schooling and the accountability movement. This book makes a useful and welcome contribution to the research literature on trust in schools.'

Megan Tschannen-Moran, Professor of Educational Leadership, College of William and Mary

'Another great read from Dean Fink and his colleagues as they examine the ins and outs of trust, mistrust, verification and the dynamics of system change. The short case studies of seven countries is a special treat as we see local context, but also generalizable insights. In the final analysis, the book gives us a new handle on school and system improvement, but you have to work smartly in your own context.'

Michael Fullan, Professor Emeritus, Ontario Institute for Studies in Education, University of Toronto

Trust and Verify

To Larry

In partial payment
for getting me
through grade 13
math.

All best wishes

Dan

Trust and Verify: The real keys to school improvement

An international examination of trust and distrust in education in seven countries

Edited by Dean Fink

IOE Press

First published in 2016 by the UCL Institute of Education Press, University College London, 20 Bedford Way, London WC1H 0AL

www.ucl-ioe-press.com

British Library Cataloguing in Publication Data:
A catalogue record for this publication is available from the British Library

ISBNs
978-1-78277-147-0 (paperback)
978-1-78277-148-7 (PDF)
978-1-78277-149-4 (ePub)
978-1-78277-150-0 (Kindle)

Typeset by Quadrant Infotech (India) Pvt Ltd
Printed by CPI Group (UK) Ltd, Croydon, CR0 4YY
Cover image ©Jay Parmar – Global Roots Photography – Events / Alamy Stock Photo; design by Rawshock

Contents

List of tables

List of figures

To the thousands of principals and teachers who trusted us enough to contribute so thoughtfully to our understanding of trust and distrust across our seven countries.

Acknowledgements

I am deeply grateful to all the authors of the country chapters for accepting my challenge and participating in this project. I truly appreciate their dedication, scholarship, and tolerance for my meddling.

To the many scholars on the topic of trust I acknowledge my indebtedness, and particularly to Megan Tschannen-Moran of William and Mary University, Keith Walker of the University of Saskatchewan, and Dimitri Van Maele of Ghent University, Belgium, who in the very early stages of this work pointed me in productive directions. I should particularly identify the work of Roy Lewicki of the Fisher College of Business, Ohio State University, and his conceptual influence on our project.

Importantly, I want to express my sincere appreciation to our computer guru Paul Hatala. In spite of his heavy workload as 'Mr. Everything' on information technology for a very large school district, he helped us set up and interpret our research instruments and was there whenever we needed advice. I'm indebted to Norm McCulla and Warren Marks for their assistance in the editing process. To Jonathan Dore and his team at the Institute of Education Press, I express my appreciation for your cooperation and encouragement. Finally, to my family and the families of the authors of this book who have tolerated our collective obsession in getting the job done, thank you.

Dean Fink
Ancaster, Ontario, Canada
September 2015

Notes on contributors

Dean Fink is a best-selling author and international consultant. A former teacher, principal, and superintendent in Ontario, Canada, Dean has worked with school leaders in 31 countries over the past 20 years.

Craig Hammonds is the director of graduate programs in education and an assistant professor at the University of Mary Hardin-Baylor in Belton, Texas. He works with the Ohio State University as a site principal investigator with Project mNET. Craig is a former public school teacher, assistant principal, and principal.

Paul Hatala is the technology-enabled learning and teaching contact for the Hamilton-Wentworth District School Board in Ontario Canada. He supports teachers and students in the effective use of technology in the classroom. He has been a science teacher at both the secondary and university levels, and presently teaches assessment and evaluation strategies to pre-service candidates at Brock University.

Warren Marks is a former teacher and school principal in New South Wales, Australia. He is now director of LEAP (Leading Educators Around the Planet), an international peer-shadowing programme for educational leaders. He is a consultant to the University of Melbourne's Graduate School of Teacher Education, lecturing in the Master of Instructional Leadership programmes.

Norman McCulla is the coordinator of the educational leadership programme at Macquarie University, Sydney, Australia. He is a former teacher and senior educational administrator in curriculum and teacher professional development. His research interests and publications focus on teachers' working lives and career path trajectories.

Eglė Pranckūnienė is the director and founder of the Centre for School Improvement in Lithuania. This independent, non-profit organization has supported school improvement in Lithuania for the past 15 years. She is involved in a variety of national educational initiatives designed to inspire better learning opportunities for all Lithuanian students. Eglė presently leads and coordinates a number of long-term educational projects, creates networks of professionals to influence educational policies and promote professional learning, and works directly with municipalities, schools, leaders, and policy makers.

Jonas Ruškus is a professor in the Social Work Department at Vytautas Magnus University, Lithuania. He has supervised a number of national research projects in inclusive education, educational monitoring and evaluation, disability, and social participation. Currently Jonas is concerned about human rights issues in education and society. He is also a member of the United Nations Committee on the Rights of People with Disabilities.

Petri Salo is a professor of adult education in the Faculty of Education and Welfare Studies, Åbo Academy University, Finland. His research interests relate to adult and popular education in the Nordic countries, schools as organizations, micro-politics, action research, and qualitative methods. He is currently researching school leadership, local leadership practices, and the importance of trust in schools.

Torbjörn Sandén is a director at the Centre for Continuing education at Åbo Akademi University and Novia University of Applied Sciences. During the last decade Torbjörn has been involved in training programmes for the principal profession. Torbjörn is a former teacher and principal. His research interest deals with educational leadership.

Lars Svedberg is an associate professor and a psychologist working at Karlstad University, Sweden. He has been teaching and conducting research in educational management for 25 years. He has written several books in social psychology, and is currently researching how superintendents interact with principals and other stakeholders.

Tom Whittingham is head of external development at the Institute of Education, University of Worcester, in the United Kingdom. A former teacher, headteacher, and local authority adviser, he has undertaken extensive leadership work and consultancy both nationally and internationally. He facilitates leadership enquiry work that brings like-minded leaders together to explore themes of mutual interest, and convenes enquiry groups that strive to improve standards and to make a difference to the communities that leaders serve.

Introduction

Dean Fink

A number of years ago I contributed a chapter to a book edited by well-known British educator Michael Fielding (2001) that looked at the ongoing efforts of the British Labour Party under Tony Blair to effect significant educational change. My contribution, entitled 'The Two Solitudes: Policy makers and policy implementers', explored the apparent inability of these usually well-meaning 'solitudes' to understand and to work harmoniously to improve learning for students in schools (Fink, 2001). Although my chapter described how the 'two solitudes' held different views on the sources of change, strategies for change, theories of action, purposes of change, and the success criteria for change, I always felt there was something missing in my analysis but I couldn't figure out what it was. Now, after almost 15 years and many trips to many places to observe and participate in change efforts, I think I know the missing ingredient: trust.

Now I know this is hardly an earth-shaking revelation, because there is an evolving body of evidence that shows the importance of trust in educational growth and development. Well-regarded researchers Janet Chrispeels and Alan Daly have concluded that 'Empirical evidence has … shown that several aspects of trust – benevolence, reliability, competence, integrity, openness, and respect – are strongly connected with school performance and student outcomes' (Daly and Chrispeels, 2008: 30). Similarly, in their much-referenced work, Bryk and Schneider (2002: 40) state that 'we have learned, based on school reform in Chicago, that a broad base of trust across a school community lubricates much of a school's day to day functioning and is a critical resource as local leaders embark on ambitious school improvement plans'. Karen Seashore Louis's study of secondary schools echoed these findings (Louis, 2007). New Zealand's Viviane Robinson concludes, after her analysis of the change literature, that 'there is compelling evidence that the level of trust among the members of a school community makes an important difference to the way they work together and to the social and academic progress of students' (Robinson, 2011: 34).

While the educational literature on trust is in its early days, other social science disciplines have provided a complex and extensive body of work on the subject over time. Trust is a key concept for economists (North, 1990; Williamson, 1993), psychologists (Tyler, 1990; Deutsch, 1958);

sociologists (Granovetter, 1985; Zucker, 1986), political scientists (Barber, 1983), and anthropologists (Ekeh, 1974). When one adds in discussions of trust and the law (Uslaner, 2004), trust and networking (Ziegler and Lausen, 2005; Schudson, 1996) and trust and organizational theory (Kramer and Tyler, 1996), among many other disciplinary specialisms, the sheer volume of the literature on trust becomes somewhat intimidating. Popular business books propagate trust as a key component of a successful economy (Covey, 2006). As Fukuyama (1996: 354) explains, 'some societies save substantially on transaction costs because economic agents trust one another in their interactions and therefore can be more efficient than low trust societies, which require detailed contracts and enforcement mechanisms'.

There also appears to be a physiological reason why some people are more trusting than others and it has to do with a chemical in the brain called oxytocin. Paul Zak, an American neuroeconomist, explains:

> The distribution of oxytocin receptors in the human brain suggests that the decision to trust another human being is largely unconscious and utilizes the 'social brain.' In humans, oxytocin receptors are massed in the amygdala, the hypothalamus (which regulates the 'autonomic' nervous system, including breathing, heart rate, etc.), and areas associated with memory. ... What this means is that oxytocin influences decision-making, but in a way that is largely outside the realm of conscious perception as the structures where it is active are outside of the large frontal cortex that distinguishes humans. Trust appears to be driven by a 'sense' of what to do, rather than a conscious determination.
>
> (Zak, 2003: 20)

While controversial, this research suggests that not only are some of us more trusting than others, and perhaps more vulnerable, but our decisions to trust or not to trust are largely intuitive.

This book started from a simple – one might even argue simplistic – observation about the relationship of trust to student success. This led to a series of helpful discussions with researchers on trust, such as Megan Tschannen-Moran of William and Mary University, Keith Walker of the University of Saskatchewan, and Dimitri Van Maele of Ghent University, Belgium, among others, then to lots of reading, and finally to invitations to an international network of friends and colleagues to participate in a project that looks at trust as fundamental to educational change. Since much of the existing educational literature on trust focuses on the importance trust plays in internal school dynamics and relationships (Bottery, 2004; Hoy and Tschannen-Moran, 1999; Kutsyuruba *et al.*, 2010; 2011; Tschannen-Moran, 2004; 2014; Walker *et al.*, 2011) we felt it was important not only to build on this work, but to go beyond it and look at the outside forces over which schools and school personnel have little or no control and that increasingly dictate new relationships, purposes, and working conditions, and seem to have altered the trust landscape within schools and classrooms.

There is a clear pattern of decision-making and policy development in most western countries. Fundamental educational issues, like what the students are to learn, when they are to learn it, how we know they have learned, and even how they are to learn, have become centralized in provincial or state governments and, in some countries, in national governments. Discussions of trust therefore need to go beyond the schoolhouse and look at the institutions that influence internal relationships: school districts, state/provincial and national governments, unions, and other mediating agencies. This increasing complexity raises a further question of more immediate relevance to the dynamics of the teaching–learning process: in what ways do relational and institutional trust or distrust affect the self-trust of principals and teachers who must respond to shifting and sometimes conflicting policy directives while still making schools work for students?

Although academics internationally are becoming increasingly active in researching trust and trust-related topics (Van Maele *et al.*, 2014), much of the foundational literature on trust in educational settings is American and reflects American values, history, policies, and attitudes. I wondered, as a Canadian, whether trusting relationships looked different in other nations, and how any differences might affect the efficacy of teachers, principals, and their students. To do this I recruited a group of knowledgeable people in seven liberal democratic western countries to address this question in their nations. All the participants in this project have had considerable experience as practitioners in schools, so they brought not only academic interests and skills to the project but a pragmatism born of years of actually having to teach, lead, and supervise educational practices in their countries. Three of the nations in our study – Australia, Canada, and the United States – have federal systems of government and thus potentially three levels of government: federal, state (or provincial in Canada), and local districts are all involved in educational policies that have a bearing on trust or distrust. The unitary systems of government in England, Sweden, and Finland have only two policy-making levels that influence schools: the national government and local districts (local authorities in England) or municipalities. Our final case is Lithuania, a post-Soviet society that has rather shallow democratic roots and is working valiantly to establish democratic institutions, a western-style economy, and a high-quality education system within a low-trust society that reflects its Soviet past. Educational policy in Lithuania is generally determined centrally by the Department of Education in Vilnius and acted upon by local municipalities.

The observation that initiated this book concerned an interesting correlation between a nation's ability to trust and be trusted and the PISA (Programme for International Student Assessment) results. Periodically, international agencies conduct surveys to compare nations on a variety of criteria, such as happiness (Helliwell *et al.*, 2013), entrepreneurialism (Bosma *et al.*, 2011), and health (OECD, 2011b), among many other issues. I find these interesting, informative, and sometimes even believable. One survey that captured my attention was conducted by Transparency International (2013). Between 2005 and 2008, its World Values Survey asked people in many countries the following question: 'Generally speaking, would you say that most people can be trusted or that you need to be very careful in dealing with people?' Two possible answers were permitted: (1) Most people can be trusted; or (2) You can never be too careful when dealing with others.

The first answer reflected people's trusting nature and the second their cautious or distrusting nature. Of the countries considered in this volume, Finland and Sweden scored highest on the trust measures. Canada and Australia followed closely, and the United States next, in that order, then Great Britain and, well behind the rest, Lithuania. A second trust measure, the Corruption Perceptions Index (Transparency International, 2013), measured the perceived trustworthiness of a nation's public sector on a scale from 0 to 100. The pattern revealed was similar to that found in the World Values Survey: Finland and Sweden both scored at 89 per cent, Canada and Australia at 81 per cent, the United Kingdom at 76 per cent, the United States at 73 per cent, and Lithuania at 53 per cent.

What struck me when I reviewed these rankings is how closely they correlated with the PISA assessment results. These results have now become the 'gold standard' by which politicians, academics, and educational officials rate school systems. While limited in scope, narrow in focus, and subject to sample distortion, PISA results have rocketed Finland to educational fame, delighted the travel industry as politicians and officials scurry off to visit the most recent superstar PISA nation, and energized and confused elections, as has recently occurred in Ontario. A few points up or down have a mesmerizing effect on policy makers. If this sounds sceptical, it is; not so much about the results, which can if used properly be very useful, but rather about the naïve and potentially destructive ways in which PISA results drive educational policy making. Education policies should be about much more than raising test scores on one-shot assessments (Levin, 2012). Sound educational policies deliver a high-quality education for all young people, regardless of socio-economic background, and at a reasonable cost.

If we put our seven countries to the tests of quality, equity, and efficiency, patterns similar to the trust measures emerge. When one averages the reading, mathematics, and science scores from the 2012 PISA exercise as one measure of quality, the results follow a familiar order: Finland ranks top (529), above Canada (522), Australia (512), the United Kingdom (502), the United States (492), and Lithuania (484). Sweden's result is an anomaly (482) when compared to its high trust scores.[1] While scores for western countries in general had declined from the 2009 PISA, with Lithuania as a significant exception, the rankings in 2009 were similar.[2]

One interesting measure of equity contained within the 2009 PISA study is the percentage of variance in student performance explained by students' socio-economic background. Once again Finland and Canada lead the way with only 8 per cent and 9 per cent of variation accounted for by family income respectively. Australia and Sweden follow at 13 per cent, with the United Kingdom and Lithuania at 14 per cent, while the United States ranks as the most inequitable of our subject nations with 17 per cent of performance variation attributable to students' socio-economic background (OECD, 2010). A second indicator of equity is student resilience: 'Resilient students are those who come from a disadvantaged socio-economic background and perform much higher than would be predicted by their background' (OECD, 2010: 62). On this measure Canada and Finland score well above the OECD average and Australia the same as the OECD average, while Sweden, Lithuania, the United Kingdom, and the United States in that order perform well below the average (OECD, 2010).[3] Finally, a third equity measure is the extent to which immigrants fit into a nation's educational system. Among the nations with larger immigrant populations (where immigrants make up at least 10 per cent of the population), the achievement of immigrant students in Canada and Australia in reading as measured by PISA is considerably higher than that of students in Sweden, the United States, and the United Kingdom.[4]

Educational expenditures seemed to reflect an inverse relationship to quality and equity (OECD, 2013a: 174), or at least a limited connection to student achievement and equitable education. Rather than looking at educational expenditures as a percentage of GDP, which reflects to some extent the relative wealth of nations, actual expenditures per pupil show more accurately how money is spent. The United States has the highest per-pupil expenditures, at US$11,828 for primary and secondary students; Finland has the lowest, at US$8,393, followed by the United Kingdom, Sweden, Canada, Lithuania, and Australia, all within the US$9,500–10,000 range (OECD, 2013b: Table B1.1a).[5] This suggests that the efficiency of schools and school districts in their use of resources rather than the total amount expended has, in general, a greater impact on high achievement and fairness of results.

There does therefore appear to be a clear pattern, on admittedly flawed measures, that suggests that high-trust countries produce higher student achievement and more equitable student results within reasonable public expenditures. To prove this conclusively was beyond our resources, since we are self-funded and beholden to no government, institution, foundation, or agency. But we were sufficiently intrigued to try in each of our countries to understand the trust dynamic and how it affected student and teacher performance at a much deeper level. To do this each member of our team surveyed samples of principals and teachers using the same 30-item, five-scale survey (see Appendices 1a and b), developed jointly and translated for non-English speaking nations. With these results, each country's researcher(s) conducted interviews and focus groups with teachers and principals using a few generic questions on trust and distrust and then more specific questions arising from the survey results.

Chapters 1 and 2 provide a conceptual framework for subsequent chapters and attempt to connect our work to the existing body of literature. After the introductory chapters, country chapters proceed in alphabetical order, with Chapter 3 on Australia, Chapter 4 Canada, Chapter 5 Finland, Chapter 6 Lithuania, Chapter 7 Sweden, Chapter 8 the United Kingdom and Chapter 9 on the United States. Authors were free to develop their chapters in ways that made sense to them and fit the unique contexts of their nations. The continuity within the project comes from the surveys, the generic interview questions, and a conceptual framework shared early on in the process and developed in detail in Chapters 1 and 2. In Chapter 10, we collectively pull together the larger themes that cut across our seven nations and detail what we think we have learned that might be useful for both policy makers and policy implementers.

It was former US President Ronald Reagan who made famous the phrase 'Trust, but verify'. Blind trust, unchecked by any kind of verification system, can prove as unproductive for individuals and organizations as can intrusive, coercive, and time-consuming verification strategies. We think both sides of this equation are important, so we have entitled our book 'Trust *and* Verify', and as the subsequent chapters will attest we think these are *the real keys to school improvement*. We believe this book provides a unique look at trust and distrust and their impact on school improvement, and, while this is not an end in itself, we hope to expand thinking and initiate an international dialogue. The time is now to pick up the challenge and, together with like-minded others in local, district, national, and international communities, to seek a productive balance between trusting our professional educators at all levels to provide a high-quality education for all children within reasonable public expenditures, and holding them accountable for the results. Our children and societies deserve and need it, now and in the future.

Notes

[1] The 2012 scores for each country in mathematics, reading, and science respectively are as follows. Finland: 519, 524, 545; Canada: 518, 523, 525; Australia: 504, 512, 521; United Kingdom: 494, 499, 514; United States: 481, 498, 497; Lithuania: 479, 477, 496; Sweden: 478, 483, 485 (OECD, 2012: 5).

[2] The 2009 scores for each country in mathematics, reading, and science respectively are as follows. Finland: 541, 536, 554; Canada: 527, 524, 529; Australia: 515, 515, 527; Sweden: 494; United Kingdom, 492, 494, 514; United States: 487, 500, 502; Lithuania: 477, 468, 491 (OECD, 2009a: 15).

[3] Only 7.8 per cent of the variation in performance of Finnish students was explained by their socio-economic situation. Rates for the other nations in our study were as follows: Canada 8.6 per cent; Australia 12.7 per cent; Sweden 13.4 per cent; Lithuania 13.6 per cent; the United Kingdom 13.7 per cent; United States 16.8 per cent (OECD, 2009b: 17).

[4] In the list that follows, the first number for each nation is its percentage of students with an immigrant background and the second number is their achievement on the PISA 2009 reading assessment. Australia:19; 520. Canada: 25; 530. Finland: 3; 540. Lithuania: 2; 470. Sweden: 12; 470. United Kingdom: 11; 490. United States: 19; 500 (OECD, 2010).

[5] If one looks at the percentage of GDP expended for primary and secondary education in 2010 the pattern is somewhat different. Australia spends 4.3 per cent of its GDP on school education, Canada 3.9 per cent; Finland 4.1 per cent; Lithuania (2011) 5.2 per cent; Sweden, 4.2 per cent; the UK 4.8 per cent; and the United States 4.0 per cent (OECD 2011a: 227, 2013b: Table B2.1).

References

Barber, B. (1983) *The Logic and Limits of Trust*. New Brunswick, NJ: Rutgers University Press.

Bosma, N., Wennekers, S., and Amorós, J.E. (2011) 'Global Entrepreneurship Monitor 2011 – extended report: Entrepreneurs and entrepreneurial employees across the globe'. Online. www.gemconsortium.org/report (accessed 28 January 2016).

Bottery, M. (2004) *The Challenges of Educational Leadership: Values in a globalized age*. London: Paul Chapman.

Bryk, A. and Schneider, B. (2002) *Trust in Schools: A core resource for school improvement*. New York: American Sociological Association.

Covey, S.M., and Merrill, R.R. (2006) *The Speed of Trust: The one thing that changes everything*. New York: Free Press.

Daly, A.J., and Chrispeels, J. (2008) 'A question of trust: Predictive conditions for adaptive and technical leadership in educational contexts'. *Leadership and Policy in Schools*, 71 (1), 30–63.

Deutsch, M. (1958) 'Trust and suspicion'. *Journal of Conflict Resolution*, 58 (2), 265–79.

Ekeh, P. (1974) *Social Exchange Theory: The two traditions*. Cambridge, MA: Harvard University Press.

Fielding, M. (ed.) (2001) *Taking Education Really Seriously: Four years' hard Labour*. London: Routledge/Falmer.

Fink, D. (2001) 'The two solitudes: Policy makers and policy implementers'. In Fielding, M. (ed.) *Taking Education Really Seriously: Four years' hard Labour*. London: Routledge Falmer, 225–37.

Fukuyama, F. (1996) *Trust: The Social Virtues and the Creation of Prosperity*. London: Penguin.

Granovetter, M.S. (1985) 'Economic action and social structure: The problem of embeddedness'. *American Journal of Sociology*, 91 (3), 481–510.

Helliwell, J., Layard, R., and Sachs, J. (eds) (2013) *World Happiness Report 2013*. Online. http://unsdsn.org/resources/publications/world-happiness-report-2013/ (accessed 19 August 2014).

Hoy, W., and Tschannen-Moran, M. (1999) 'Five faces of trust: An empirical confirmation in urban elementary schools.' *Journal of School Leadership*, 9 (3), 184–208.

Kramer, R.M., and Tyler, T.R. (1996) *Trust in Organizations: Frontiers of theory and research*. Thousand Oaks, CA: Sage.

Kutsyuruba, B., Walker, K., and Noonan, B. (2010) 'The ecology of trust in the principalship'. *Journal of Educational Administration and Foundations*, 21 (1), 23–47.

— (2011) 'Restoring broken trust in the work of school principals'. *International Studies in Educational Administration*, 39 (2), 81–95.

Levin, H. (2012) 'More than just test scores', *Prospects*. DOI: 10.1007/s11125-012-9240-z. Online. http://roundtheinkwell.files.wordpress.com/2012/09/more-than-just-test-scores-sept2012-2.pdf (accessed 20 August 2014).

Louis, K.S. (2007) 'Trust and improvement in schools'. *Journal of Educational Change*, 8 (1), 1–24.

North, D.C. (1990) *Institutions, Institutional Change, and Economic Performance*. Cambridge and New York: Cambridge University Press.

OECD (2009a) *PISA 2009 Results: What students know and can do*. Vol. I. Paris: OECD Publishing. Online. www.oecd.org/pisa/pisaproducts/48852548.pdf (accessed 27 January 2016).

— (2009b) *PISA 2009 Results: Executive summary*. Paris: OECD Publishing. Online. www.oecd.org/pisa/pisaproducts/46619703.pdf (accessed 27 January 2016).

— (2010) *PISA 2009 Results: Overcoming social background: Equity in learning opportunities and outcomes*. Vol. 2. Paris: OECD Publishing. Online. www.oecd.org/pisa/pisaproducts/48852584.pdf (accessed 12 November 2013).

— (2011a) *Education at a Glance: Indicator B2. What proportion of national wealth is spent on education?* Paris: OECD Publishing. Online. www.oecd.org/edu/skills-beyond-school/48630884.pdf (accessed 23 January 2012).

— (2011b) *Health at a Glance 2011: OECD indicators*. Paris: OECD Publishing. Online. www.oecd-ilibrary.org/social-issues-migration-health/health-at-a-glance-2011_health_glance-2011-en;jsessionid=285ee3vywsbbe.x-oecd-live-02 (accessed 28 January 2016).

— (2012) *PISA 2012 Results in Focus: What 15-year-olds know and what they can do with what they know*. Paris: OECD Publishing. Online. www.oecd.org/pisa/keyfindings/pisa-2012-results-overview.pdf (accessed 16 August 2014).

— (2013a) *Education at a Glance 2013: OECD indicators*. Paris: OECD Publishing. Online. www.oecd.org/edu/eag2013%20%28eng%29--FINAL%20 20%20June%202013.pdf (accessed 5 June 2014).

— (2013b) *Education at a Glance 2013: Annexes and indicators*. Paris: OECD Publishing. Online. www.oecd.org/edu/educationataglance2013-indicatorsandannexes.htm (accessed 28 January 2016).

Robinson, V. (2011) *Student-Centered Leadership*. San Francisco, CA: Jossey-Bass.

Schudson, M. (1996) *The Power of News*. Cambridge, MA: Harvard University Press.

Transparency International (2013) 'Corruption Perceptions Index'. Online. http://cpi.transparency.org/cpi2013/results/ (accessed 16 August 2014).

Tschannen-Moran, M. (2004) *Trust Matters: Leadership for successful schools*. San Francisco, CA: Jossey-Bass.

— (2014) *Trust Matters: Leadership for successful schools*. 2nd ed. San Francisco, CA: Jossey-Bass.

Tyler, T.R. (1990) *Why People Obey the Law*. New Haven, CT: Yale University Press.

Uslaner, E.M. (2004) 'Trust and corruption'. In Lambsdorf, J.G., Taube, M., and Schramm, M. (eds) *The New Institutional Economics of Corruption*. London: Routledge, 76–92.

Van Maele, D., Forsyth, P.B., and Van Houtte, M. (2014) (eds) *Trust and School Life: The role of trust for learning, teaching, leading, and bridging*. Dordrecht, Netherlands: Springer.

Walker, K., Kutsyuruba, B., and Noonan, B. (2011) 'The fragility of trust in the world of school principals'. *Journal of Educational Administration,* 49 (5), 471–94.

Williamson, O.E. (1993) 'Calculativeness, trust, and economic organization'. *Journal of Law and Economics,* 30 (1), 453–86.

Zak, P. (2003) 'Trust'. CAPCO Institute Journal of Financial Transformation, 7 (April), 13–21. Online. www.neuroeconomicstudies.org/images/stories/documents/CAPCOTrust.pdf (accessed 22 January 2016).

Ziegler, C., and Lausen, G. (2005) 'Propagation models for trust and distrust in social networks'. *Information Systems Frontiers*, 7 (4/5), 337–58.

Zucker, L.G. (1986) 'Production of trust: Institutional sources of economic structure, 1840–1920.' *Research in Organizational Behavior*, 8, 53–111.

Chapter 1

Trust and mistrust: Competing models of policy and practice

Dean Fink

Driving through the Romanian countryside a few years ago with my associates, Tavi, Anca, and our driver Marion, I felt like a time traveller being transported from the twenty-first century to the eighteenth. As we rolled along the two-lane highway from Galati, a large and rather run down industrial city on the Danube River, to Piscu, a small rural village 12 miles away, we passed men and women, young and old, labouring in fields with huge ploughs pulled by oxen that reminded me of the pictures in my history textbook on eighteenth-century Britain. There were few cars or trucks, only locals in donkey carts, and small wooden houses, some with thatched roofs, and all with outside toilet facilities. As we approached Piscu we could see one larger building with a shiny roof that gleamed in the sunlight: this was the village school. The school building in Piscu, with the exception of this new roof of sheet metal, needed repair. As I stepped into the main foyer I immediately noticed new strip carpeting that seemed incongruous in such an old school building. I was then introduced to Elena, the school's principal.

Actually I should say reintroduced, because I had no recollection of the first time we had met, when she was part of a larger group of Romanian school principals who had participated in a workshop sponsored by the Open Society Foundation in which I also took part. Frankly, she was not at face value a particularly memorable person. Elena was in her late forties, perhaps early fifties, very plainly dressed, quite softly spoken, and not a person to stand out in a group; in fact she was the antithesis of the charismatic leader. As we toured her school I watched her closely, and without understanding the language observed how teachers and students responded to her. She was like a ballet dancer, floating from student to student, teacher to teacher, with a word of encouragement here, a suggestion there, evoking smiles and nods as she progressed. Everywhere we went in the school we were met with displays of children's work, even in the boys' washroom. With the help of my interpreter and my many years of experience observing children's work,

I was able to appreciate that the work of the children in Elena's school was of a very high quality. As I went from classroom to classroom, I found that most children past the age of ten could converse with me in passable English. They of course asked about my country, Canada, and they all knew about Niagara Falls. I was then ushered into a meeting of the staff that included the head of their parents' council, who happened to be Elena's predecessor. The staff had the usual complaints one might hear in any staff meeting anywhere about government mandates, insensitive inspectors who knew nothing about the challenges of rural schools, and deteriorating working conditions. They made very sure I knew how much they appreciated Elena and each other.

What made this school and staff different from most is that this faculty hadn't been paid in two months. In addition, any repairs or upgrades to the school had to be funded and undertaken by the local community. This agricultural village had collected the money and provided the manpower themselves to put a new roof on the school and lay the new carpet throughout, because external pressure on the central government obliged them to squeeze public service expenditures in a drive to create a suitable climate for western corporate investment. In spite of all of its difficulties and obstacles, this village school in Piscu was an island of learning and hope in which the teachers continued to work together industriously and effectively with only vague promises of a payday. Why? The teaching staff trusted Elena as their leader of learning, they trusted each other, they trusted their community to support the school, and the community trusted them and invested what they could in them. The strength of this school resided in its rich and interconnected network of internal relationships: between the leader and her staff, between and among the teachers, between the school and the community, and ultimately between the adults and the children. This was social capital in action. By supporting and trusting each other professionally and personally, and sharing a carefully articulated and acted-upon sense of purpose focused on developing deep and broad learning for all the children of this struggling community, Elena and her school community collectively worked to lead this next generation of children out of Piscu's historical cycle of menial labour and endemic poverty despite the odds against them.

While this example of the relationship of student success to social capital is anecdotal and easily dismissed, research by Carrie Leana (2011: 5) and her colleagues demonstrates rather convincingly that 'when relationships among teachers in a school are characterized by high trust and frequent interaction – that is social capital is strong – student achievement scores improve'. Policies that try to change individual behaviours by hectoring, fear-mongering, and reward and punishment strategies have short-term efficacy but virtually no sustainability. Conversely, policies that focus on peer pressure to effect change within organizations and cultures have a far greater chance of long-term success (Rosenberg, 2011). Investments in social capital, therefore, can change schools and educational systems (Levin, 2010).

The professional model

When one looks into formal definitions of social capital, however, the sources and meanings can become quite obtuse. Some researchers, like Bourdieu and Wacquant (1992: 119), stress an organization's external links by defining social capital as 'the sum of the resources, actual or virtual, that accrue to an individual or a group by virtue of possessing a durable network of more or less institutionalized relationships of mutual acquaintance and recognition'. With the exception of its immediate community and some help from an outside foundation, the external sources for the little school in Piscu were either non-existent or working in ways that undermined its internal social capital. Nonetheless, external sources of social capital such as school districts, state departments, and even federal departments of education, as well as unions and relevant social agencies, all contribute to – or, unfortunately, as our research will show, in many cases inhibit – the development of a school's social capital. Robert Putnam (1995: 67) focuses more on internal sources when he describes social capital as 'features of social organization such as networks, norms, and social trust that facilitate coordination and cooperation for mutual benefit'. Schools like Piscu can function well, based on these internal sources of social capital, for a time, but they need external sources of social capital to sustain high levels of efficacy. Adler and Kwon (2002) provide a more comprehensive definition of social capital that combines its internal and external features when they state 'Social capital is the goodwill available to individuals or groups. Its source lies in the structure and content of the actor's social relations. Its effects flow from the information, influence, and solidarity it makes available to the actor' (Adler and Kwon, 2002: 23). They explain that 'goodwill' means the 'sympathy, trust and forgiveness others have towards us' (Adler and Kwon, 2002: 18) and highlight the following qualities of social capital:

- Social capital can substitute for other sources of capital (such as financial capital).
- Social capital is collective, not located in individuals as human capital is.
- It does not depreciate with use, but grows and develops with use.
- It is not amenable to quantifiable measurement.
- It needs maintenance, and must be renewed and reconfirmed.

Woven throughout most discussions of social capital is the concept of trust. Some researchers see it as the very essence of social capital and others view it as a product of social capital. Adler and Kwon (2002) explain:

> There is . . . some confusion in the literature as to the relationship between trust and social capital. Some authors equate trust and social capital (Fukuyama, 1995; 1997), some authors see trust as a source of social capital (Putnam *et al.*, 1993), some see it as a form of social capital (Coleman, 1988), and some see it as a collective asset resulting from social capital construed as a relational asset (Lin, 1999).
>
> (Adler and Kwon, 2002: 23)

Still others, for their part, consider trust to be a motivational source of social capital (Knoke, 1999). The question, however, of whether trust is in fact social capital, as Fukuyama suggests, or a source of social capital, a form, a collective asset, or a motivational tool tends to lead us to an irresolvable 'chicken-and-egg' kind of controversy. For the purposes of this book our answer is that it is all of these: social capital equates to trust; it is also a form, a source, a collective asset, and motivational, depending on the context and situation.

Definitions of trust abound in the literature on the topic but almost all seem to reflect three fundamental concepts: honesty, reliability, and caring (Tschannen-Moran, 2004; Kutsyuruba *et al.*, 2010). Another word that also permeates the trust literature is 'vulnerability'. In trusting, one makes oneself vulnerable to other people, organizations, institutions, or even to an idea or ideology. The more one trusts the more one has confidence in the other, and the more vulnerable one becomes if trust is betrayed. Conversely, distrust reflects a lack of confidence in the 'other', and the more one distrusts the less vulnerable one becomes.

Roy Lewicki and his colleagues define trust 'in terms of confident positive expectations regarding another's conduct, and distrust in terms of confident negative expectations regarding another's conduct' (Lewicki *et al.*, 1998: 439). They explain that they define the term 'another's conduct':

> … in a very specific, but encompassing sense, addressing another's words, actions, and decisions (what another says and does and how he or she makes decisions). By 'confident positive expectations,' we mean a belief in, a propensity to attribute virtuous intentions to, and a willingness to act on the basis of another's conduct. Conversely, by 'confident negative expectations,' we mean a fear of, a propensity to attribute sinister intentions to, and a desire to buffer oneself from the effects of another's conduct.
>
> (Lewicki *et al.*, 1998: 439)

Social capital, then, as exemplified by schools like the one in Piscu where we can detect 'confident positive expectations regarding another's conduct' (ibid.), has trust not only as its essence, but as a source, a form, a collective asset, and a motivational tool. Social capital within an organization alone, however, is not enough to sustain excellence in a school or district. Without external support, including paydays, and ongoing professional learning, even Elena and her staff will wear down.

Andy Hargreaves and Michael Fullan (2012) contend that social capital and its offshoot, decisional capital, when combined with human capital produce a powerful professional capital that predicts enhanced educational performance and sustained educational improvement. They contend that making 'decisions in complex situations is what professionalism is all about. The pros do it all the time. They come to have competence, judgement, insight, inspiration, and the capacity for improvisation as they strive for exceptional performance' (Hargreaves and Fullan 2012: 5). As our subsequent discussions will suggest, the nature and extent of individual and group decision-making is ultimately determined by the degree to which policy makers deem policy implementers trustworthy.

Another source of trust is in the expertise, credentials, and experience of the people in whom we invest our children, our money, our property, and even our bodies. It is really important to me when I get my knee replaced that I can trust my surgeon's knowledge, skills, experience, and talent to get me vertical and mobile. This is human capital, but it alone is not enough. My surgeon, for all his expertise, is part of a team, and I trust that this team knows how to work together and make the right decisions for my benefit. The three kinds of capital come together as professional capital in education when schools and governments adopt what Fullan (2011) calls the right drivers for growth and improvement: capacity-building among staff members, group work, and a focus on pedagogy and systemic solutions.[1] Unfortunately, many educational change efforts have focused almost exclusively on developing human capital with little regard for social and decisional capital. As Leana (2011: 2) argues, 'enhancing teacher human capital should not be the sole or even primary focus of school reform'. This blind faith in the power of human capital and the ideology behind it has its roots in economics and value-added metrics.

The production model

From the perspective of the prevailing economic philosophy that has captured educational thinking at the highest levels in many countries, my story of Piscu makes no sense. Elena and her staff were not acting rationally or in their own interests by working diligently for children without pay. According to public choice theory, people are driven by self-interest as opposed to public service (Burch, 2009). Social capital is a sociologist's fantasy; only human and financial capital mean anything. To economists of the utilitarian school, there has to be a payoff. Giving to charity is undertaken to get a warm feeling, Mother Theresa liked the publicity, Nelson Mandela was merely a power seeker, and acting altruistically is designed to satisfy personal needs for esteem, applause, and so on. Besides, things like trust, collaboration, and social capital are difficult, if not impossible, to measure and therefore not susceptible to scientific inquiry.

In the 1960s when Milton Friedman first came to prominence, he was a member of the University of Chicago economics department. Prominently displayed in the department was a sign that stated 'Science is Measurement'. By reducing economics to that which was measurable and ignoring the human costs of an ideology that asserted that government has a very limited role to play in the economy except to create a climate for investment, and everything else, including education, health care, and social security, can best be handled by the private sector, these neo-liberals gave an intellectual veneer to hyper-individualism and a rationale for ignoring social needs and economic inequities. Friedman was, and his followers still are, providing leadership to countries like the United States, the United Kingdom, and New Zealand, and to international organizations such as the International Monetary Fund and World Bank. Even though the applications of their economic theories in Pinochet's Chile and Suharto's Indonesia failed miserably, caused untold horror for vast numbers of people (Klein, 2007), and have directly contributed to the economic disasters of 2008 and 2009 (McLean and Nocera, 2010; Stiglitz, 2010), Friedman's true believers and their supporters, although shaken by recent economic events

(Cassidy, 2010), remain convinced that where society has a choice, private interests always trump public interests.

Influenced by the Chicago School's unshakable belief in the 'efficient markets hypothesis' and the 'rational expectations theory', lawmakers in most western countries have relaxed government regulations on banks and other financial institutions over the past 20 years. The former theory assumes that the prices of stocks, houses, and other assets accurately reflect all available information about economic conditions. The market, therefore, is rational, and humans and their governments and social safety nets get in the way of this perfectly operating system. Advocates of this point of view hold that most aspects of society should be subject to unfettered market forces and commodified, including education, health care, pensions, and even fighting wars, as the activities of the Halliburton conglomerate and other private contractors in the Iraq war attest. The neo-liberals oppose impediments that may encumber the operation of the market, like taxes to pay for public services and the education of other people's children, government regulations, public debt to support a social agenda, and unions that obstruct 'labour flexibility'. The second theory, the 'rational expectations theory', insists that all economic players, from everyday citizens to well-paid CEOs and investors, are all deeply knowledgeable about the economy and act wisely on that knowledge, and if they haven't succeeded it is because they lacked the intelligence, diligence, or positive attitude to do so (Ehrenreich, 2009). Success and failure in this Darwinian world characterized by the survival of the fittest is the result of individual strengths and weaknesses as opposed to any societal or economic advantages or inequities. To the business guru Tom Peters, for example, we each must become a brand. As he explains, 'To start thinking like your own favorite brand manager ask yourself. . . . What is it that my product or service does that makes it different? . . . Being CEO of Me Inc. requires you to act selfishly—to grow yourself, to promote yourself, to get the market to reward yourself' (Peters, 1997: n.p.). By reducing everything to a commodity, privatized interests and desires, rather than social roles and obligations, define one's personal life and social relationships. An entire industry built around motivational speakers and literature has created the ethos in many organizations that one must always be positive and promoting oneself (presumably to the disadvantage of others), and failure, or feelings of unhappiness, unfairness, and being put upon by the organization are the byproduct of personal negativity and presumably lack of character. As Zig Zigler, an American Christian motivator, declared, 'It's your own fault. Don't blame the system, don't blame the boss – work harder and pray more' (quoted in Ehrenreich,

2009: 115). Sadly, the bank failures, industry buyouts, gutted retirement savings plans, and bizarre housing markets have proven the first theory to be profoundly untrue, and as for the second, even the high rollers didn't know what was going on, let alone the average worker, and all the positive thinking and prayers in the world won't refurbish pensions or get back foreclosed houses or undo social distress (McLean and Nocera, 2010; Cassidy, 2010).

When the neo-liberal economists' fondest dreams are translated into education, everything is measureable and everything has a price. Language has first to be altered and manipulated (Fink, 2010: 1). 'The use of new language is important. The new public management organizations are now "peopled" by human resources that need to be managed, learning is re-rendered as a "cost-effective policy outcome" and achievement is a set of "productivity targets"' (Ball, 2008: 43). It is a production paradigm of how education should work: teachers are merely human capital, not professionals to whom society entrusts its children's education; principals (school heads) are managers of the productivity of this 'workforce', not leaders of learning; and the results of these efforts are neatly and simplistically codified into easily understood and manipulated numbers based on the bottom line – students' test scores (Leana, 2011). These value-added metrics look at annual increments in test scores and glibly draw conclusions about teachers' competence, principals' leadership, and district and even state departments' efficacy by ignoring the complexities of teaching and leading and reducing these activities to commodities to be measured. Like the stock market or a quarterly report, a school's success goes up or down dependent on these numbers, and in more recent times, particularly in some areas of the United States, teachers and principals' salaries fluctuate accordingly. Often the answer to declining or stalled test scores is a quick injection of outside expertise or one-shot workshops. More systemic problems have produced short-term expedients like Teach for America in the United States, or Teach First in the United Kingdom, which place relatively untrained and inexperienced young people from elite universities into challenging schools. In the extreme, government agencies take over schools, fire the existing staff, and presumably create a renewed and flourishing school with the same children and parents. Unions and particularly teacher tenure have increasingly come under attack as barriers to school reform based on the assumption that teachers don't want to improve and that experienced teachers are tired, incompetent, or just complacent, and that they deprive students of a quality education (Nagourney, 2014). The ideology upon which this production model is based is shot through with mistrust of the teaching profession. As Michael Fullan has indicated, this model of educational change emphasizes the wrong drivers: multiple and often fragmented change initiatives; perseverance on accountability at all levels to drive and verify change among individual teachers, leaders, and schools; and massive investment in and blind confidence that 'the wonders of the digital world will carry the day v/s instruction' (Fullan, 2011: 5). Evidence described in the preamble to this book from nations, such as Sweden, the United States, and the United Kingdom, that have bought into this change model indicates that these drivers of change and the 'low trust' paradigm upon which they are based are clearly not working. Not only is the production creed not working in education, it may well be the cause of our world's economic lethargy. Mark Carney, Governor of the Bank of England, has said of the extreme free-market orthodoxy among business leaders and policy makers that 'Just as any revolution eats its children, unchecked market fundamentalism can devour the social capital essential for the long-term dynamism of capitalism itself' (Carney, quoted in Burman, 2014: n.p.).

What is really worrying is how completely the neo-liberal ideology has captured political thinking around the world. Even political parties that style themselves democratic, liberal, or labour parrot the three fundamental policy pillars of neo-liberalism – 'privatization of the public sphere, deregulation of the corporate sector and lower corporate taxes paid for with cuts to public spending' (Klein, 2014: 19). Major international organizations such as the World Trade Organization (WTO), the International Monetary Fund (IMF), the World Bank, and the Organization for Economic Cooperation and Development (OECD) are thoroughly engaged in spreading these values. Any one of these policies can undermine state-supported education and the professional model; taken together they will spell its doom. To the corporate world, there is too much money to be made in education to leave it to governments.

While neo-liberals lead this production model, there are many others who have joined the parade for their own reasons, and end up supporting the libertarian philosophy that propels it. Michael Apple (2006) argues that a 'perfect storm' in education has connected the neo-liberals' privatization agenda with neo-conservatives' nostalgia for times past when, supposedly, schools had standards, students worked hard, and dedicated teachers toiled dutifully for the love of teaching and meagre remuneration; these drives are connected also to religious fundamentalists and evangelicals' desire to 'return to (their) God in all our institutions' (Apple, 2006: 9). Like large corporations, quasi-commercial religious institutions preach a prosperity gospel of self-sufficiency that proclaims that God meant for 'true believers' to be affluent: '[Y]ou can have all the stuff in the mall, as well as the beautiful house and car, if only you believe that you can. But always, in a hissed undertone, there is the darker message that if you don't have all that you want, if you feel sick, discouraged or defeated, you have only yourself to blame. Positive theology ratifies and completes a world without beauty, transcendence, or mercy' (Ehrenreich, 2009: 146). Combine these forces with a growing cadre of middle class technocrats who are more interested in forms, functions, and efficiency than human beings and we can see a powerful coalition of supporters of the production model of education who would really like to replace public education with an education marketplace, or at least change the system in ways that meet their world view.

Their motives may differ, but this coalition advocates for schools such as charter schools (or Swedish-style 'free' schools, or British-style academies and more recently free schools) that are not constrained by local democratic governments, national or state curricula, or teacher certification, and that supposedly employ tougher standards and offer plenty of testing and evaluation. Most importantly members of this coalition seek to avoid teacher unions and their advocacy for job protection, tenure, and better working conditions such as smaller class sizes. Moreover, performance pay, presumably based on value-added test scores, is an important part of this agenda.

Educational critics routinely describe educators who suggest that poverty, inadequate health care, and poor facilities or materials contribute to students' difficulties in school as whiners, quitters, incompetent, and worse. Powerful and efficacious concepts such as trust, respect, optimism, intentionality, commitment, and compassion no longer permeate the educational discourse. These unfashionable words and ideas are now considered soft, 'touchy-feely', left-wing, 'wussy', and effeminate and it is held that they should not obscure the tough judgements necessary to oblige reluctant teachers and principals to change and 'reform' their ways. The problem for the technocrats who claim to live in the 'real world' or 'in the trenches' and who now seem to dominate educational policy in many nations is that these 'soft' words and concepts like trust are hard to quantify or codify, and are not compatible with military and business metaphors. In place of words that speak of healthy and productive human interactions, we get a steady drumbeat of market-based words, phrases, and concepts that describe rigorous, demanding, and macho forms and functions, like 'accountability', performance management, the 'bottom line', and 'more bang for the buck' (or payoff for the pound). It is far easier to mouth slogans about 'no child left behind', or a 'world-class education', or to decry the alleged plethora of 'bad teachers' than it is to come to grips with the deeper causes of school failure. In summary, the production model demands that schools operate on sound business principles, make themselves accountable to their customers, and show a profit or growth over the previous reporting period.

In some respects, however, there are some aspects of this production model that can and should inform and improve the professional model of education. Schools and school systems should and must be efficient in terms of effective use of resources; they need to be responsible for the growth and development of each child and they must be accountable and transparent to the child's parents and the community in general. For most countries, the ideal is not exclusively the professional model or the production model but a unique blending of the two. Some countries have merged aspects of these two paradigms more effectively than others, and subsequent chapters will explicate how this merging has occurred in different contexts.

While ideological, tactical, and strategic differences divide the professional and production models, the real difference between the two comes down to trust. Can society trust teachers and principals as professional educators to prepare young people for the challenges of life in a changing world, and can teachers and principals learn to trust and work cooperatively with others in their professional networks who strive for the same goals but in different ways? Conversely, if teachers and principals are seen to be untrustworthy, how did this happen and what can be done to change this perception? Similarly, if policy makers have failed to gain the trust of the people who must carry out their policies – teachers and principals – how did this happen, who is or was responsible, and how can the situation be rectified? Before we address these big questions on a country by country basis, it is worth looking a little more deeply into the meanings of our book's title, 'Trust and verify'.

Notes

[1] I applaud and appreciate Michael's recognition of the 'wrong and right drivers', but for me his choice of the term 'drivers' is problematic. It implies that someone has determined a direction and holds the reins that 'drive' his or her minions towards preconceived goals. You can drive cars, you can drive horses, and you can drive golf balls, but I doubt that you can do more than 'move' people temporarily from one place to another using coercive methods. For long-term sustainable change, policy makers and implementers need to work together and be mutually supportive in pursuit of agreed-upon goals. Perhaps 'initiators' is a better term. I may be accused of quibbling but semantics is important.

References

Adler, P., and Kwon, S. (2002) 'Social capital: Prospects for a new concept'. *Academy of Management Review,* 29 (2), 17–40.

Apple, M. (2006) *Educating the Right Way: Markets, standards, God and inequality.* New York: Routledge.

Ball, S. (2008) *The Education Debate.* Bristol: The Policy Press.

Bourdieu, P., and Wacquant, L. (1992) *An Invitation to Reflexive Sociology.* Chicago: University of Chicago Press.

Burch, P. (2009) *Hidden Markets: The new education privatization.* New York: Routledge.

Burman, T. (2014) 'Why the establishment is worried about inequality'. *Toronto Star*, 25 October. Online. www.thestar.com/news/world/2014/10/25/why_the_establishment_is_worried_about_inequality_burman.html (accessed 21 January 2016)

Cassidy, J. (2010) 'After the blowup: Laissez-faire economists do some soul searching – and finger-pointing'. *The New Yorker,* 11 January. Online. www.newyorker.com/magazine/2010/01/11/after-the-blowup (accessed 3 August 2014).

Coleman, J. (1988) 'Social capital and the creation of human capital'. *American Journal of Sociology,* 90 (supplement), S95–S120.

Ehrenreich, B. (2009) *Bright-sided: How the relentless promotion of positive thinking has undermined America.* New York: Metropolitan Books.

Fink, D. (2010) 'Words that work ... or do they? Online. http://deanfink.wordpress.com/2010/07/29/words-that-work-or-do-they/ (accessed 21 January 2016).

Fukuyama, F. (1995) *Trust: The social virtues and the creation of prosperity.* London: Hamish Hamilton.

— (1997) 'Social capital and the modern capitalist economy: Creating a high trust workplace'. *Stern Business Magazine,* 4 (1), 17.

Fullan, M. (2011) 'Choosing the wrong drivers for whole system reform'. *Seminar Series,* 204. Melbourne, Australia: Centre for Strategic Education, pp. 3–19.

Hargreaves, A., and Fullan, M. (2012) *Professional Capital: Transforming teaching in every school.* New York: Teachers College Press.

Klein, N. (2007) *The Shock Doctrine: The rise of disaster capitalism.* Toronto: Knopf, Canada.

— (2014) *This Changes Everything: Capitalism vs. the climate.* Toronto: Alfred A. Knopf.

Knoke, D. (1999) 'Organizational networks and corporate social capital'. In Leenders, A., and Gabbey, S. (eds) *Corporate Social Capital and Liability.* Boston: Kluwer, 17–42.

Kutsyuruba, B., Walker, K., and Noonan, B. (2010) 'The ecology of trust in the principalship'. *Journal of Educational Administration and Foundations,* 21 (1), 23–47.

Leana, E. (2011) 'The missing link in school reform'. *Stanford Social Innovation Review,* Fall 2011. Online. www.ssireview.org/articles/entry/the_missing_link_in_school_reform (accessed 28 August 2014).

Levin, B. (2010) 'Governments and education reform: Some lessons from the last 50 years'. *Journal of Education Policy,* 25 (6), 739–47.

Lewicki, R., McAllister, D., and Bies, R. (1998) 'Trust and distrust: New relationships and realities'. *Academy of Management Review*, 23 (3), 438–58.

Lin, N. (1999) 'Social networks and status attainment'. *Annual Review of Sociology,* 25, 467–87.

McLean, B., and Nocera, J. (2010) *All the Devils are Here: The hidden history of the financial crisis*. New York: Portfolio/Penguin.

Nagourney, A. (2014) 'California Governor appeals court ruling overturning protection for teachers'. *New York Times*, 30 August. Online. www.nytimes. com/2014/08/31/us/california-governor-fights-decision-on-teacher-tenure.html (accessed 30 August 2014).

Peters, T. (1997) 'The brand called you'. *Fast Company,* August/September. Online. www.fastcompany.com/28905/brand-called-you (accessed 21 January 2016).

Putnam, R. (1995) 'Bowling alone: America's declining social capital'. *Journal of Democracy*. 6 (1), 65–78.

Putnam, R.D., Leonardi, R., and Nanetti, R.Y. (1993) *Making Democracy Work: Civic traditions in modern Italy*. Princeton, NJ: Princeton University Press.

Rosenberg, T. (2011) *Join the Club: How peer pressure can change the world*. New York: W. W. Norton.

Stiglitz, J. (2010) *Freefall: America, free markets and the sinking of the world economy*. New York: Norton.

Tschannen-Moran, M. (2004) *Trust Matters: Leadership for successful schools*. San Francisco, CA: Jossey–Bass.

Chapter 2

Trust *and* verify

Dean Fink

One evening in the late 1990s, as part of my PhD research (Fink, 1997), I recorded the comments on educational leadership of seven female former teachers at a school in which I was an original staff member in the early 1970s, Lord Byron High School. Each of these women had moved on to significant leadership roles in secondary schools, school districts, and the Ministry of Education of Ontario. They were part of a larger women's network that emerged from Lord Byron in the 1970s. The school district had initiated the school with the express purpose of challenging the structures of secondary education, the curriculum, teaching and pupil assessment methods in Ontario, and, most importantly, the treatment of students. In the context of Ontario at the time, the philosophical, pedagogical, curricular, organizational, and structural innovations introduced at Lord Byron were revolutionary and intimidating to groups who sought to preserve the status quo in the educational system (Fink, 2003). For those of us who joined the teaching staff, it was an exciting and stressful time in our careers because we were trying to do things differently for students without much guidance or external support, while playing defence against powerful community and district forces of continuity and retrenchment. We bonded together out of both necessity and the conviction that we were on to something that would make a difference for our students and students in other schools.

For women in secondary education in the 1970s, leadership was out of the question: the prevailing ethos was that women were too emotional and not tough enough to run a large, complicated secondary school. Most schools and school systems encouraged and rewarded power, competition, control, domination, and linear, analytic rational thought. The school district in which Lord Byron was located was a totally male-dominated, patriarchal system, especially at the secondary level, where 80 per cent of teachers and almost all the senior leaders were male. The prevailing metaphors were those of male dominated team sports like football. Ironically all of the first department chairs at Lord Byron were men, because no qualified women applied, which spoke eloquently to the state of women's leadership in the school district at that time.

One woman remembered seeing the department chairs at Byron work together as a council to solve problems in a collaborative way and saying to herself 'I can do that. It was more collaborative and there was discussion. It wasn't a decision made by a principal, which everybody carried out. My guess is that women are good at that kind of leadership and prefer it.' Another participant in my group interview stated:

> The principal had a philosophy but he was open to anybody's input. I remember it was significant that he was going to let women wear pant suits. I just remember it being an issue for working women. You just had a sense if you took something to him, an idea, it was going to be heard. I think that in three years we were willing to say as women 'we must go further'. I almost felt that was the ethos that was there – readiness to accept and an invitation to proceed.
>
> (Female former teacher at Lord Byron High School)

As the women explained, they felt comfortable, trusted, and empowered to aspire to formal leadership roles.

In this environment, the women of Lord Byron – with the active support of the school leadership and male staff members – helped each other professionally and personally. They were there for each other at the 'birthing of babies' and the seeking of advancement. Since there were no women in the original chairs group, for instance, they asked why not, and encouraged their colleagues to apply, which over the ensuing years many did with success. One male staff member said he envied the women's group 'because they really talked about interesting things'. Since the group had a tradition of doing a quilt for the birth of each member's new child, this male member joined them after the group made a quilt for his newborn. Sexist jokes and gender-based language were discouraged at Byron by men and women alike.

The movement spread throughout the district. In the early 1980s, two members of the group, the aforementioned man and a female leader, helped to found an organization in the school district which dealt with gender-based issues in the region. One of its successes was a district policy on inclusive language and a review of curriculum to ensure gender equity, and today, of the 19 secondary principals' jobs available, 12 are held by women. As Margaret Mead is alleged to have said, 'Never doubt that a small group of thoughtful committed citizens can change the world; indeed, it's the only thing that ever has'.[1] The Byron women didn't change the world, but they certainly changed their school and school district over time.

Lord Byron was a school built on trust: trust in a philosophy, trust in the leadership, and above all trust in each other. Trust that if we made mistakes (and we made lots of them), there was someone there to support us, prop us up, and help us to move on. The school leadership created an ethos in which teachers learned from mistakes 'because mistakes were open and acknowledged'. At Byron we decided if we made mistakes we were allowed to learn from those mistakes. One teacher provided a personal example:

> [W]hen I look back probably one of the things that made (the principal) a good leader was that he could talk about what you had done and said – he would remember and come back a couple of weeks later and say 'how did such and such work out' and I would say, it was either 'great' or it 'bombed'. If it bombed, he would say 'did all of it bomb or did only part of it bomb? Do you have to change it all'? It became a questioning routine so that it got you thinking again as to the evaluation of it and then you would start over again and make the changes you needed.
>
> (Female former teacher at Lord Byron High School)

Experimentation implies making mistakes. In highly visible and antagonistic environments, mistakes become magnified, publicized, and criticized (Fletcher *et al.*, 1985; Hargreaves *et al.*, 1992). When this happens the experimenters pull back to the 'tried and true', and learning ceases. Experimentation leads to higher levels of learning only if it is sustained by a culture characterized by three types of trust: institutional, relational, and self-trust. Just for a moment let us try a short mental experiment.

Trust and distrust

Have you ever thought about how much we blindly trust institutions and the people who run them that we don't know and probably will never encounter? Mentally retrace your steps this morning from the time you got up to your arrival at your workplace. If you are like me the first thing you did after waking is to turn on the light, then head to the bathroom to take care of nature's call and have a shower or bath. Then you dress, and have breakfast before you drive to work. Each step of the way you trusted faceless people to ensure your accommodation had electrical power for lights and hot water, other nameless souls who made sure the water was there when you turned it on and the sewers worked to eliminate waste. You dressed in clothes made in many places around the world by anonymous people, and then sat down for breakfast or picked up something at a fast food stop on your way to work. Regardless, at breakfast you are obliged to trust one of a few major international corporations, such as Nestlé, Nabisco, Kraft, General Foods, or Kellogg's, a local (or in some cases, like Wal-Mart, international) supermarket chain or a fast food franchise. You have to trust that your government's regulatory schedule and enforcement ensures high-quality and hopefully nourishing food, to say nothing of its backing the currency you used to buy it.

Once in your car, you have to trust that other drivers will follow the rules of the road, that your car operates according to the manufacturer's specifications, and that your country's distribution system has sufficient reasonably priced gasoline (petrol) available to keep your car on the road. While you may trust all these institutions you probably trust some more than others. For example, I have high trust in our water system, only modest trust in our electrical system (because we have frequently experienced both blackouts and brownouts), and I have very low trust in the companies who make processed foods.[2] I would diagram my levels of trust this way:

<table>
<tr><td>FOOD
MANUFACTURER</td><td>ELECTRICAL
SERVICE</td><td>WATER
SUPPLY</td></tr>
<tr><td>*LOW*
TRUST</td><td>*MODERATE*
TRUST</td><td>*HIGH*
TRUST</td></tr>
</table>

Figure 2.1: Levels of trust

Now let us continue to think about our morning. As I drive to work I am always conscious that some drivers are not as cautious as I am. While I'm not paranoid, I drive with a certain amount of distrust in the skills of my fellow drivers. Distrust is a natural and sometimes necessary human response; in fact we are taught from an early age 'don't talk to strangers', 'buyer beware', and my father's best piece of advice, which prevented me from doing stupid things on more than one occasion: 'if it sounds too good to be true, it probably is'. As I pass a gasoline (petrol) station I notice that the price has gone up significantly overnight. Since this is the beginning of a long weekend I suspect the petroleum industry is out to make a swift windfall profit. I am hugely distrustful of the monopolistic practices of this industry. When I arrive at work, sitting on my desk is a report on education by a right-wing newspaper. Since this particular newspaper is often critical of publicly supported education and manages even in its news reports to suggest that most public services should be privatized, I read the report on education with a certain amount of scepticism and distrust. I would diagram my levels of distrust this way:

Figure 2.2: Levels of distrust

My purpose in describing these little vignettes is to suggest that trust and distrust are not opposite ends of a single continuum – trust is good and distrust is bad – but two different but interconnected constructs that guide our behaviour in daily life and have application in our understanding of educational leadership and change strategies.

In the preamble to this book I observed that countries that ranked highly on international trust surveys also performed exceptionally well on international assessments of student performance and that students of lower-trust nations tend to perform at mediocre or unsatisfactory levels. Based on this evidence, one could simplistically conclude that policy makers at all levels of the educational enterprise should develop policies that trust teachers, principals (heads), and school district officials to get on with the job of educating students. Moreover there is an impressive body of evidence from multiple disciplines to suggest that institutions that extend trust to their employees unleash the latter's initiative, creativity, and innovation. At the same time, it would be naïve to suggest that all teachers, principals, or senior officials are sufficiently competent, motivated, or energetic to create optimal learning environments for all students. Distrust, therefore, becomes a logical and perhaps necessary aspect of policy making at all levels of the educational enterprise and manifests itself in verification systems like standardized tests, various reporting procedures, and state inspections of schools and teachers.

Trust/distrust matrix

In the previous chapter I introduced definitions of trust and distrust articulated by Roy Lewicki and his colleagues (Lewicki *et al.*, 1998). They defined trust 'in terms of confident positive expectations regarding another's conduct, and distrust in terms of confident negative expectations regarding another's conduct' (Lewicki *et al.*, 1998: 447). At one end of the trust continuum, high trust is almost 'blind' trust in another person, organization, or institution, such as my trust in the water supply. In this position people have total confidence in the 'other', and they have made themselves totally vulnerable to their intentions. If for some reason my water supply became contaminated I'd feel a real sense of betrayal, whereas if my electrical power went off I would feel less vulnerable because I have flashlights (torches), candles, and portable radios stashed in accessible places. At the other extreme, low trust, a person has little reason to trust and has no expectations for positive results from the relationship, and limited vulnerability. I don't expect much from most processed foods so I try as best I can to avoid them. Similarly, high distrust is a stance in which people feel totally vulnerable to the other and have absolutely no confidence in the goodwill or intentions of the other, and must take every precaution to protect themselves. Canada, where I live, is a 'car culture'. Our train system is quite under-developed compared to that of most European countries and we are very dependent on – indeed, wedded to – our automobiles for transportation. Therefore we are quite vulnerable to the whims and wiles of the petroleum industry. In a low distrust stance, people anticipate no 'sinister intentions' directed at them and feel only mildly vulnerable if at all to the conduct of the other. I know my fellow drivers are not 'out to get me' and I'm confident that if I stay alert and act with caution I should be able to avoid any trouble on our roads. When combined, the two concepts – trust and distrust – produce the following matrix that provides a useful way to describe diverse contexts and complex conditions internationally.

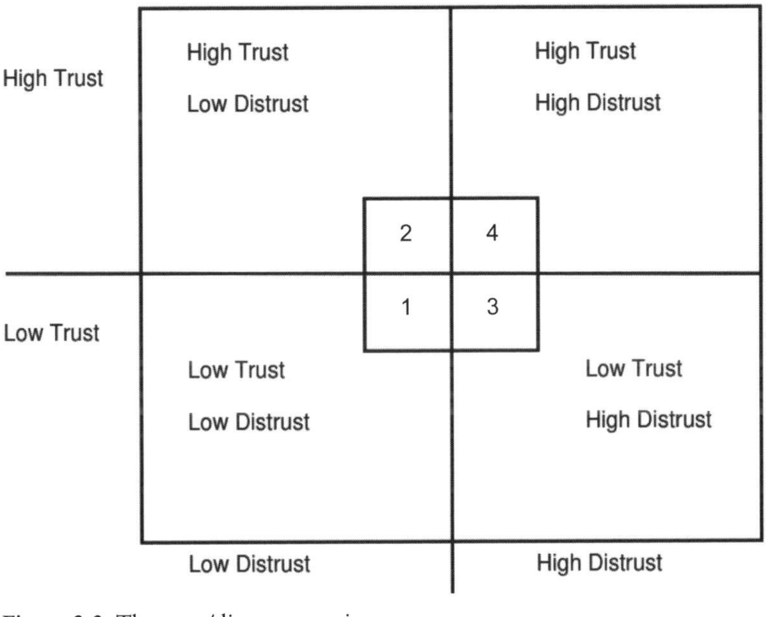

Figure 2.3: The trust/distrust matrix

The quadrants

Each of the quadrants in this matrix describes a theoretical stance that reflects the interactions of the two constructs, trust and distrust. Depending on the issue and context, a person may find themselves operating from all four positions simultaneously. I may operate in quadrant 1 with my local government, quadrant 2 with my wife, my physician, and best friend, quadrant 3 with my telephone and lawn care companies, and quadrant 4 with my grandson's school.

Quadrant 1

Low trust/low distrust describes relationships that are characterized by limited interdependence. In this quadrant there is little anticipation of positive relationships but at the same time little concern that the relationship could be harmful. It is in a sense an 'arm's-length' relationship. For example, a school might have infrequent and distant connections to a private contractor of psychological services, but the service will be bound to provide appropriate services based upon society's ethical and legal requirements. Rousseau and his colleagues (1998) call this *deterrence-based trust* because it 'emphasizes utilitarian considerations that enable one party to believe that another will be trustworthy, because the costly sanctions in place for breach of trust exceeds any potential benefits from opportunistic behaviour' (Rousseau *et al.*, 1998: 399). Relationships in this quadrant require leaders to be *vigilant* to determine whether continuation of the relationship is advantageous to the leader's organization.

Quadrant 2

High trust/low distrust are what a person would aim for in any relationship, whether personal or institutional. *Identification trust,* or what Rousseau and his colleagues (1998) call 'relational trust', derives:

> ... from repeated interactions over time between trustor and trustee. Information available to the trustor from within the relationship itself forms the basis of relational trust. Reliability and dependability in previous interactions with the trustor give rise to positive expectations about the trustee's intentions. Emotion enters into the relationship between the parties because frequent, longer term interaction leads to the formation of attachments based upon reciprocated interpersonal care and concern.
>
> (Rousseau *et al.*, 1998: 399)

Failure to maintain trust can, in the extreme, result in deep feelings of betrayal by trustees and relationships redefined in terms of distrust. Relationships that fit into this quadrant oblige leaders to be *facilitating, empowering, and empathetic* to maintain and strengthen the connections.

QUADRANT 3

Low trust/high distrust situations can be described as *security-based trust*. In situations of this nature, sensible people avoid engagement with others with whom they not only anticipate no positive outcomes of the relationship (low trust) but actually fear negative consequences (high distrust). Relationships are often based on what Solomon and Flores (2001: 4) describe as 'cordial hypocrisy': the strong tendency of people in organizations, because of loyalty or fear, to pretend that there is trust when there is none, being polite in the name of harmony even while cynicism and distrust are acting as poisons, eating away at the very existence of the organization. There are times, however, when there is no alternative to engaging with individuals or institutions that fit this description. Anyone who has been audited by their country's revenues services, or negotiated a contract with an aggressive and adversarial organization or individual, will understand. As Lewicki and his colleagues explain 'If they must interact, distrusting parties may devote significant resources to monitoring the other's behavior, preparing for the other's distrusting actions, and attending to potential vulnerabilities that might be exploited' (Lewicki *et al.*, 1998: 447). The present negotiations between western countries and Iran would fit this description. It is impossible to ignore Iran, so western nations must enter into some kind of relationship with the country. Recognizing past history however suggests that Iran is a country that is difficult to trust. Lewicki and his colleagues add that 'we see cell 3 as an uncomfortable condition for sustained working relationships' (ibid.). When the parties have low trust and high distrust but are interdependent nevertheless, they must find some way to manage their distrust. Leaders who deal with relationships in this quadrant become *gatekeepers*, admitting policies, practices, and procedures that fit with their own organizations' mission and goals while actively opposing or, failing that, subverting those that are destructive of important school values.

QUADRANT 4

High trust/high distrust situations might be described as 'let's make a deal' or *calculus-based trust*. This form of trust relationship is based on rational choice. Trust emerges when the trustor perceives that the trustee intends to perform an action that is beneficial. The perceived positive intentions in calculus-based trust derive not only from the existence of deterrence but from the presence of credible information, such as certification or references from reliable sources, regarding the intentions or competence of another. 'Such "proof sources" signal that the trustee's claims of trustworthiness are true' (Rousseau *et al.*, 1998: 399). A principal's hiring of a teacher for a school is one example of calculative-based trust. 'Trust and verify' might be the motto of leaders who operate in this quadrant. Leaders who extend trust to others must also do their *due diligence* to ensure that their trust is extended appropriately.

Both quadrants 1 and 4 have a calculative dimension to them. In each case a person makes a rational decision to remain aloof from another person or institution (in quadrant 1) or stay involved (in quadrant 4). Conversely, quadrants 2 and 3 have a heavily emotive quality, because people in quadrant 2 situations feel deeply and have a heavy investment in trust, and because in quadrant 4 there exist deep feelings of distrust that are hard to change. Let me illustrate the applicability of this matrix to school leadership by looking first at institutional trust.

Institutional trust

Institutional trust refers to the degree to which an organization's various constituencies continue to have confidence in its competence, integrity, and sustainability. A school leader, for example, might identify totally with the vision and directions of the school's district (quadrant 2), agree in general with the government's educational directions but retain significant reservations and caveats (quadrant 4), and profoundly disagree with and distrust the efforts of the teachers' union to assume important management rights that the leader believes will undermine the leadership of the school (quadrant 3), all while remaining vigilant toward changes in safety regulations that might have some relevance to the leader's school (quadrant 1). The leader's trust or distrust and feelings of vulnerability in each scenario will determine his or her leadership strategies. For example, the leader may become an active member of a regional committee to achieve district goals, while getting involved with a state or provincial principals' (or heads') association to negotiate with the government about the implementation of its policies. At the same time, the leader at the local level may actively confront the union's representatives, while remaining observant but not actively involved in the process of safety regulation changes. Our matrix, populated with the preceding examples, now looks as follows:

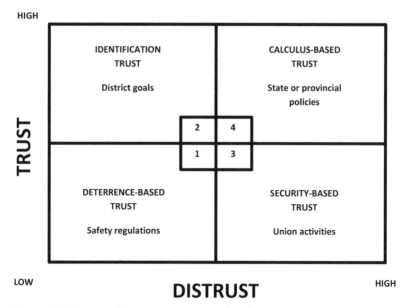

Figure 2.4: The trust/distrust matrix, populated

Now let's look at the matrix from the perspective of a policy maker. Whether at a national, state, district, or school level, a leader initiates policies intended to improve the quality of education. Policy makers have two big problems: how do they get the policy implemented in ways they intend, and how do they verify that the policy has been implemented and in fact does what it is intended to do? Rather than a blanket approach that focuses on one quadrant or another, policy makers who want to achieve the purposes of their policy need to devise at least four separate but related strategies to engage the policy implementers in each quadrant. Typically 20 per cent of a group will support and trust a change initiative (Peshwaria, 2013). This suggests that the overall strategy must proceed in ways that maintain the trust of those who identify with the change by supporting their efforts and developing verification systems that provide information on efficacy while promoting creativity and innovation.

A significant percentage of a population charged with implementing a change, perhaps as high as 60 per cent, will assess the change based on their own values and experience, consider the trustworthiness of the policy developers, and 'calculate' whether the policy or direction is something worth supporting and investing with their time, energy, and discretionary commitment. Maintaining or developing trust, timely, transmitting reliable and credible information concerning the change, and deploying verification systems that enhance rather than inhibit the policy's implementation are essential strategies for attracting the support of this group. For example, the policy of linking teachers' salaries and other benefits to a verification system based on test scores, adopted in some US states and advocated by the Obama administration but seen by many teachers as inherently unfair, has little chance of convincing the 60 per cent, and no chance of attracting the remaining 20 per cent who are either indifferent (quadrant 1) or viscerally opposed (quadrant 3).

While trust building and information sharing may influence some individuals or organizations that remain somewhat indifferent to the proposed direction, it is probably a waste of time and energy to perseverate on quadrant 1. Powerful individuals or adversarial organizations in quadrant 3, such as unions, parents' organizations, political groups, and community agencies, are however a different story. They will not be mollified by anything short of surrender. While they might engage in 'cordial hypocrisy' and pretend to support a policy and direction, they can undermine or even sabotage any change efforts. This is where political processes of negotiation and coalition building kick in, and the parties involved move from the more relational contracting in quadrants 2 and 4 to classical contracting. A long-term classical contract is a formal arrangement, usually involving lawyers, in which the participating parties specify in considerable legal detail the rights and duties of each party and what will happen in all envisaged contingencies as defined within the contract. Conversely, a relational contract, typical of quadrants 2 and 4, is one in which many of these factors are left implicit. The mechanism of enforcement is not recourse to the contract or the courts. It is the need that each party has to go on dealing with the other (Kay, 1991).

Relational trust

Our matrix does not only apply to institutional trust but also can apply to everyday relational trust or distrust. There are a few people with whom you identify and trust implicitly. For example I trust my spouse, my children, and grandchildren, as well as friends of long standing, unconditionally. This is what Bryk and Schneider (1996) call organic trust, and it is in many ways unquestioning or blind trust (high trust, low distrust). It is more emotional than cognitive, and betrayal of this kind of trust can be personally devastating. There are however people who over time I have come to trust implicitly because of our repeated trusting interactions. This is the essence of *relational trust*. It is 'formed through the mutual understandings that arise out of the sustained associations among individuals and institutions' (Bryk and Schneider, 1996: 6). A more calculating stance, on the other hand, in which one is inclined to trust but still withholds total trust, is deemed one of *calculative trust*, or trust and verify (high trust, high distrust). There are still others that I just wouldn't trust, and if I have to deal with them I do so cautiously and carefully and find ways to verify and, if necessary, ensure their trustworthiness (low trust, high distrust). This, to Bryk and Schneider, is *contractual trust*. Finally there are many people in this world with whom I have limited contact, and whether I trust or distrust them is a matter of little consequence (*indifferent trust*) to me or to them (low trust, low distrust).

Themes of honesty (or dishonesty), transparency, competence, and respect for others define *relational trust* and the judgements and decisions that result. The same sequence follows in virtually all our interpersonal engagements. Whenever we have entered into a new relationship, whether it was meeting a new teacher on our first day in school or encountering the boss at our first job, the unspoken questions in our minds were: do I trust this person? Do I have confidence in his or her leadership? What will my relationship with this person become? How will I respond? Similarly, relational trust answers the implicit questions that staff members have of their leaders: How well do you know me and care about me as a person? Do you truly respect me? What do you know about my interests, my family, my aspirations, my fears, and the support I may need to do my job well? Do you really listen to me at a deep level? Are you open to influence or do you just pretend to be interested? Do you treat me with civility and friendliness? Are you with me for the long haul or are you using me to advance your own career?

The degree to which relational trust exists in a school, a district, or even a school jurisdiction will determine staff members' willingness to commit time and energy beyond their contractual obligations to provide extra help to students, coach teams, organize students' events, festivals, concerts, and attend to the myriad activities outside the classroom that make schools vibrant and engaging places for students. Similarly, teachers' commitment to engaging in collegial efforts that contribute to enhanced student performance is directly correlated to their feelings of efficacy and well-being derived from relational trust (Forsyth *et al.*, 2006).

For me and many of my colleagues, Lord Byron was a turning point in our careers because it enabled and encouraged us to trust in ourselves and our personal potential to excel. As the financial tycoon Warren Buffet has observed, 'Trust is like the air we breathe. When it is present no one really notices. But when it is absent, everybody notices' (quoted in Covey *et al.*, 2012: 12). Over time, as I have chronicled elsewhere (Fink, 1997; Fink, 2003), Lord Byron experienced an 'attrition of change'. Lord Byron regressed to the mean and became like every other school as factions emerged, philosophical differences surfaced between true believers and sceptics, external contexts changed, and trust in colleagues, leadership and ideals eroded. In time the initiating leaders moved on and these internal difficulties resulted in Lord Byron as a public institution losing the trust of its community, and in the early years of the twenty-first century the district totally reorganized and even renamed the school. Distrust in the school, in colleagues, and in self, replaced trust.

Self-trust

A touchstone of western philosophy from the Greeks to the present is the aphorism 'know thyself', phrased by Lao Tzu (1905: 44) as 'He who knows others is wise; he who knows himself (or herself) is enlightened'. Institutional and relational forms of trust have a direct bearing on our ability to trust and 'know ourselves' as professional educators. If I return to the four-quadrant matrix again, there were areas of my professional practice where I felt supremely confident. I had high trust and little distrust (quadrant 2) in my ability to teach a secondary school history class that engaged my students. My students' results on examinations and day-to-day feedback reinforced my *self-confidence*. As my father used to say, however, confidence is a short trip to arrogance, and perhaps I should have been just a bit more reflective. Did I engage all the students, both males and females, high and low performers, and so on? Did I trust myself and verify as well? This is *reflective self-trust*, a saner and less arrogant position (quadrant 4). There are some aspects of my teaching and leading roles where I knew I wasn't very good. As a principal I was not terribly interested in budgets and I knew my ability to control a budget was suspect, therefore I made sure that I had an assistant who was trained and empowered to do those things where my confidence in myself was at best *insecure trust* (quadrant 3). Finally there were areas of practice in which I had little interest, ability, or involvement, manifesting *disinterested or apathetic trust* (quadrant 1), where engaging would have distracted me from my main concern for students' learning. I suspect we all operate in all four quadrants at the same time depending on the issues and challenges before us , but self-trust resides in quadrants 2 and 4 and self-distrust lingers in quadrants 1 and 3.

Quadrants 2 and 4 reflect a person's confidence or self-efficacy in what they are doing. In quadrant 2 (high trust, low distrust) there is little self-checking, and the potential to become overconfident. In quadrant 4, high trust but high distrust in one's efficacy, emerges the self-monitoring or verifying notion often called reflective practice. Quadrant 1, low trust and low distrust in one's efficacy and worth, and quadrant 3, low trust in others and oneself and high distrust in one's efficacy and others' support, are both breeding grounds for burnout. In the first case, burnout expresses itself in apathy, withdrawal, and indifference, whereas in the second case burnout victims can appear angry, aggressive, and cynical. Dmitri Van Maele and Mieke Van Houtte in their 2015 study on teacher burnout state that the lack of trust 'associates with distinct components of teacher burnout, namely, emotional exhaustion, depersonalization, and a sense of reduced personal accomplishment (see Maslach *et al.*, 2001)' (Van Maele and Van Houtte, 2015: 4). They connect trust and burnout when they 'conclude that those school leaders who are not discerned by their teachers as demonstrating benevolence, reliability, competence, openness, and honesty in their actions and attitudes risk a higher level of emotional exhaustion, and burnout, to occur within their teaching staffs. While teacher–principal relationships were most predictive of emotional exhaustion, collegial trust relationships appeared to matter most for teachers' feelings of depersonalization' (ibid.).

What, then, is self-trust? As a former history teacher, I find history instructive and biography particularly useful to understand the factors that influenced historical figures when they faced issues of monumental importance. Why, for instance, did an inexperienced President, John Kennedy, trust his own judgement and hold back from a direct attack on the missile sites the Russians were constructing in Cuba in 1962, when most of his senior advisors and his military leaders advocated a direct attack? By trusting his own judgement over the advice of more experienced and seasoned professionals he probably averted a potentially catastrophic conflict with the Soviet Union (Case, 2012). Why did Josef Stalin trust his own judgement and blindly ignore all the advice of his advisers and the compelling evidence that the Germans would attack Russia in 1941, and as a result of his stubbornness leave his country woefully unprepared when the attack eventually came (Beevor, 2012)? Why did George III continue to trust policies that eventually led to the Americans breaking away from the British Empire in 1776 when every piece of evidence suggested that these policies were failing (Tuchman, 1984)? The answer, I suspect, is wrapped up in the character of the decision-maker, the context in which they operated, and the degree of mutual trust that existed between these leaders and their closest advisers.

One of my favourite books, *Team of Rivals* by Doris Kearns Goodwin, is a detailed study of how Abraham Lincoln and his cabinet – which included three of his rivals for the presidency in 1860, each of whom considered himself better suited for the highest office than the untested, somewhat ungainly, poorly educated lawyer from Illinois – navigated their way through the innumerable crucial decisions that led to a successful conclusion to the American Civil War. Kearns Goodwin explains that her book is a story about how Lincoln:

> ... possessed an acute understanding of the sources of power inherent in the presidency, an unparalleled ability to keep his governing coalition together, a tough minded appreciation of the need to protect his presidential prerogatives, and a masterful sense of timing. His success in dealing with the strong egos of men in his cabinet suggests that in the hands of a truly great politician the qualities we generally associate with decency and morality-kindness, sensitivity, compassion, honesty, and empathy – can also be impressive political resources.
>
> (Kearns Goodwin, 2006: xvii)

She goes on to explain that in spite of great personal sorrow, innumerable military and political setbacks, and countless 'Black Swans' (Taleb, 2007: xix), he persevered. 'When resentment and contention threatened to destroy his administration, he refused to be provoked by petty grievances, to submit to jealousy, or to brood over perceived slights. Through the appalling pressures he faced day after day, he retained an unflagging faith in his country's cause' (Kearns Goodwin, 2006: 749).

What was the essence of self-trust? At the very heart of Lincoln's entire presidency was:

> ... an indomitable sense of purpose that sustained him through the disintegration of the union, and through the darkest months of the war ... His conviction that [the United States was] one nation, indivisible, 'conceived in Liberty, and dedicated to the proposition that all men are created equal', led to the rebirth of the union free of slavery.
>
> (Kearns Goodwin, 2006: xvii)

As the Civil War evolved Lincoln had come to the conclusion that the war was also about ending slavery as well as restoring the union, but he resisted pressure for quick action, and waited for the right time militarily and politically to issue the emancipation proclamation in 1863, freeing the slaves in the states in rebellion. Similarly, school and district leaders' decision-making must be guided by an 'indomitable sense of purpose' as leaders of learning. As I have written elsewhere, they must be 'passionately, creatively, obsessively and steadfastly committed to deep learning for all students – learning for understanding, learning for life, learning for a knowledge society' (Fink, 2005: xvii).

Lincoln had an 'intuitive sense of when to hold fast, when to wait, and when to lead' (Kearns Goodwin, 2006: 501). John Kennedy waited an excruciatingly long time, in spite of considerable pressure to act decisively, to allow the Russians to contemplate the consequences of their actions in Cuba and find a way to back down. People who trust themselves and their decisions seem to know just the right time to take action and when to withhold judgement.

Like Kennedy, Lincoln surrounded himself with strong, thoughtful people who were not afraid to disagree with him, and to offer alternative approaches to decisions. He, in turn, was sufficiently open-minded to consider their advice. For example, while Lincoln had made the decision to issue an emancipation proclamation because it was politically, militarily, and – perhaps most important – morally right, he listened intently to the various views of his cabinet colleagues, particularly to his Secretary of State, William Seward, and opted to postpone the declaration until after the North had achieved a military victory. As Lincoln later observed 'The wisdom and view of the Secretary of State struck me with very great force. It was an aspect of the case that, in all my thought upon the subject, I have entirely overlooked' (Lincoln, quoted in Kearns Goodwin, 2006: 468). Conversely, disagreeing with Stalin was not just a career-ending move; it was often a life-ending decision. George III surrounded himself with like-minded people from the landed aristocracy and collectively their group-think lost the American colonies.

Lincoln's self-trust depended on his ability to trust and engender trust. When Kearns Goodwin described him as possessing the qualities of 'kindness, sensitivity, compassion, honesty, and empathy' (Kearns Goodwin, 2006: xviii), she described a person whose leadership promoted trust and confidence. This ability was a powerful political tool that united his supporters, won him an election in 1864, and, had he lived, might have rebuilt trusting relationships with the South. Sadly his premature death enabled less trusting and compassionate politicians to reverse his policy of 'With malice towards none; with charity for all' and open the door for a century of division, racism, and distrust between and among the former protagonists.

What then can we learn from Lincoln about self-trust? While not all of his decisions turned out successfully – many failed ignominiously – and although he was quick to accept the blame and take steps to rectify the situation, we can discern his dedication to a clear and transcendent moral purpose, his willingness to encourage divergent opinions among his advisors, his fine sense of timing, and, above all, his ability to trust and engender trust in others while ensuring results. He held his leaders to account and fired more than a few. Lincoln's self-trust, therefore, reflects our theme, trust <u>and</u> verify.

Verify

The greatest challenge for those of us at Lord Byron was to convince our colleagues in other schools that breaking out of traditional forms and structures of education in Ontario provided a superior learning experience for young people. We tried, through many talks, workshops, publications, and tours of our school, to build relational and institutional trust but we had few assessment tools available at the time and little extant research to help us and others to trust our approach. As a result it would only take one anecdote about a misstep by a Lord Byron student or teacher to fuel a full-scale crisis of confidence in our approach. Then again, for many who questioned what we were doing no amount of data or research would have convinced them to alter their opinions. A knowledgeable colleague who later became a principal and provincial leader captured this idea this way:

> We were like Thomas Kuhn's (1962) paradigm pioneers. We didn't have the statistically validated basis for what we were doing; some of us acted based on experience. My feeling after 25 years or so is the precepts we enunciated clearly enough in 1970 to 1974 have been validated in the following 30-odd years.
>
> (Former Lord Byron teacher)

In the intervening years the balance between trust and verification has shifted. For most of my career as a practitioner I was trusted as a professional to do the best job I possibly could for my students, which led me to a great deal of experimentation, and to continuous efforts to get better. As nations and states have become more enamoured with the production model of education, and chastened by some of the negative effects of blind trust, the balance in most countries has now shifted to the verification side of the equation, with a concomitant loss in experimentation, risk taking, and arguably improvement. Education has become a victim of what Michael Powers (1999) has called the 'audit society' – 'institutionalized pressures for audit and inspection systems to produce comfort and reassurance, rather than critique' (Powers, 1999: xvii).

As has been argued previously, that verification as a manifestation of distrust, mistrust or doubt is a natural and often necessary human activity.

McAllister (1997: 104) explains 'First and foremost, in contrast to present enthusiasm among management scholars for exploring the virtues of trust, it is important to recognize that unabated enthusiasm for trust poses risks. ... there are times when distrust is very much appropriate and trusting would be foolhardy'. Accountability and results are important in schools, school systems, and life in general. I would never hire service people to repair a household utility without checking them out, nor would I invest in something before doing very careful homework. As a school principal, I must admit I trusted some teachers more than others and tended to evaluate the performance of some more rigorously than that of others. Similarly, some students required more supervision than others. These decisions didn't require elaborate verification systems but rather intuitive checking based on experience and training.

But how do you know that a school is delivering optimal learning experiences for all students regardless of who the students are? Our matrix is useful here.

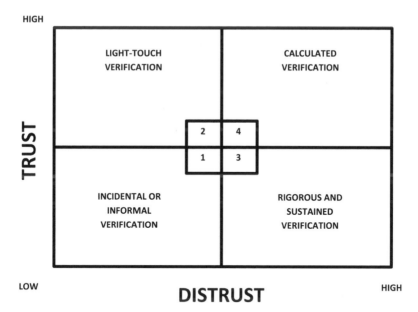

Figure 2.5: Trust, distrust and verification

One-size-fits-all verification systems are very expensive, and often counterproductive. As shown in Figure 2.5, schools in a high trust/low distrust position would require a very *light touch* approach (quadrant 2), assuming there are no egregious indications of deteriorating results (defined in terms of quality, equity, and effectiveness). Ofsted (Office for Standards in Education), the British inspection system, has in recent years adopted such a light-touch approach to more successful schools. While one may disagree (and many do) with how Ofsted assigns schools to lighter or more rigorous inspection protocols, the principle has merit. On the other hand, schools that show negative changes in achievement results, or that experience leadership shifts or parental concerns, might require *calculative verification* (quadrant 4) to determine whether in fact the school has experienced problems and needs support. How this is done is dependent on available data, supervisory resources, or the urgency of the situation. Low trust, high distrust schools exhibit many of the traits of failing schools and require ongoing, *rigorous, sustained verification* (quadrant 3), accompanied by systemic help, support, and encouragement. Both verification and support are important. The tendency in some countries to 'name and shame' schools is not only counterproductive, it is institutional malpractice. Schools of this nature need to be built up, not torn down: they already know they are in difficulties. Fear may move people for the moment but it can't motivate for the long term. Finally, schools that are not directly connected to but impinge upon your system, or schools in other jurisdictions, like free schools, charter schools, or schools that have programmes of interest, might require *informal or incidental verification* (quadrant 1). These are forms of checking to see whether and how they might be affecting your school or system, or whether their programmes fit with what your school or system is doing. General awareness of one's environment and problem seeking is good management practice. Determination of a verification system, therefore, should involve more than a simplistic ranking of schools based on test scores and crude value-added measures: it should take into account the social context of the school, the school's climate, student engagement, and the range of characteristics of successful schools.

While this matrix might be useful way to categorize different levels of checking, it doesn't attend to the big questions about verification and checking. As Michael Powers puts it:

> What we need to decide as individuals, organizations, and societies, is how to combine checking and trusting? What kind of activities should be checked? How much explicit checking is enough? How does checking affect those who are checked and when does the demand for monitoring become pathological? Can the benefits of checking be clearly demonstrated?'
>
> (Powers, 1999: 2)

How we verify in our respective countries, states, and provinces is more than a function of the availability of technical devices such as achievement tests, and rather depends on how trusting we are and what accountability measures we can accept. For example, I'm confident that the very intrusive British inspectoral system would find little traction in most Canadian provinces, especially among educators who would fight like fury against such a paternalistic system. Too much trust leaves policy makers vulnerable politically and professionally, and too much verification strips policy implementers of their autonomy and stifles creativity and innovation. The challenge is to find the 'sweet spot' between trusting and verifying.[3]

Over the past 20 years our societies have gradually turned away from traditional professional models of public service delivery and the presumed inefficiencies of hierarchical bureaucracies, and replaced them with production models and the discipline of the marketplace, with its focus on cost controls, financial transparency, and decentralized management systems. As a result, the idea of audits, with their insistence on a dispassionate statistical accountability that purports to ensure fiscal competency, honesty, and transparency in the business world, has gradually replaced the interpersonal supervisory functions and social science evaluative methods of traditional professional models. The result is concentration on short-term outputs as opposed to long-term outcomes, which tends to perpetuate the short termism that is inherent in the production model. This has resulted in the replacing of local systems of evaluation and improvement with disengaged and arguably low-trust national, state, or provincial measures.

Both trust and verification are keys to school improvement. Teachers and leaders need to feel trusted as professionals, and to trust the policies and practices of their larger institutional settings. They also require indicators to determine the efficacy of their teaching and leading for students and as benchmarks for growth and development. To change, redirect, and sustain educational practices, policy makers need the support and trust of those who carry out their policies in schools and classrooms, as well as ways to determine whether these policies are working on behalf of students. At the same time, taxpayers justifiably insist that governments hold the educational system, its schools, and their personnel accountable for the use of tax dollars. Educators at all levels, both policy makers and policy implementers, therefore, face the twin pressures of balancing trust with verification. In the following seven chapters, we attempt to describe and explain how seven western nations try to find their 'sweet spot'.

Notes

[1] There are no direct sources for this quote attributed to Mead, but the formulation has been widely reported and reproduced. It can be found at www.brainyquote.com/quotes/quotes/m/margaretme100502.html.

[2] For a detailed discussion of cigarette manufacturer Philip Morris and its control of Nabisco, Kraft, and General Foods, and of R.J. Reynolds's control of Nestlé in the production of processed foods, see Moss (2013).

[3] 'Sweet spot' is a sporting reference: in baseball, golf, or racquet sports, the sweet spot is the perfect place on the bat, club, or racquet to hit the ball accurately and with maximum velocity. A Wikipedia definition (accessed 4 October 2014) states: 'The sweet spot is the location at which the object being struck, usually a ball, absorbs the maximum amount of the available forward momentum and rebounds away from the racket, bat, club, etc. with a greater velocity than if struck at any other point on the racket, bat or club'. See http://en.wikipedia.org/wiki/Sweet_spot_%28sports%29.

References

Beevor, A. (2012) *The Second World War.* New York: Little, Brown and Company.

Bryk, T., and Schneider, B. (1996) 'Social Trust: A moral resource for school improvement'. Online. https://ccsr.uchicago.edu/sites/default/files/publications/socialtrust_amoralresourceforschoolimprovement.pdf (accessed 8 August 2015).

Case, R. (2012) *The Years of Lyndon Johnson: The passage of power.* New York: Alfred A. Knopf.

Covey, S.M., Link, G., and Merrill, R. (2012) *Smart Trust: Creating prosperity, energy and joy in a low-trust world.* New York: Free Press.

Fink, D. (1997) 'The Attrition of Change'. Ph.D. diss., Open University.

— (2003) *Good Schools/Real Schools: Why school reform doesn't last.* New York: Teachers College Press.

— (2005) *Leadership for Mortals: Developing and sustaining leaders of learning.* Thousand Oaks, CA: Corwin.

Fletcher, C., Caron, M., and Williams, W. (1985) *Schools on Trial: The trials of democratic comprehensives.* Milton Keynes: Open University Press.

Forsyth, P.B., Barnes, L.L.B., and Adams, C.M. (2006) 'Trust-effectiveness patterns in schools'. *Journal of Educational Administration*, 44 (2), 121–41.

Hargreaves, A., Fullan, M., Wignall, R., Stager, M., and Macmillan, R. (1992) *Secondary School Work Cultures and Educational Change.* Toronto: Ministry of Education.

Kay, J. (1991) 'The economics of mutuality'. *Annals of Public and Cooperative Economics*, 62 (3), 309–18. Online. www.johnkay.com/1991/09/30/the-economics-of-mutuality (accessed, 11 January 2013).

Kearns Goodwin, D. (2006) *Team of Rivals: The political genius of Abraham Lincoln.* New York: Simon & Schuster.

Kuhn, T. (1962) *The Structure of Scientific Revolutions.* Chicago: University of Chicago Press.

Lao Tzu (1905) *The Sayings of Lao-Tzu.* Trans. Giles, L. London: John Murray. Online. www.sacred-texts.com/tao/salt/salt10.htm (accessed 28 September 2014).

Lewicki, R., McAllister, D., and Bies, R. (1998) 'Trust and distrust: New relationships and realities'. *Academy of Management Review*, 23 (3), 438–58.

Maslach, C., Schaufeli, W.B., and Leiter, M.P. (2001) 'Job burnout'. Annual Review of Psychology, 52 (1), 397–422.

McAllister, D.J. (1997) 'The second face of trust: Reflections on the dark side of interpersonal trust in organizations'. *Research on Negotiation in Organizations*, 6, 87–111.

Moss, M. *Salt, Sugar, Fat: How the food giants hooked* us. New York: Random House.

Peshwaria, R. (2013) 'Trust: The currency of leadership'. *Forbes*, 22 September. Online. www.forbes.com/sites/rajeevpeshawaria/2013/09/22/trust-the-currency-of-leadership (accessed 11 January 2014).

Powers, M. (1999) *The Audit Society: Rituals of verification*. Oxford: Oxford University Press.

Rousseau, D., Sitkin, S., Burt, R., and Camerer, C. (1998) 'Not so different after all: A cross-discipline view of trust'. *Academy of Management Review*, 23 (3), 393–404.

Solomon, R., and Flores, F. (2001) *Building Trust: In business, politics, relationships, and life*. Oxford: Oxford University Press.

Taleb, N.N. (2007) *The Black Swan: The impact of the highly improbable*. New York: Random House.

Tuchman, B.W. (1984) *The March of Folly: From Troy to Vietnam*. New York: Ballantine Books.

Van Maele, D., and Van Houtte, M. (2015) 'Trust in school: A pathway to inhibit teacher burnout'. *Journal of Educational Administration*, 53 (1), 93–115.

Van Maele, D., Forsyth, P.B., and Van Houtte, M. (2014) (eds) *Trust and School Life: The role of trust for learning, teaching, leading, and bridging*. Dordrecht: Springer.

Chapter 3

Australia: Halfway to anywhere?

Warren Marks and Norman McCulla

Australia is a nation of contrasts. It is a young country, but also a very old country. One of the oldest continents on earth, Australia is the planet's sixth largest country by landmass after Russia, Canada, China, the USA, and Brazil. It is the world's largest island. Its indigenous people, Aboriginal Australians, have continuously inhabited the land for at least 50,000 years, developing a deep spiritual connection with it, not as one people but as many separate peoples, moving from place to place and teaching their young people the song-lines by which to navigate country and the skills by which to survive. And yet Australia is a young country by European standards. Caught up in European colonization patterns in the seventeenth and eighteenth centuries, it could have quite easily been Dutch, or French, or claimed by a mix of colonizing powers as various maritime explorers passed by.

If you were to enter 'the world by night' into Google, you would no doubt soon find a map of the world showing the key population centres as patches of illumination at night. The USA, the United Kingdom, and much of Europe can be seen to be quite densely populated throughout. Australia on the other hand, for all its landmass, is characterized by isolated dots of light that are soon equated with the seaboard state capital cities. From its settlements in the early 1800s the nation grew not as a single entity but as a clutch of distinct colonies. As settlers, roads, and railroads pushed inland even the width of the railway lines varied between states, necessitating for many years a change of trains at the border. In this context of the emergence of disparate systems, early schooling was the province predominantly of the wealthy, with a strong connection to either the Church of England or the Catholic Church. The advent of mass public education in the 1870s and 1880s saw each of the states claiming responsibility under its constitution for school education. Each has vigorously maintained and defended that responsibility ever since.

New South Wales (NSW), the largest state by population, and Victoria, the second largest, established government school systems in

1880 and 1872 respectively, severing those states' educational ties with the church. The Church of England schools, beyond a small number of prestigious schools that remained independent, threw their lot in with the government in NSW. The quid pro quo was that time would be set aside during the school week for Special Religious Education, wherein clergy or their nominees could lead scripture classes. The practice continues to the present. The Catholic Church, on the other hand, opted for its own system of low-fee schools staffed for the most part by nuns and priests.

The emphasis from the beginning in the public education systems was on the inputs to education. No matter where children attended school, whether it was in the inner-city or in a more remote rural area, the focus was on having a high quality school building, staffed by trained teachers, with equal provision of education resources such as desks, blackboards, and teaching resources. The grand, sandstone school buildings of inner Sydney are a testimony to the optimism of the 1890s and the beginning of the new century, and to the status of public education in the community.

It followed that to assure the quality of these inputs, centralized control and local surveillance were essential. Local surveillance was undertaken by Inspectors of Schools, who assured the quality of the inputs, monitored the learning outputs of students, and promoted teachers onto the relevant promotion lists. The content of the curriculum was prescribed. In New South Wales in 1965, for instance, all Year 4 students learnt the names of all the major rivers in the state and the towns on them. Class sizes were large. Textbooks were the link between the syllabus and the classroom.

For the purposes of this chapter, we can pick up the story after the Second World War, when both class sizes and the numbers of students completing secondary education grew exponentially. The Catholic system found it increasingly difficult to staff and maintain their schools without government support. A watershed moment was reached in 1962 when the Commonwealth government opened the door to what was termed 'state aid' for non-government schools. This was closely followed in 1967 by an announcement from the national Liberal Party that it would provide per-capita payments to students attending non-government schools. Thus it came about that the Commonwealth government, which did not and does not operate a single school, is the prime source of funding (alongside parental fees) for non-government schools in Australia. The state governments were and still are the principal source of funding for government schools.

There are several outcomes from these decisions. First, Australia now has one of the highest proportions of non-government schools in the world, despite the fact that these schools are also funded from the public purse. Around 34 per cent of students now attend non-government schools and pay tuition fees. The proportion of non-government schools is also growing at the expense of government schools. In 2009, 3.48 million students (including part-time students) attended school in 9,529 institutions across Australia. Of these, 2.29 million students (66 per cent of the total) attended 6,802 government schools, and 1.19 million students (34 per cent) attended 2,727 non-government schools. Of the non-government schools, 1,705 were classified as Catholic schools and 1,022 as independent (OECD, 2011).

Two very distinct paradigms characterized Australian school education after the Second World War: one typified by government-sponsored expansion, the other by free-market choice and competition. Schools in Australia up until the Second World War had been fairly well insulated from economic matters. The decades immediately following the war were, of urgent necessity, expansionist ones for Australia. Secondary schooling was made more readily available for all young people. Education was seen as the means of fuelling growth and expansion. Post-war reconstruction and a baby boom precipitated a burgeoning number of secondary schools. Governments were prepared to spend to stimulate and promote growth. A tangible expression of this expansionist mood was the encouragement of schools to make many more local decisions about curriculum (the 'school-based curriculum' movement). Funding for teacher professional development was ramped up accordingly. Progressive education philosophies became more dominant in primary schools, focusing on a better understanding of how children learn and on approaches that enabled student learning. The curriculum changed from being content driven to become more process oriented. The overall management of schools in the government and Catholic systems remained centralized. The local government school, which most students could be expected to attend, was seen as a cornerstone of the local community and community life. It was a high-trust environment for which, in retrospect, many principals and teachers found themselves unprepared. Then, almost dramatically, it all changed.

Moving into the 1980s, Australia (like other western nations) faced a major challenge: the age of splendid isolation was over. Due to the forces of globalization sweeping around the planet, Australia's industries and companies needed to change and become more competitive. Education was no exception. Teachers, it was now said, needed to be more accountable for what it was that students were learning, and more subservient to economic need. Without teachers and schools adopting a more economic lens through which to view their profession, it was said that Australian students would not be competitive on the global market. As a consequence teachers, and particularly government school teachers, were often discredited and sometimes vilified in the public media under a 'declining standards' rhetoric, thus fuelling a drift of students to the independent ('private') school sector as middle-class parents in particular sought 'the best' for their sons and daughters.

In response to pressures for fiscal accountability, the curriculum was again centralized, changing to a more prescriptive, outcomes-based model. Management responsibilities were increasingly devolved to schools within the confines of a regulated and accountability-driven environment oriented on the one hand to competition, parental choice, and free markets and on the other to the surveillance of teachers and their work. Economic policy has increasingly determined education policy. The paradigm that was introduced then extends to this day. Economic rationalism led to a constant restructuring of organizations, including education bureaucracies, to make them more 'dynamic'. Private sector discourse (with terms like 'strategic planning', 'alignment', and 'performance management') was introduced to public sector instrumentalities. At the same time, the prime responsibility for personal welfare shifted from the state to the individual in matters of health, retirement savings, and education. The market rather than the common good became the prime driver and definer of education policy.

One by one since the 1980s, these pieces of the jigsaw that constitutes today's Australian education system have fallen into place, against a backdrop of what appear superficially to be competing centripetal and centrifugal trends. Australian education, always organized at the level of the states as we have seen, has now shown some tendencies to become more centralized at the national level in terms of the setting of standards for curricula and teacher quality. Prior to this development some states and territories had their own standards, but others did not.

After numerous failed attempts at developing a national curriculum (Reid, 2005), Australia now has one through the work of the Australian Curriculum Assessment and Reporting Authority (ACARA). Established in 2009 under a Labor government, ACARA has taken (as might be expected) an understandably conservative approach to the design of the national curriculum, with English, Mathematics, Science, and History at the forefront, with students then moving progressively on to other learning areas (ACARA, 2014). A recent review of the national curriculum has made significant recommendations, not least of which is to reduce the sheer volume of curriculum content. While the idea of a national curriculum appears to have political and popular support, its efficacy has yet to be determined.

Of no small significance is the role that ACARA plays in national assessment. Australia, along with any number of other nations linked together economically in a globalized world, has been seduced into thinking that the quality of its schools, its teachers, and the learning of its students can be measured by standardized tests of literacy and numeracy and ranked on the proliferation of league tables that compare school with school and country with country. In Australia, the use of the high-stakes National Assessment Program – Literacy and Numeracy (NAPLAN) has reached epidemic proportions, though the instrument is strongly criticized for the way in which it both distorts and narrows the curriculum (Dinham and Scott, 2012; Boston, 2009). In 2016, the tests will be based on the Australian curriculum for the first time. As far as the political process is concerned, angst and apoplexy are words that come to mind to describe our political leaders whenever Australia appears to be slipping down the international league tables (as it appears to be doing at present). In addition to this apparent general slippage for Australian students as judged by international measures (PISA, TIMMS, and PIRLS), the underperformance of Aboriginal students relative to the wider school population remains an ongoing issue and a social justice concern in Australian education (OECD, 2013). Teacher quality is often held to be the problem that underlies such slippage, rather than the quality of the educational service provided. The validity of using isolated test results to assess whole schools and indeed entire school systems is seldom questioned in the public domain.

Parents, in choosing a school for their child, are able to access details of every school in Australia via the *My School* website (www.myschool. edu.au). A glance at this website will show the weight that is placed on the outcomes of NAPLAN and in like-for-like comparisons between schools. Also featured is the funding base for each school. A major question with which Australia now grapples is just how self-managing a school should be. The issue of securing an ongoing fair and equitable basis for school funding in Australia remains unresolved as of this writing.

In giving a broad and generalized overview of these trends in Australian education, we would probably conclude that the centripetal and centrifugal tendencies, far from being contradictory, are mutually supportive. Outcomes-based curricula, assessment and basic skills testing, teaching standards and performance management schemes are all mechanisms that provide frameworks for teaching through which the individual work of teachers can be placed under surveillance. While unquestionably they offer a degree of assurance concerning teachers' work and student learning, they have a downside inasmuch as schools cannot compete on an equal basis, due to funding arrangements; we can also be concerned about the extent to which compliance, regulation, and reporting dominate and standardize school practice. It is not so much that such schemes exist that is a problem; rather we must consider questions about who uses them, for what purposes, and to what outcome.

Political philosophers may well argue that these building blocks have been put in place quite deliberately and systematically over time, utilizing windows of political opportunity (Mackinac Center for Public Policy, 2014). The public discourse, preoccupied by concerns about the economy and increasing societal change, has opened up spaces to create the neo-liberal paradigm of choice and market-driven schools. An outcome of this marketization of schools has been the shifting of the social perception of schools from public good to private, individuated service for personal advantage (Campbell *et al.*, 2009; Connell, 2013; Thomson, 2013).

Interestingly, it would appear that teachers' and principals' reactions to and perceptions of these changed policy agendas are a crucial element for governments and educational jurisdictions. Until now, little has been really known about how these agendas are impacting on such educators' senses of professionalism, resilience, creativity, and moral purpose as they go about their daily work. The following analysis of the data arising from the Australian sample in this international study gives some insights into this.

The trust study

The research conducted in Australia utilized two data gathering strategies:

- First, an international online survey (the Trust Connection Questionnaire) formed the substantial basis for this research.
- Second, individual email 'interviews' with a small number of selected principals were informed by the survey responses.

A total of 490 Australian educators responded to the international Trust Connection Questionnaire, of whom 333 (67.95 per cent) were school leaders and 157 (32.05 per cent) teachers. The respondents were predominantly public schools employees (88.08 per cent) and were relatively evenly split between primary and secondary schools, with the majority of respondents being female (see Table 3.1).

Table 3.1 Questionnaire cohort demographic information

	%	
	Leaders	Teachers
School type		
Primary	56.41	44.00
Secondary	41.03	50.67
Special Education	2.56	5.33
School Sector		
State	84.00	92.16
Private	1.50	1.31
Catholic	14.46	6.54
Gender		
Male	39.76	25.83
Female	60.24	74.17

To standardize the research, identical surveys were used internationally in each location studied. To explore the relationship between what should be happening in schools and what was actually happening in schools, the survey sought two responses to each item: respondents were asked to describe both the ideal situation (i.e. what should be happening), and the real situation (i.e. what is happening).

Following the collection and collation of the survey data, interviews were conducted by email with nine selected high-performing principals. Of these nine, six were male and three female; five headed primary and four secondary schools; and three worked in city, four at metropolitan, and two at rural locations. Each of these principals has been promoted by merit selection in the last five years. Five of the nine principals interviewed have recently been promoted to more senior positions, demonstrating the expertise of this particular interview cohort. Each interviewee had been recognized for their leadership capacity by either their state principals association or by a national professional association, and each one had been involved in an international leadership programme. Participation in the interviews was voluntary. Anonymity and confidentiality were guaranteed.

The questionnaire

Relevant statistical techniques were used to analyse the data collected from the 490 respondents and to identify the relationships between the variables. The data was analysed using descriptive and comparative statistics. Correlation, factor analysis, and multivariate analysis were used to analyse the mean scores. The software used for the management, indexing, and searching of the data was the Statistical Package for the Social Sciences (SPSS 22.0 for Windows, 2013).

The interviews

Responses were assembled, sub-clustered, categorized, and organized to permit contrasting, comparing, analysis, and patterning. The analysis of this qualitative data rested on effective data coding (open coding, axial coding, and selective coding) that compressed and ordered data to permit the drawing of coherent conclusions.

Study results: The trust story 'down under'

Declining levels of trust in Australian society

There appears to be a general perception that trust levels in Australian society are declining. When responding to the question 'Do you consider that you operate in a high or low trust society?' the majority of the 'interview principals' (66.6 per cent) indicated that they saw trust in Australia as being in decline. A female secondary principal declared that 'there is declining trust in our society ... with a significant dose of cynicism'. A male primary principal added:

> We live in a society where trust is being challenged at every level. Political events from broken promises ... to the exposure of corruption in politics has left the population disillusioned ... trust in significant institutions has also been damaged – the Catholic Church, the banks and associated financial industries, major supermarket chains, and land developers ... People of certain ethnic and racial backgrounds are openly distrusted.
>
> (Male primary school principal)

Although the views represented here come from the relatively small number of principals interviewed in the study, they may well be representative of the general tenor of public discourse about trust within contemporary Australian society. Support for this perception comes from eminent social researchers who indicate that people in Australia seem less certain today about who to trust and how far to trust (Mackay, 2007; Salt, 2007; McCrindle, 2009).

Institutional trust 'down under'

'Institutional trust refers to the degree to which an organization's various constituencies continue to have confidence in its competence, integrity, and sustainability' (Fink, 2015: 153). In Australia the institutional hierarchy above the school will usually be perceived as having two layers: the first is bureaucratic (i.e. the head/central office) and the second is political (i.e. the Minister for Education). The extent to which teachers and leaders trust either the educational bureaucracy or the educational ministry will demonstrate the level of 'institutional trust'.

In this study, 'institutional trust' is explored through six core educational criteria: equity for students; professional autonomy for teachers; professional respect for teachers; the role of teacher unionism; the level of teacher remuneration; and the assessment of teacher professional competency.

Equity and trust

A significant aspect of the Australian cultural identity is grounded in the concepts of 'mateship', 'equality', and getting 'a fair go' (Mackay, 2007). Australians value these traits and see themselves as *egalitarian*. In education these values manifest themselves in terms of educational *equity*: a fair distribution of educational resources and educational opportunity irrespective of family background, socio-economic status, racial grouping, religious affiliation, or cultural heritage. The most recent national statement of the educational aspirations for all Australian students, *The Melbourne Declaration* (MCEETYA, 2008: 7), requires that 'Australian schooling promote equity and excellence'. This concept of equity lies deep within the Australian psyche.

Against this cultural backdrop it is interesting to note the responses to the research question about whether 'state government policies support quality public education for all, regardless of the family income'. Responses revealed a discrepancy between the *ideal* and the *real* situation. Somewhat surprisingly, around 30 per cent in the survey did not see equal support and opportunity for all as a very important ideal. This may well be an indicator of a growing neo-liberal philosophy that rejects the idea of wasting resources on those unlikely to benefit, and would appear to conflict with the more traditional Australian emphasis on egalitarian values. A majority of leaders (71.1 per cent) and teachers (61.6 per cent), however, did agree that, *ideally,* there should be equitable support and opportunity for all. When commenting on the actual situation in schools, the majority (61.9 per cent of leaders and 71.1 per cent of teachers) disagreed, or at best were uncertain, that equity in resourcing and opportunity existed. It would seem that whilst a majority of leaders and teachers support government policies/practices that espouse equity, these cohorts do not see equity as being delivered in the school setting. There is a basic discrepancy between the ideal and the real that was to be repeated in many of the findings of this research.

This finding would also seem to be validated by the national testing evidence which shows that significant equity-related differences exist between the performance of students from indigenous and non-indigenous groupings, from high and low socio-economic backgrounds, and from remote and city locations (ACARA, 2014; Dinham, 2011).

Professional autonomy and trust

As in many countries around the world, Australia's education system currently espouses a philosophical commitment to having local schools and local principals exercise greater autonomy in relation to decision-making and financial control. The continuum that has *total centralization* at one end and *total localization* at the other has shifted well towards the latter. At present, the notion of local school autonomy is being touted by politicians (both state and federal) as the panacea for all that ails education. The argument supporting this movement is that local principals (and schools) want the greater flexibility in terms of resourcing and staffing that supposedly comes with greater local control.

In the context of this political agenda, respondents were asked to comment on the statement that 'schools need complete autonomy to pursue a school improvement agenda'. The majority of leaders (64.8 per cent) and teachers (70.8 per cent) did not support the ideal that autonomy is needed in order to pursue school improvement. As the political dialogue is continually prefaced (and justified) by the comment that it is teachers and leaders who want this greater autonomy this finding runs contrary to that claim. Indeed this finding suggests that greater autonomy is not necessarily an ideal that Australian teachers and leaders crave at all.

When responding to the real situation in schools, the opposition to greater autonomy being a benefit for school improvement rose to 78.5 per cent for leaders and 84.6 per cent for teachers. There would seem to be little trust in government policies that espouse greater local autonomy as a process that leads to school improvement. Local autonomy would seem to be viewed as a political agenda implemented through a 'top-down' model, and not (as is often claimed by political leaders) as a 'bottom-up' response to calls from the profession.

Professional respect and trust

The litmus test for institutional trust in Australia (and possibly globally) is the level of support that is forthcoming from the employing authority when a teacher/leader comes under external professional criticism (e.g. from the media). There is probably no more sensitive area in the institutional trust relationship. Therefore it is interesting to note the response to the statement 'the school district (system) backs the teachers when their professionalism is questioned by the press and other media'.

In the ideal situation a small majority of leaders (56.5 per cent) and a minority of teachers (45.5 per cent) agreed support should be forthcoming. This is a surprising result. Even in the ideal world, agreement with this basic concept is low. When considering the *real* school-based situation the response was even more negative, with leaders (73.7 per cent) and teachers (81.5 per cent) indicating that there would be little likelihood of support for the teacher/leader from the system. Teachers and leaders appear to have very little trust that they will receive support in these circumstances. This lack of trust would seem likely to have a destabilizing and negative effect on confidence within the teaching profession.

Unionisms and trust

Trade unions have long been a core component of the Australian workforce. Teaching in Australia is a highly unionized profession, with teacher unions maintaining a high profile as strong industrial advocates for teachers' salaries and working conditions. Teacher unions have also been vocal on professional and policy-related matters. Unlike in other countries, Australian teacher unions are *inclusive*, in that teachers and principals belong to the same union. Over the past two decades unions generally have been losing membership and political power, and have been subjected to increasing criticism and scrutiny. Teacher unions are no exception to this trend.

The survey sought feedback on whether 'unions are an agency for school improvement' (Question 4), and whether 'unions protect all teachers' (Question 5). As an *ideal* only a small majority of leaders (53.8 per cent) and a greater proportion of teachers (66.9 per cent) agreed that unions should be an agency for school improvement. When responding to the *real* situation in schools, leaders (77.0 per cent) and teachers (63.0 per cent) either disagreed or were at best uncertain that unions actually promote school improvement.

When responding to the proposition that 'teacher unions protect all teachers regardless of their competence', there appeared to be uncertainty about automatic support for teachers, with the most popular response category being 'uncertain' (leaders 32.9 per cent and teachers 46.9 per cent). There would seem to be a marginal level of trust that unions would support their members. This may indicate a growing view that incompetence should not be defended or protected, or it may simply indicate that unions are not trusted in such situations. Unions in Australia are under pressure to assure workers that they can effectively protect and advocate on their behalf.

Teacher remuneration and trust

Trust in the employing authority to deliver salary justice is very low, as indicated in the responses to the statement that 'the State is prepared to pay for quality teaching' (Question 10). Only 10.0 per cent of leaders and 10.3 per cent of teachers agreed with that statement. Both teachers and leaders exhibited a negative trust relationship with their employers in relation to salary justice.

Professional competency and trust

As in many other counties, standardized testing has in Australia become a major political and media issue. Rightly or wrongly, tests at both a national and international level are viewed as indicators of the efficiency of systems, schools, and teachers. In the ideal world both leaders (88.8 per cent) and teachers (90.8 per cent) strongly agreed that 'teachers' assessment (should) include more than just test scores'. However when asked about the real world, 62.8 per cent of leaders and 60.2 per cent of teachers saying by contrast that teacher assessments are in fact linked predominantly to student test scores.

Conventional wisdom and experience would indicate that assessments of principal effectiveness are also linked primarily to student performance in national standardized testing. The *My School* website (www.myschool.edu.au) includes, along with other data, detailed information about the basic skills test results of every school in Australia. The principal of any so-called 'under-performing school' is placed under pressure to improve results. Teachers and leaders appear to believe that their professional competency is now increasingly being assessed by students' test scores; they simply do not trust institutional and political rhetoric to the contrary.

Summary: institutional trust

The findings from the survey indicate that teachers and leaders have deep concerns with institutional trust. If, as Fink (2015: 155) states, institutional trust is measured by 'the degree to which an organization's various constituencies continue to have confidence in its competence, integrity, and sustainability', it would seem that in Australia the level of trust that teachers and leaders have towards their institutions could be classified as low.

This low institutional trust may have its basis in the Australian culture, which gives preference to mateship over authority, to collectivism over individualism, and to cooperation over competition (Mackay 2007). This brings us to the other side of the trust-coin: relational trust. Are Australian schools faring any better in the relational (as opposed to the institutional) trust domain?

Relational trust 'down under'

Fink (2015: 155) describes relational trust as comprising 'the themes of honesty ... transparency, competence, and respect for others'. Relational trust is the heart and soul of people-centred organizations such as schools. The relational trust that now operates between teachers and principals (as 'workers' and 'the boss') in Australian schools is a complex issue, as the traditional values of mateship, egalitarianism, collectivism, and anti-authoritarianism attempt to co-exist with global movements towards privatization, marketization, individualism, aspirationalism, and competition. It is against this cultural context that we now explore the level of relational trust between teachers and leaders.

Teachers working in a high-trust environment

Both conventional wisdom and research (Hattie, 2009; Leithwood and Jantzi, 2008; Wallace Foundation, 2012) conclude that teachers working in high trust environments will be more professional and that the school will be more effective. This belief was re-enforced in the survey when the vast majority of leaders (96.0 per cent) and teachers (93.1 per cent) strongly agreed that in an ideal world, 'working in a high-trust environment makes a teacher a more effective professional in promoting student learning'. However, when considering a *real-world* setting, the level of agreement decreased to 68.5 per cent for leaders and 61.5 per cent for teachers: hardly an overwhelming vote of confidence. Why would 30 to 40 per cent of respondents not agree that a high-trust environment produces higher teacher professionalism and higher student outcomes? This is one of the inconsistencies in the findings about trust in Australian schools that is worthy of further investigation.

Teacher collaboration, teamwork, and trust

Being cognizant of the literature (e.g. Wahlstrom and Louis, 2008; Stoll, 1998; Harris and Spillane, 2008) that supports teacher collaboration as an effective strategy that produces better outcomes than teachers working in 'splendid isolation', the researchers examined the result of three survey items. The first item asked: 'to what extent is *collaboration* used by teachers?'. Just 11.3 per cent of leaders and 23.9 per cent of teachers believed that supportive time and space for collaboration was actually provided in schools. This finding seems to contradict the professional rhetoric claiming that teacher collaboration is highly valued and widely used. Might the global trends associated with neo-liberalism (i.e. the cult of competitiveness and individualism) be impacting negatively upon teacher collaboration?

The second, associated item explored teamwork. When considering an ideal setting there was strong support (from 71.4 per cent of leaders and 77.7 per cent of teachers) for the concept of teamwork. However when describing the real world, support for the statement that 'teachers in my school work together in teams' dropped dramatically to 38.9 per cent for leaders and 56.9 per cent for teachers. This finding aligns with the previous finding, such that in practice there seems to be less collaboration or teamwork happening in Australian schools than the literature recommends (Harris and Spillane, 2008; Harris, 2009), or that is desired by teachers and leaders.

The third area related to teachers' support for each other. Not surprisingly, when contemplating the ideal-world situation, there was very strong agreement (leaders 90.4 per cent and teachers 98.5 per cent) that teachers' 'support of each other's teaching is crucial to school improvement'. However once again, in evaluating the real world the level of agreement fell dramatically, to 54.4 per cent for leaders and to 63.1 per cent for teachers. It would appear that whilst teachers' support for one another's teaching is highly valued (by both cohorts), the reality is that in practice it happens far less than would be desired.

Trust between teachers and leaders

Relational trust between the leader and the teachers is generally accepted as a core determinant of trust levels within that school. But what should/does that trust look like? Blind trust in leaders (i.e. 'it is best to trust the leadership of those in charge by going along with what they want') would not usually be seen as a strong indicator of relational trust. Accordingly blind trust received support from just 14.4 per cent of leaders and 15.3

per cent of teachers. What, then, are the building blocks of relational trust between teachers and leaders?

There are certain role characteristics and personality traits of leaders (i.e. dimensions of leadership) that are commonly accepted in the research literature as being important in building relational trust (Robinson *et al.* 2008; Louis *et al.*, 2010; Hallinger, 2011; Dinham, 2008; Darling-Hammond, 2011). This current research explored nine such qualities which teachers most desire in their leaders, in order to create high relational trust in their school.

Leaders who are competent

Teachers want their leaders to be competent educators. In the ideal-world situation posited in the survey, a very large majority (95.0 per cent of leaders and 92.3 per cent of teachers) agreed that 'teacher trust of their leader [would be] conditional upon the leader's competency'. In describing the real-world situation in schools, support for this statement fell to 69.4 per cent for leaders and 64.6 per cent for teachers. This almost 30 per cent drop-off would seem to indicate that leaders do not (or cannot) easily deliver on educational competency in schools.

Leaders who show concern for teachers' welfare

When responding to the proposition that leaders need to 'know and show concern for staff members' personal circumstances', there was a dramatic difference between the attitudes of teachers and leaders. In the ideal-world situation 44.6 per cent of teachers strongly agreed that leaders would need to show concern for teachers' welfare. This appeared to be a surprisingly low support level. However the level of support from leaders themselves was even lower, at just 9.6 per cent. The discrepancy between the two cohorts was re-enforced in describing the real-world situation, where 60.1 per cent of leaders disagreed that there was a need to show personal concern for teachers, while 53.9 per cent of teachers strongly agreed that good leaders needed to show such concern. Something that teachers believe to be central to a trusting relationship was not seen as a priority by leaders.

Leaders who are good 'gate-keepers'

Deeply ingrained in teacher folklore and supported by research is the need for a 'good leader' to protect and buffer the staff from the political and bureaucratic demands that teachers believe detract them from their core business of teaching and learning. Accordingly, in describing the ideal world, there was alignment between the cohorts, as 80.1 per cent of leaders and 80.7 per cent of teachers agreed that 'good leaders are good gatekeepers'.

However in describing the real-world situation, just 39.8 per cent of leaders and 52.3 per cent of teachers agreed that leaders do actually provide 'a buffer to protect teachers and children from the negative effects of some government and/or district policies'.

Leaders would appear to have difficulty in simultaneously being good gatekeepers and faithful deliverers of their political masters' agendas. This dilemma would appear to be impacting negatively upon the building of positive, trusting relationships between leaders and teachers.

LEADERS WHO ARE KNOWLEDGEABLE ABOUT PEDAGOGY

Does the leader really know what he/she is talking about in relation to teaching and student learning? In considering the ideal-world setting leaders (77.7 per cent) and teachers (77.0 per cent) agreed that leaders should be 'knowledgeable about effective teaching practices and contemporary learning theories'. In the real-world setting the level of agreement dropped consistently for both cohorts: for leaders to 59.5 per cent, and for teachers to 51.1 per cent, so that over half of the research participants did not see leaders as sufficiently 'knowledgeable'. In an era that promotes the importance of instructional leadership for improved student outcomes (Hattie, 2009; Robinson *et al.*, 2008) this is a major concern. The demands of the leadership role may well take the leader away from teaching/learning and much more towards management (Dinham, 2008) which would appear to be impacting negatively upon relational trust.

LEADERS WHO 'WALK THE TALK'

Teachers want leaders to 'walk the talk'. Leaders can often be seen as being strong on rhetoric but weak on integrity, action, and moral purpose. In the ideal world 90.8 per cent of leaders and 70.7 per cent of teachers agreed that leaders should 'act with integrity: walk the talk'. However this situation changed dramatically when describing the real-world school setting, with just 66.4 per cent of leaders and 42.3 per cent of teachers believing that leaders do actually succeed in this challenge. This finding would seem damaging to relational trust as over 50 per cent of respondents do not believe that their leaders 'act with integrity... (and)... walk the talk'.

LEADERS WHO ADDRESS TEACHER VULNERABILITY

Teachers tend to see themselves as being on the lowest rung of the educational hierarchy. Teachers are the foot soldiers, principals are local lieutenants, the bureaucracy is filled with lieutenant colonels, and the politicians are the major-generals. Teachers naturally see themselves as the most vulnerable in this chain and when times are tough teachers turn to their in-school leader (the principal) for support. In an ideal world, 85.3 per cent of leaders and a much lower 55.4 per cent of teachers agreed, leaders should 'address teachers' feeling of vulnerability'. In the *real-world* situation however only 57.2 per cent of leaders and a very low 31.6 per cent of teachers agreed that leaders do actually address teacher vulnerability. This finding highlights two significant issues: (1) the sizeable gap between leaders and teachers on this important personal welfare issue; and (2) the fact that almost 70 per cent of teachers do not feel supported by their leader in times of vulnerability. This perceived of lack of support must impact negatively upon relational trust.

LEADERS WHO ARE OPEN AND HONEST

Honesty (incorporating *openness*) is a quintessential component in developing a trusting relationship. Every cultural group, religious group, friendship group, and family group knows the indispensable value of honesty in building and sustaining trust. Workplaces are no exception. In describing the ideal world, 92.7 per cent of leaders and 80.0 per cent of teachers agreed that 'trustworthy leaders at all levels say what they mean and mean what they say'. However in describing the real world the agreement levels dropped dramatically, to 63.1 per cent for leaders and 47.7 per cent for teachers. This indicated that less than half of all teachers agree that their leaders are honest ('say what they mean and mean what they say'). This finding would seem to have deep significance for the relational trust between leaders and teachers.

Equally disturbing was teachers' assessment of their leaders' *openness*. In response to the statement that 'district and school leaders admit mistakes openly and promptly', 42.2 per cent of leaders (a low self-ranking in itself) but just 10.0 per cent of teachers agreed that leaders admit mistakes openly. The fact that 90 per cent of teachers believe that school leaders do not openly and promptly admit mistakes must be a significant inhibitor to relational trust and consequently to effective and productive school relationships.

LEADERS WHO SHARE DECISION-MAKING

Schools, like most modern organizations, have moved philosophically into a model that favours more distributed and shared decision-making (Harris and Spillane, 2008; Leithwood and Mascall, 2008). In considering the *ideal world*, this form of decision-making was fairly well supported, with 67.0 per cent of teachers and 76.5 per cent of leaders agreeing that 'school leaders (should) share decision-making with staff members'. In describing the real-life school situation this changed dramatically, with only 53.1 per cent of leaders and a very low 31.5 per cent of teachers agreeing that shared decision-making actually happens. The perception is that real decision-making power still resides with the leader alone. This finding raises significant questions about the true level of shared or distributed leadership and collaborative decision-making in schools.

LEADERS WHO ACT ON POOR PERFORMANCE

Leaders taking direct disciplinary action against poorly performing teachers are often viewed as engaging in a risky behaviour. It is assumed that other teachers will defend and support any colleague who is under performance assessment pressure, and that this may negatively affect teacher–leader relational trust. However, the finding from this research would suggest something quite different. In fact the majority of teachers (61.5 per cent) believed that strong action by leaders on underperforming teachers actually enhances relational trust in the school setting. In a sign of growing professional confidence, teachers are apparently seeking stronger quality-control action. This is good news for school leaders.

Summary: Relational trust

Teachers look for leaders who are competent educators; show concern for the welfare of the staff; are good gatekeepers; display good pedagogical knowledge; walk the talk; address teacher vulnerability; are open and honest; share decision-making; and act on poor performance. In Australia leaders would seem to be showing a mixed capacity to deliver on these qualities. There are encouraging signs with leaders taking action on poor performing teachers.

School effectiveness and school improvement: The big issue

Like most countries, Australia is committed to school effectiveness and school improvement as driving philosophies. These agendas combine to form a highly visible educational and political mantra. What, then, is the impact of trust on school effectiveness and school improvement? This is obviously a question of the deepest significance for educational jurisdictions, governments, unions, teachers, principals, and principals' associations.

On the issue of *school effectiveness*, there was very strong agreement (leaders 98.4 per cent and teachers 90.8 per cent) that in the ideal-world setting 'schools [would] operate most effectively on behalf of children within a culture of trust'. But when describing the real world, the agreement level for both cohorts decreased significantly, to just under 70 per cent (leaders 68.4 per cent and teachers 69.4 per cent). Although it is disturbing that any teachers or leaders (let alone almost one in three) would disagree with the claim that schools actually operate most effectively within a climate of trust,

70 per cent agreement with this maxim is still a very positive affirmation that school effectiveness is seen as being aligned to a culture of trust.

On the issue of *school improvement,* there was a marked difference in responses between the two cohorts. As an ideal, the proposition that 'school improvement depends on the school leader's ability to build trusting relationships with all staff members' was supported by just 49.2 per cent of leaders but by 99.2 per cent of teachers. Teachers felt very strongly that high relational trust had to exist in order to create conditions for school improvement, whilst principals were not so convinced. This finding represented the largest difference of opinion between teachers and leaders on any of the 30 items in the questionnaire. When asked to comment on the real situation in schools most teachers (63.9 per cent of those who responded) continued to see this relational trust issue as having a greater impact on school improvement than did leaders (46.9 per cent).

Educational leadership literature abounds with statements of the need for the principal to build high trust and cultivate positive relationships with staff in order to facilitate school improvement (Hattie, 2009; Robinson *et al.*, 2008; Wahlstrom and Louis, 2008; Hallinger, 2011; Wallace Foundation, 2012). Trust is seen as a prerequisite for building school improvement and as the glue that bonds the staff to the school's vision (for effectiveness and improvement). However this finding would suggest that it may in fact be the case that *teachers* in Australian schools value the effect of high relational trust on school improvement more than *leaders* do. Might teachers, through this value that they place on relational trust, be an untapped (and under-utilized) source for greater school effectiveness and school improvement?

Principals' perspectives: The interviews

Nine purposively selected principals engaged in a deep reflective email discussion with the authors to provide additional insights. The participants were chosen on grounds of their high performance and constituted a representative cohort (see above). Discussion centred on 10 questions. Four questions related to institutional trust and six questions related to relational trust. The questions were informed by the survey responses and were intended to capture aspects of institutional and relational trust from a principal's perspective:

1. Do you consider that you operate in a high or low trust society?
2. Do you consider that you operate in a high or low trust education system?

3. Do you consider that you operate in a high or low trust school?
4. As a professional educator do you feel trusted?
5. As a professional educator, do you have any evidence that you are distrusted?
6. How does being trusted (or distrusted) affect your willingness to change your practice?
7. How does the profession need to regain or sustain trust?
8. What or who in your education system do you trust or distrust?
9. Do you consider the level of trust in your school affects student outcomes?
10. How should your efficiency be verified by your 'supervisor'?

Trust in Australian society

The majority of these interviewed leaders (66.6 per cent) felt that trust was in decline across the nation, citing instances of loss of trust in politicians, the political process, political parties, religious institutions, financial institutions, corporations, unions, and schools. If trust is in decline, what might that mean for teachers and leaders in schools? The unquestioning trust that the community once placed in teachers, schools, and other institutions was not seen to exist in modern Australia.

Principals feeling trusted by the system

Responding to the question 'Do you consider that you operate in a high or low trust education system?', the majority (66.6 per cent) indicated that they saw institutional trust (between systems and schools) as being quite high:

> I feel trusted within the education system. I feel that I have the authority to make most of the decisions I need to make to ensure I am doing the best I can for students ... I feel that when I am able to articulate my visions well and substantiate them with credible purpose and planning, the system supports me in the delivery of the vision.
>
> (Male primary school principal)

The same cohort who indicated that trust in the Australian society was in decline was now indicating that the system trusted them to run their own school. This is a more positive response on the idea of institutional trust than was indicated by the wider 'leaders' cohort in the survey. It may be worth noting however that the survey leader cohort (333) included both principals (192) and deputy principals (141).

Principals feeling trusted within their schools

Principals were almost evenly divided on the question of the extent to which they felt their staff to trust them: 55.6 per cent felt that they had 'high trust' with the staff; 44.4 per cent that they had 'low trust':

> Although I have given staff no reason to distrust me personally, an undercurrent of 'us versus them' and distrust sits just underneath the surface.
>
> (Male primary school principal)

The leadership qualities that teachers identified in the survey as contributing to high trust (effective gatekeeping, knowledge of pedagogy, addressing poor performance, walking the talk, sharing decision-making, and, most importantly, openness and honesty) might be extremely valuable for leaders to consider when looking to develop greater trust.

Principals feeling professionally trusted

Although the survey did not ask leaders if they felt 'trusted', 100 per cent of the interviewed principals reported feeling 'highly trusted' by colleagues, parents, and educational authorities:

> I feel that my school community trust me to ensure their children are learning in a safe and encouraging environment ... I feel my staff trust me to support their teaching and their own professional learning ... I feel students trust me completely ... I feel that the employer trusts me as a principal with educational practice and decisions.
>
> (Male primary school principal)

Principals here in the interviews self-reflect that they felt trusted by various levels of the education community. Teachers and leaders in the survey indicate that a much lower level of trust is the reality.

Principals feeling distrusted

Although 100 per cent had indicated feeling 'trusted', 66.6 per cent also reported feeling *distrusted*. This seems contradictory, but when explored more deeply these feelings of *distrust* were found to relate primarily to groups outside the school:

> Having spoken to colleagues, we are all increasingly facing a barrage of complaints and vilification on social media and comments in a community. They are often personal and attack

decisions made that are made for the benefit of many. The general media often portray issues of poor academic results, sensationalise issues and demonstrate how teachers are not doing the right thing. They then often blame all who are connected with education for social ills.

(Female secondary school principal)

Although trusted within the confines of their school these principals reported a sense of distrust emanating from outside (i.e. from community groups, the media, and even the unions).

Principals' willingness to change practice

The majority of this cohort (88.8 per cent) indicated that high trust towards them was a positive influence giving them confidence to take risks and to change practice:

As an educator, feeling trusted encourages risk-taking and reflective practice in a safe environment. Where educators feel unsafe about admitting areas for development, they will not change current practice.

(Female primary school principal)

It would seem that principals need to feel trusted by teachers before they take the steps to initiate change.

Principals' judgement on regaining/sustaining trust

The interviewed principals identified nine desirable actions to build trust:

- eradicate nepotism in promotion systems
- confront poor teacher performance
- focus primarily on student learning
- focus on evidence-based teaching
- provide evidence-based advice
- articulate a clear professional purpose
- articulate a clear and consistent set of professional values
- confidently confront media-based 'teacher bashing'
- confidently portray teaching as a high-quality profession.

Who do principals trust?

Principals indicated that there were three groups of people who they trusted:

- those whose actions matched their words (which correlates with teachers' trust for leaders who 'walk the talk')

- those with proven confidentiality, ethical behaviour, and moral purpose (which again correlates with teachers' expectation of leaders who can gain teachers' trust)
- principal peer colleagues (as opposed to staff or supervisors).

The latter was the group whom respondents said they trusted most.

Principals and student outcomes

All the principals in the interviewed cohort expressed the belief that high trust has a positive effect on student outcomes:

> The level of trust in a school has a direct impact on professional practice, teachers' abilities to engage in reflective practice and as direct result, impacts upon student's outcomes.
>
> (Female primary school principal)

It is worth recalling that in the survey it was teachers (63.9 per cent agreement), not leaders (46.9 per cent agreement), who more strongly supported the view that high relational trust has a positive influence on learning. The 100 per cent agreement from the interviewed principals that high trust has a positive influence on student outcomes adds weight to the teacher responses as reported in the survey.

Principals' performance assessment

The employer's line supervision and performance assessment was seen by principals as 'a matter of trust'. They felt that such supervision must include qualitative face-to-face discussions in addition to the quantitative use of student outcome data:

> To verify such results the supervisor needs to be in the school to see the school in operation rather than merely relying on websites and newsletters.
>
> (Female secondary school principal)

The interviewed principals were clearly indicating that trust needs to permeate all levels of the education process, including their own performance assessments. The principals believed that what might superficially appear to be a form of 'institutional trust' (i.e. the line supervision of the principal) should in fact be seen as falling within the domain of 'relational trust'.

In general, the principals interviewed indicated that they felt: (1) trusted by the education system, their peers, and most teachers; (2) distrusted by forces outside of the school (e.g. media and politicians); (3) confident to implement change when they were trusted; (4) insistent that performance assessment should be based on relational trust; and (5) convinced that high trust in schools impacts positively to promote high student outcomes.

Summary

Supported by various political forces, the globalization movement of the twentieth and twenty-first centuries have thrust a 'splendidly isolated' Australia into a highly competitive free-market world. This movement has permeated all sectors of society. Unsought by educators, the movement has created a measure of disquiet in the Australian education community. As a result (and as this study would indicate) Australian education appears to be undergoing a crisis of identity.

The once confident and comfortable professionalism of educators seems to be being replaced by a sense of professional uncertainty. Some would argue that under the previous 'splendid isolationism' the profession had become too confident, too comfortable, and too complacent, and that checks and balances needed to be restored. Australian education has certainly been 'modernized' by the movements towards privatization and marketization. There is little doubt that Australian schools have become far more dynamic, corporate, goal-centred, results-driven, and competitive. However it could also be argued, as from the findings in this study, that these changes have come at the price of a decline in the professional confidence of, and public trust in, the teaching profession.

In bringing about these changes, educators have not appreciated politicians (or media celebrities) posing as educational experts in order to continually discredit and devalue the profession. As this study has also shown, this tendency is eroding educators' perception that they are trusted. Though trust is a key component of highly effective schools and of a confident, self-assured teaching profession (Day and Gu, 2010), it would seem that trust within the Australian education system has been a casualty of the changes. Trust has obviously 'slipped down the rankings' along with student outcomes.

In the *institutional domain,* the levels of trust that Australian teachers and leaders have towards their institutions are generally lower than might be expected, and are characterized increasingly by a lack of confidence in, a lack of co-operation with, and sometimes overt cynicism towards components within the hierarchy (e.g. politicians and bureaucrats).

In the *relational domain,* although trust levels are again lower than might be expected, there are some more positive signs, with leaders and teachers (in particular) articulating a commitment towards trust that they perceive as a vital element for improving school effectiveness and student achievement. Much appears to hang on the extent to which principals 'walk the talk' with moral purpose, act with integrity, honesty, and openness, display pedagogical knowledge and leadership, support efficient staff, act on inefficiency, and succeed as gatekeepers who protect and buffer the staff from a somewhat hostile external environment.

Overall the data from the study provides mixed results. Clearly there are principals navigating changing political circumstances in ways that develop trust among their staff and in their local communities. Yet there are also principals who are distrusted by their staff, who distrust the institutions they work for, and who believe that trust in their teachers and relational leadership is not of high importance. These are contradictory messages indeed. They play out against the backdrop of an Australian education landscape characterized on the one hand by centripetal forces, which tend to centralize curriculum, assessment, and teacher standards, and on the other by centrifugal forces, which tend to devolve local school management. These forces operate within a marketplace that remains characterized by parent choice and positioning directed toward individual gain. Add to this the apparent reality that Australia is slipping down the international student performance league tables. The panaceas for this in the political debate focus on the development of human capital: improving the quality of teachers and the teaching of literacy and numeracy. This has becomes a complex mix indeed.

Key questions arise: How might policy frameworks enable trust to be cultivated between principals and their staff? How might principals be identified, supported, and developed so that they lead with moral purpose, developing strong and effective relationships with staff and community? Certainly there is evidence in the study that teachers on the ground are looking for this kind of leadership and are no longer prepared to work with other teachers who are not fully committed to their profession.

Conclusion

In 1947 Sydney artist Norman Lindsay published a novel entitled *Halfway to Anywhere*, a rollicking look at the frustrations and foibles of adolescence and growth to maturity. It seemed to us to be an appropriate metaphor on which to end our interpretation of the data and our reflections on current developments in Australian education.

Our analysis confirms that we are indeed at a tipping point concerning policies for the future of Australian education. Without a clearly defined and consistent moral purpose to schooling at the policy level, one centred on trust rather than surveillance, we could well be 'halfway to anywhere'.

In the absence of such a clearly defined moral purpose, it is left to school principals to attempt to define one, to reflect it in school culture and ethos, and to interpret for their staff the ways in which external culture impacts upon their school and to adapt it accordingly. There is evidence in this study that the approaches adopted by principals are both variable and contextual, and that the policy frameworks in which they operate, as well as the socio-cultural milieux in which they work, may well be inhibiting rather than enabling them in their efforts to develop the trusting relationships in which good schools are known to operate.

Despite these trends there are at the time of writing some encouraging signs emerging. There is a questioning of the ideal role of the Commonwealth in school education. There are moves to create a better architecture of professional standards, ones centred on aspiration and demonstration, at higher levels of professional performance,[1] and an interest in states such as New South Wales in linking teacher salaries directly with these standards. There is some willingness to at least discuss what a world-class curriculum actually might be: perhaps one that truly develops the human capital of all the nation's young people. There are signs that principals in government schools are embracing greater levels of authority in making local decisions (Lazenby, 2015). There are, to be sure, issues still to be resolved in ensuring greater equity in funding to the nation's schools. Yet perhaps there will come a day when the political process might sufficiently trust the teaching profession to self-regulate its professional standards and career path progression. There is a willingness to consult with and among the education community that remains a cornerstone of Australian education. In the short term, however, the litmus test of the state of trust relationships in education, as reported in this chapter, indicates that Australia is very much at a crossroads in education and indeed 'halfway to anywhere'. Wise policy decisions are now called for.

Notes
[1] See the Australian Institute for Teaching and School Leadership; http://aitsl.edu.au/.

References

ACARA (2014) 'Australian curriculum'. Online. www.australiancurriculum.edu.au (accessed 6 December 2014).

Boston, K. (2009) 'Our early start on making children unfit for work'. *The Sunday Times*, 26 April.

Campbell, C., Proctor, H., and Sherington, G. (2009) *School Choice: How parents negotiate the new school market in Australia*. Crow's Nest, NSW: Allen & Unwin.

Connell, R. (2013) 'Why do market "reforms" persistently increase inequality?' *Discourse: Studies in the Cultural Politics of Education*, 34 (2), 279–85.

Darling-Hammond, L. (2011) 'Quality teaching: What is it and how can it be measured?' Online. http://edpolicy.stanford.edu/sites/default/files/events/materials/ldhscopeteacher-effectiveness.pdf (accessed 23 February 2015).

Day, C., and Gu, Q. (2010) *The New Lives of Teachers*. New York: Routledge.

Dinham, S. (2008) *How to Get Your School Moving and Improving: An evidence-based approach*. Melbourne: ACER Press.

— (2011) 'Let's get serious about teacher quality: the need for a new career architecture for Australia's teachers'. Dean's Lecture Series, University of Melbourne, MGSE, 27th September.

Dinham, S., and Scott, C. (2012) 'Our Asian Schooling Infatuation: the problem of PISA envy'. *The Conversation*, September. Online. https://theconversation.edu.au/our-asian-schooling- infatuation-the-problem-of-pisa-envy-9435 (accessed 10 March 2015).

Fink, D. (2015) 'Trusting our schools: The "soft" side of decision making'. In Chitpin, S., and Evers, C. (eds) *Decision Making in Educational Leadership: Principles, policies and practices*. New York: Routledge, 148–62.

Hallinger, P. (2011) 'Leadership for learning: Lessons from 40 years of empirical research'. *Journal of Educational Administration*, 49 (2), pp. 125–42.

Harris, A. (ed.) (2009) *Distributed Leadership: Different Perspectives*. Dordrecht, Netherlands: Springer.

Harris, A., and Spillane, J. (2008) 'Distributed leadership through the looking glass'. *Management in Education*, 22 (1), 31–4.

Hattie, J. (2009) *Visible Learning: A synthesis of over 800 meta-analyses relating to achievement*. London: Routledge.

Lazenby, S. (2015) *Established Principals: Developed or deserted?* Paper presented at the International Confederation of Principals 'Leading Educational Design' conference, Helsinki, 4 August.

Leithwood, K., and Jantzi, D. (2008) 'Linking leadership to student learning: The contributions of leader efficacy'. *Educational Administration Quarterly*, 44 (4), 496–528.

Leithwood, K., and Mascall, B. (2008) 'Collective leadership effects on student achievement'. *Educational Administration Quarterly*, 44 (4), 529–61.

Louis, K.S., Dretzke, B., and Wahlstrom, M. (2010) 'How does leadership affect student achievement? Results from a national US survey'. *School Effectiveness and Improvement,* 21 (3), 315–36.

Mackay, H. (2007) *Advance Australia — Where?* Sydney: Hachette Publications.

Mackinac Centre for Public Policy (2014) 'The Overton window: A model of policy change'. Online. www.mackinac.org/12887 (accessed 12 January 2015).

McCrindle, M. (2009) *The ABC of XYZ: Understanding the global generations*. Sydney: University of New South Wales Press.

MCEETYA (2008) *Melbourne Declaration on Educational Goals for Young Australians*. Canberra: Ministerial Council on Education, Employment, Training and Youth Affairs.

OECD (2011) *OECD Reviews of Evaluation and Assessment in Education: Australia*. Paris: OECD Publishing. Online. www.oecd.org/australia/48519807.pdf (accessed 9 January 2015).

— (2013) *Education policy outlook: Australia. Paris.* OECD Publishing. Online. www.oecd.org/edu/EDUCATION%20POLICY%20OUTLOOK%20 AUSTRALIA_EN.pdf (accessed 8 April 2015).

Reid, A. (2005) *Rethinking National Curriculum Collaboration: Towards an Australian Curriculum.* Canberra: Commonwealth Department of Education, Science and Training.

Robinson, V., Lloyd, C., and Rowe, K. (2008) 'The impact of leadership on student outcomes: An analysis of the differential effects of leadership types'. *Educational Administration Quarterly,* 44 (5), 635–74.

Salt, B. (2007) *The Big Picture: Life, work and relationships in the 21st century.* Prahran, Victoria: Hardie Grant Books.

Stoll, L. (1998) 'School culture'. *School Improvement Network's Bulletin,* 9, Autumn.

Thomson, P. (2013) 'Romancing the market: Narrativising equity in globalising times'. *Discourse: Studies in the Cultural Politics of Education,* 34 (2), 170–84.

Wahlstrom, K., and Louis, K. (2008) 'How teachers experience principal leadership: The roles of professional community, trust, efficacy, and shared responsibility'. *Educational Administration Quarterly*, 44 (4), 458–95.

Wallace Foundation (2012) 'The school principal as leader: Guiding schools to better teaching and learning'. Online. www.wallacefoundation.org/knowledge-center/school-leadership/effective-principal-leadership/Documents/The-School-Principal-as-Leader-Guiding-Schools-to-Better-Teaching-and-Learning.pdf (accessed 29 January 2016).

Chapter 4

Canada: At the tipping point

Dean Fink

There are four grand themes in Canadian history that provide a contextual framework for understanding contemporary Canada and its educational scene. From a European or Asian perspective, Canada is a 'new kid on the block'. In the sixteenth and seventeenth centuries, agents of the government of France founded settlements on the St Lawrence River in what is now the province of Quebec. From these bases, French fur traders, missionaries, and explorers fanned out across North America and mapped much of what is now Canada and large parts of the present United States. Over the following centuries France and Great Britain fought for control over North America until finally in 1763 Britain absorbed France's North American settlements into its empire. In spite of their forced inclusion in the British Empire, the former French colonists retained their language rights, religion, and legal system – rights that persist to the present. Within the following three decades the cessation of the American Revolution precipitated the migration of thousands of citizens of the 13 former British colonies who had supported the losing side into what are now Ontario and New Brunswick. The mass migration of 10,000 Tory refugees, as the American history books describe them (and United Empire Loyalists, as Canadians venerate them), into Upper Canada provided the initial settlements along the St Lawrence River, Lake Ontario, and Lake Erie and their surrounds that later became the province of Ontario. In 1791 the British government, in an act of union, created Upper Canada (Ontario as it is now), an English-speaking and largely Protestant colony, and Lower Canada (now Quebec), a French-speaking Catholic community.

In addition to the Loyalists of central Canada, 33,000 American refugees arrived on the shores of Nova Scotia in 1783, leading to the creation of New Brunswick in 1784. Even though the British had tried to rid the Maritime colonies of the 'French fact' before the American Revolution, through their expulsion of the Acadians in 1755, these resilient former French colonists began drifting back from Louisiana and from their hiding places in the deep woods of New Brunswick after 1783, resettling in what is now New Brunswick.[1] This is today the only Canadian province with an officially bilingual school system; it has one Minister of Education and two

Deputy Ministers of Education, one for each of the French and English non-denominational public school systems. It is a testament to the persistence of the Acadians in British North America over the past 250 years that New Brunswick still celebrates both the French and English languages.

Within this admittedly sketchy description lie the seeds of three of the four grand Canadian themes – the relationship between French Catholics in Canada and the English-speaking remainder of the country; the influence of the north–south geographic pull and the very large part that the United States, intentionally or unintentionally, plays in Canadian affairs; and the historic ties between Canada and Great Britain, exemplified by Canada's continuing connection to the British crown.

Now fast forward 50 years to the early 1860s, and the fourth theme comes into play. Throughout the first half of the nineteenth century, the United States inexorably pushed its frontiers to the Pacific and into Alaska, and many American politicians looked avariciously to the north to the British colonies that now stretched like a ribbon along the American border. Emerging from its Civil War with perhaps the largest, most professional army in the world, America manifested an expansionism that became a very real concern for Canadians. As a result, in 1867, for protection as well as for economic and political reasons, Ontario, Quebec, Nova Scotia, and New Brunswick formed a Canadian Confederation. By 1870, a nascent colony on the west coast of North America, what is now British Columbia, had expressed interest in joining this confederation on the condition that the Canadian government would build a railway to join the west to the east. As a result, from the 1880s until well into the early twentieth century there flourished an age of railroad building in Canada that led in turn to massive multicultural immigration, which continues to the present and has had a significant influence on Canadian educational policy (Mehta and Schwartz, 2011). The advent of railways and immigrants in the nineteenth century resulted in the settlement of the vast open spaces of what are now the prairie provinces of Alberta, Saskatchewan, and Manitoba. Nation building, quite as much as railroad building, required the development of institutions in the east and west, as well as customs and infrastructure to bind together a massive land mass; thus we perceive the fourth theme: Canada, a nation in defiance of geography.[2]

To adapt to its geographical challenges, Canada – like the United States and Australia – adopted a federal system of government, with considerable powers residing in the individual provinces. Education remained firmly in provincial control, as it still does. The provinces, usually led by Quebec, vigorously resist any attempts by federal authorities to encroach on provincial educational responsibilities. Unlike in Australia and the United States, the Canadian federal government has no education department and exerts very little influence over K–12 educational policies. Interestingly, however, education from province to province is much more similar than different. Students, teachers, and school officials experience little difficulty when moving from province to province. This compatibility has resulted from formal and informal agreements built up over the years among the provincial governments on issues as they arise. There is no common core curriculum, and it is doubtful that one will ever be established, considering the provinces' concern for their autonomy, but issues of mutual concern in education, such as curriculum compatibility, have usually been hammered out in a spirit of mutual trust and cooperation.

Both the north–south pressure exerted by the United States and the historic tug of British influences have played a large part in Canadian educational policy and practices over time. Since 90 per cent of Canada's 34 million residents live within a few hours' drive of the American border, they experience the power and pervasiveness of America media and economic imperialism. If the United States sneezes, Canada catches a cold. In education, this tie continues to be a blessing and a curse. Canadian educators benefit from the tremendous research power of American scholarship, and the willingness of American educators 'to try things'. American educational gurus propagating their latest ideas often keynote Canadian educational conferences. Popular American educational publications sit on bookshelves in virtually every Canadian school and district office. Historically, Canadian educators have tended to sit back, weigh the validity of these new ideas and practices, and 'cherry pick' the most appropriate for their schools. The curse of American influence comes often at the policy level, when Canadian politicians borrow ideas, policies, and practices that arguably are better suited to the American context than the Canadian experience.

Throughout the nineteenth century, the British approach to education dominated the Canadian scene. With the exception of Quebec (a recurrent Canadian theme) where the Catholic Church controlled most of the educational system, schools in other parts of Canada began as North American versions of the British public schools, restricted for the most part to educating the children of the more affluent and elite. The American introduction of free, publicly supported and locally controlled education in the nineteenth century gradually made its way into Canada and over time became the dominant model in all the provinces and territories. New Brunswick became the first province in Canada to create a public non-denominational school system with the Schools Act of 1872. Private education, which includes both religious and exclusive private schools, enrolls only 5.6 per cent of Canadian students (Statistics Canada, 2001). In some provinces, such as Ontario, as a result of Canada's constitutional bargain to accommodate Quebec's French Catholics, Catholic schools are considered public because they receive full funding from the province.

While British influence has waned over time, the advent of modern communications has brought vestiges of the contemporary British model to Canadian shores. In recent years, for example, Ontario has successfully replicated aspects of the British literacy initiative, albeit with a significant difference: Ontario abandoned the 'naming and shaming' British approach and provided significant support to schools and districts, and trusted its professionals to work to improve the system (Levin *et al.*, 2008).

Historically this professional model of education has dominated, and to a greater or lesser degree still dominates, Canadian educational policies and practices. Mehta and Schwartz (2011) comment, with specific reference to Ontario's government but also with applicability to other provincial governments, that 'the fact that teaching has historically been a respected profession in Canada, one that continues to draw its candidates from the top third of secondary school graduates, meant that government had a solid basis for believing that trust would pay off' (Mehta and Schwartz, 2011: 159). But as the subsequent discussion will reveal, Canadian education may now be at a tipping point. The production model, as exemplified by the powerful influences of both the United States and Great Britain, has crept in and created an alternative reality with which Canadian educators struggle. Will Canada continue to maintain and improve its historically high-trust professional model, or continue along the slippery slope to a full-scale low-trust production model along the lines of its American neighbour and its British mother country?

The Canadian sample

If one believes international comparisons of nations, Canada in 2016 is a happy, prosperous, trusting (Delhey and Newton, 2005), and trusted nation.[3] Its educational system ranks among the very best on international comparisons and is held up as a model for other nations (Tucker, 2011). While Canadians can be justifiably proud of their educational systems, our research suggests that snapshot measures of educational progress such as PISA hide some deep and troubling tensions within the Canadian educational scene. To assess the Canadian 'condition' we surveyed principals and teachers in three school jurisdictions, one in each of New Brunswick in eastern Canada, Ontario in central Canada, and British Columbia in western Canada, and followed up the survey results with interviews both in person and through social media. While finances, geography, and logistics made a statistically representative sample impossible, we attempted to develop as representative a sample as possible. All three school district are geographically large, socially, economically, and ethnically diverse, and reflect the challenges of their region of Canada. Income differentials are greater in British Columbia and Ontario than in New Brunswick.[4]

Our sample includes 141 principals and assistant principals, and 360 teachers. Both groups are almost equally balanced among the three provinces. The teacher sample is numerically similar between elementary and secondary teachers, whereas the principals group includes 41 per cent secondary principals and assistants and the elementary panel 59 per cent. Females comprise 75 per cent of the teacher sample and 60 per cent of the principals group. Our principal respondents are chronologically older than the teacher respondents; 75 per cent of the principals were born in the 1950s and 1960s whereas over 50 per cent of the teachers who answered our survey were born in the 1970s and 1980s. The principals sample is far more experienced in education, with 55 per cent having over 21 years' experience in education, whereas among our teacher respondents only 28 per cent had spent over 21 years as professional educators.

What did stand out for both groups is how little time they had spent in their present schools. For example, 50 per cent of the teachers had spent less than five years in their present schools. Interestingly, 95 per cent of our teachers had fewer than 5 years' experience working with their present principal. This is partly explained by the fact that 75 per cent of the principals had been in their posts for fewer than five years. These data suggest that such limited mutual exposure of leaders and teachers could well affect the development of trusting relationships. As one very young teacher stated, 'the challenge for me as a new educator is that I have a hard time trusting someone if I haven't had adequate time to do so'. There are two explanations for the relatively limited time principals have been in their schools. First, one-third of all principal and assistant principal appointments are fairly recent. Secondly, school districts in both Ontario and British Columbia routinely rotate principals and assistant principals from school to school as the need arises.[5] Unlike the United Kingdom and many school districts in the United States, leaders are hired to the district, not to a specific school (Fink, 2010). A number of school districts in New Brunswick hire principals on five-year renewable contracts that also contribute to a turnover of school leaders.

The eastern provinces of Canada, including New Brunswick, are the least advantaged and have suffered more than other Canadian provinces from the 2008 economic downturn. Many of their citizens over this period have moved to other parts of Canada and to the United States. As a result New Brunswick has gone from 172,000 students in 1972 to 95,000 currently. The New Brunswick educational jurisdiction in our sample has experienced major structural and policy changes, and is one of a number of newly created school districts. A colleague who has observed his province's school system for many years as a teacher, administrator, and academic explains:

> There have been three different Governments in the past decade and each apparently needs to make its personal mark. Ten years ago the Conservative government enlarged 5 Anglophone districts to 12 and reinstated school boards which were abolished by the previous Liberal Government. ... The current Conservative government has reduced the 12 Districts to four Anglophone, and three French speaking districts. This reorganization was allegedly to save money which is to be reinvested in education. The combining of three or four districts into one meant that procedures had to be re-examined and a consensus reached. Invariably there were conflicts, numerous staff displacements and confused teachers who indicated they didn't know who to call for help in any of the districts. A lot of teachers and support staff were negatively affected and lingering resentment remains.
>
> (Rod Campbell, personal communication)[6]

A principal within New Brunswick' reorganized system echoed this view:

> [O]ur district is under a relatively new amalgamation of four districts. Bigger is not better in our situation. I felt connected, forward thinking and completely trusting of our district leaders prior to amalgamating. This is not the case in such a large district. Perhaps that will change over time but in the last two years of the amalgamation I frequently do not know, let alone trust the people in leadership positions. Providing updated organizational charts doesn't help!
>
> (Female school principal, New Brunswick)

Many of the issues described in New Brunswick also affect education in Ontario. This province has also suffered from the 2008 recession. With the province serving as the manufacturing centre of Canada, Ontario's government has found itself rescuing overextended companies, dealing with closing companies, trying to hold onto businesses that threaten to move to low-tax, low-environmental-regulation states and countries, and building up a worrying debt in the process. Once again educators find themselves facing cutbacks, increased audits, and complaints about the role and power of unions. Many fear a return to the 1990s when neo-liberal influences imported from the United States led to massive cuts in educational spending, dramatic reductions in the number of school jurisdictions, tax credits for parents with students in private schools, removal of principals from the teachers' unions, high-stakes testing including a pass/fail literacy exam for all 15 year olds, as well as a heavy emphasis on teacher accountability and the imposition, in spite of massive professional protests, of most of the trappings of a production model of education.

The return to power in 2003 of a Liberal government, led by a premier who styled himself as the 'education premier' after eight years of turmoil in the education sector, reversed the thrust to the political right through reinvestment in education, including full-day kindergarten, improving pay and working conditions for teachers and principals, and returning in part to the more professional model of education that Ontario educators had historically experienced. At the same time, the government retained provincial control of educational funding and provincial testing and continued to exclude principals from membership in teacher unions. From 2003 to 2010, the government worked closely with various educational organizations, especially unions, to build a climate of trust and mutual support that some have described as 'the best of times', and that led to significant growth and development in measured provincial educational achievement and in international acclaim (Mehta and Schwartz, 2011; Hargreaves and Shirley, 2012). Suddenly, in 2012, for political and economic reasons the government and 'the education premier' passed legislation to freeze all educators' salaries and roll back long-standing benefits such as retirement gratuities and eligible sick days. The general feeling among teachers and principals was one of deep betrayal. In the words of an elementary principal 'I think that the biggest loss was the fact that teachers didn't feel valued any more by the Province.' This led to an extended job action in which teachers adhered to the letter of the collective agreement and refused to go beyond their contracted classroom duties. As his cabinet colleagues have since admitted, the premier handled the wage freeze and accompanying belt tightening ineptly (pers. comm.). When the government sought to win an important seat in a by-election that would have given it a majority in the legislature, teacher unions and other educational professionals worked collaboratively to defeat the government's candidate, who ultimately finished third in a three-party race. Subsequently, the premier resigned and was replaced by a popular former education minister. She recently secured a majority government with considerable help from the education sector. Educators are now wondering how she is going to deal with a massive provincial debt while regaining the trust and support of the education profession that her party once enjoyed. This is the climate in which we conducted our research.

If the educational climates in Ontario and New Brunswick are at least somewhat hopeful, the educational context in British Columbia (BC) is rife with distrust and acrimony. Historically, British Columbia, like Ontario, has followed a professional model of educational policy development. As Michèle Schmidt of Simon Fraser University explains:

> When closely examining the history and legacy of British Columbia education, it becomes evident that teachers and teacher leaders have long enjoyed a measure of professional autonomy. This ... is a result of a strong *British Columbia Teachers' Federation (BCTF)* that advocates social justice and collective action to achieve these aims—aims that are often incongruent with shifting governmental policies that advocate a form of entrepreneurial capitalism. Therefore an ideology of political activism and democratic social justice exists that underscores the teacher's sense of status and professional autonomy. Underscoring this professional identity has been increasing resistance among teachers toward globalization, marketization, and aspects of accountability in defense of a highly guarded professional value system such as teacher autonomy, democracy, and the values of a liberal education.
>
> (Schmidt, 2010: 6–7)

The clash of these two perspectives on educational purposes and policies became toxic after 2002 when a new Liberal government stripped teachers' rights to negotiate class size and class composition from existing contracts. While court case after court case has ruled in the teachers' favour and called for monetary redress, the government has found various legal and procedural ways to avoid fulfilling the courts' mandate. A BC teacher among our survey respondents describes the systemic nature of distrust fostered by the ongoing conflict thus:

> The current government has created a system of distrust among all of the stakeholders by lying, refusing to fund, and forcing

changes that are not in the best interests of the child. Trustees do not trust the government and are forced to do things because of government policy. This trickles down and creates friction between the board and the principals. Principals then create mistrust between themselves and the teachers because they are following 'board policy' which is in fact government policy...

(Teacher, British Columbia)

While the surface issues appear to be monetary in nature, and to be expected given the inherent tension between the government's efforts to hold the line on its budget and the teachers' and other public servants' demands for fair treatment, there is an underlying issue concerning the privatization of the educational system, as the government increasingly supports religious private schools and even some high-priced selective private schools. Ironically one of the attractions of private schools is small class sizes, which is a core issue in the present dispute with public school teachers.

Principals appear to be caught in the middle of this ongoing tug of war. Removed from the teachers union in 1987:

... school leaders inevitably find themselves competing with market driven Government agendas and negotiating their practices to align with special interest groups, the union, the Ministry of Education, parents, and the public and local boards of education, rather than their own vision of what they perceive is needed within their schools.

(Schmidt, 2010: 16)

Principals thus see themselves as marginalized, caught between a government that seems intent on promoting an American-style production model of education and an inflexible teachers' union that is insistent on maintaining autonomy by limiting its cooperation with schools, local districts, and the province (Day and Schmidt, 2007). After a long and bitter strike, British Columbia teachers are back on the job but with still no resolution to the issue of teachers' rights to negotiate working conditions.

In spite of all this controversy and unrest, British Columbian students, along with students from Alberta and Ontario, compare very favorably on international comparisons of student achievement, and on measures of high school and university completion (Conference Board of Canada, 2014). British Columbia appears to be a case in which schools and students seem to thrive in a low-trust environment. One teacher's explanation for this connects to Mehta and Schwartz's (2011) discussion of how Canada's immigration policies actually benefit the nation's educational achievement profile:[7]

> Education begins at birth! Without dedicated support and involvement of parents in the HOME, few students will ever reach their full potential. There is a reason, easily identifiable, as to why many of our foreign students excel, without whom BC would be at best mediocre in international rankings. Parental involvement (not in schools), dedicated teachers and administrators that care about their students and staff are all part of a strong country and economy. Take away one and the whole system falls.
>
> (Teacher, British Columbia)

This raises numerous questions. Are all groups of students and types of schools actually thriving? Is the environment as toxic as it appears? Are there other factors that allow teachers and principals to get on with the job in spite of the provincial scene? To address some of these we were able to survey principals and teachers with the help and support of the school district's administration, before the rotating strikes, lockouts, and full-scale strike began. The strike however, and all of the surrounding drama, have prevented further efforts to pursue details through interviews in British Columbia.

Our findings present something of a good news/bad news story. The good news is that trusting relationships at the school level remain fairly strong. A closer examination of many schools in our study would provide examples of both identification trust and calculative trust. The bad news is that the relationships between policy implementers at the school level and policy makers at both district and provincial levels, and between principals and teacher unions, are looking increasingly like 'security trust' (low trust, high distrust), a condition that threatens the connections that have enabled Canadian education to be held up as a model for other nations and states (Mehta and Schwartz, 2011; Hargreaves and Shirley, 2012; Tucker, 2011). In spite of turbulence in all three provinces, and structural impediments that have made long-term trust building difficult, however, our data suggests that relationships between principals and teachers and among teachers remain fairly strong. The maintenance of these bonds of relational trust among the various players in educational systems will become even more crucial in the years ahead to sustain the Canadian educational system's quality, equity, and efficiency in a political and ideological climate that, judging by events in the United States and England, delivers none of these. We therefore probed the sources of relational trust at the school level.

Relational trust

Almost every teacher agreed that their trust was 'conditional on the leaders' competence'. An experienced elementary teacher described a principal who inspired her best work this way:

> I have worked with several different principals over the years, the best principal that I had worked with me. He was always visible in the building and knew what was going on. He would address issues directly with teachers and ask how he could help if he could see you may need assistance with anything. He was friendly, yet demanding, and you didn't mind going above and beyond to do extra because he always encouraged you and you just wanted to. He was easy to respect and gave respect back, he was thoughtful and would leave you encouraging letters and notes. He knew all of the students and interacted with all of them. He would walk through your classroom on a regular basis just to check in. He would encourage you to grow professionally, and was always inviting teachers to get involved in professional development of some kind.
>
> (Female elementary school teacher)

Equally important was a leader's 'concern for a teacher's personal circumstance'. Another experienced elementary teacher who suffered from chronic headaches and debilitating fatigue contrasted her treatment by two different principals:

> I had been suffering some ongoing health issues but was dealing with them privately and quietly. I had not used the yearly allotment of sick days by any means but certainly had used more than usual. One day I was asked by the new Principal if I 'had a minute'. Thinking he wanted to talk about the recent PD (professional development) session I had provided for the staff I entered his office. Then I found out he wanted to discuss my absences. I listened as he recited the number and asked me why. I honestly answered, but I sensed the tone was changing as paperwork was produced that showed a history of the staff absences for the school from head office. At some point, he turned his back on me and I realized that the discussion was ended. I was confused. The next day in my mailbox was a formal note mentioning the number of absences and suggesting I use the board's psychological services in my own time.

... I figured the previous Principal had probably put me on her radar for absences and I wanted to be proactive in dealing with this rather than reactive. When I knew details of surgery, she was very understanding, and actually quite concerned for my welfare. For the first time in a long time, I felt valued, supported and understood. Now that I am better, I realized how a supportive Principal can help in health recovery.

(Female elementary school teacher)

Over 75 per cent of respondents believed that a trustworthy leader must 'act with integrity': be open and above board and, in a word, transparent. A secondary teacher explains, 'Trust is lost when transparency turns opaque. Changes have been made throughout this year to the courses that I teach, without a single word of collaboration or forewarning. It's been a long year of being the "last to know" regarding changes that affect me greatly.' The same percentage trusted leaders of learning who were 'knowledgeable about effective teaching practices and contemporary learning theories'. A female elementary teacher in Ontario explained:

If a Principal 'protects the good teachers' and supports or provides support to weaker teachers then ultimately the pupils will benefit in the end. I have had great Principals that support in seemingly invisible ways, for example, tell you a story of how they screwed up and how they fixed it so you can use that experience to further your own situation OR I have had a Principal come into my room and micro-managed. Some Principals are very visible in the classroom and others are not and good Principals seem to know what is going on even if they aren't in your room all the time.

(Female elementary school teacher, Ontario)

A secondary teacher pulls these themes together, but refers also to another high-priority theme for teachers: the leader as gatekeeper. Over 70 per cent agreed that 'school leaders must act as gatekeepers' to protect teachers from the negative effects of some district and/or provincial policies:

To me, trust must be earned. A principal must show his/her staff that they understand their role, and are consistent in filling it. They should be knowledgeable when it comes to policy and/or legal matters, and they should show backbone. Weakness and 'flip flopping' with decision making in a principal is like blood in the water. It all boils down to perception ... it is in my opinion that trust is becoming much more difficult as policies change, and staff are expected to keep losing/gaining momentum with the 'flavour of the month' being presented by the politicians to ensure that the votes keep pouring in for them.

(Female secondary school teacher)

Shared decision-making, a phenomenon that has generated an entire genre of educational writing, was mentioned by 68 per cent of respondents. Fifty-five per cent felt a trustworthy leader 'addressed poor teacher practice promptly and effectively'.

In a second set of questions, we asked teachers to determine whether they agreed that schools and districts met their expectations. The greatest differential between the ideal and real situations was found when teachers were asked whether they believed leaders act expeditiously on poor teacher practices. While 55 per cent agreed it was important and should happen in the ideal world, only 28 per cent believed that it actually happened in their real-world setting. Only half of the teachers felt that school leaders acted with integrity, were honest and transparent in their dealings, and interceded as gatekeepers to balance the multiplicity of top-down initiatives that are experienced in the three provinces surveyed. Well-known researcher Douglas Reeves has argued that trustworthy leaders maintain a 'focus' on a few high-leverage initiatives to prevent 'initiative fatigue' among their colleagues (Reeves, 2011: 1). Leaders gain trust by courageously and sometimes cleverly carrying out their gatekeeping role, helping the staff to maintain its focus on students' learning. Over two-thirds of the principal respondents saw themselves as gatekeepers in support of students' learning.

The principals' group, as one would expect, almost unanimously agreed on the importance of building trusting relationships in schools, being knowledgeable about educational issues, showing concern for the personal issues of staff members, and clearly focusing on the welfare of students. Items relating to transparency in communications revealed the greatest discrepancies between teachers and school leaders. For example, while 90 per cent of principals believed they were transparent in their dealings with staff, only 46 per cent of teachers would agree. Similarly 77 per cent of principals said that they shared decision-making with staff, but only 54 per cent of teachers agreed. While over 75 per cent of principals attested that they addressed poor teacher practices 'promptly and effectively', not unexpectedly, only 28 per cent of teachers felt that this happened in their schools. In most situations, issues of just cause and due process require competence issues to be dealt with privately, and staff in general might never find out how the principal dealt with a situation. On a more positive note, however, 86 per cent of school leaders reported that teachers rallied 'behind their school leaders in difficult situations'.

When asked if a leader's trust in teachers should be conditional on teaching performance and results, school leaders were evenly split between agreement and disagreement. Subsequent interviews however suggested that a teacher's perceived competence does affect a school leader's trust, whether this happens consciously or unconsciously. One experienced Ontario principal stated:

> I try to have (professional) relationships with everyone. If you go all the way back to the old stuff we used to do on situational management; tell, sell, participate, delegate. I delegate to some but not to everybody. I participate with some. I tell others what to do, and persuade others what is necessary to do. I think more principals have to understand that situational management still has to occur.
>
> (School principal, Ontario)

When asked the same question a well-respected elementary principal in New Brunswick replied:

> It's a really simple litmus test for me. Is their focus in the best interest of the students? They can make mistakes; they can do things that aren't necessarily the best pedagogical decisions, things that I can work with. But if I believe that they're doing what they believe is the best thing for students and they're putting the students first, I will trust them implicitly and work with them.
>
> (Elementary school principal, New Brunswick)

Another eastern elementary principal pursued a similar theme:

> Relationships build trust, and gut instinct helps; the history that you have with a teacher directly, or through reputation. Relationship, relationship, I can't beat that drum enough, and it does take effort and time. I have been one year at this new school and I think the trust is growing. I don't lie, and I do try to say yes, or as close as possible to support teachers. I listen a lot, and ask them questions. I go to the socials, and don't dance on the tables. With different degrees of relationships come different degrees of trust. Those I trust more, I do not verify their work as often. I ask for less proof of data and evidence of student learning.
>
> (Elementary school principal)

A secondary principal in a new and innovative school declared, 'I see a teacher or a leader valuing all kids, particular those at-risk kids that I love so much, or those reluctant kids, I trust them more than the teacher that doesn't have a lot of time for kids that struggle.' While teachers and principals tend to see their relational worlds somewhat differently, our study indicates that both respondent groups have much in common when dealing with powerful and influential policy makers – provincial governments and teachers' unions.

Institutional trust

Levin (2010) suggests that governments in general have misdirected many of their investments in educational change into policies that focus on altering educational structures that have minimal impact on school improvement, rather than directing their money and attention into what really makes a difference, the work of teachers and principals (Hargreaves and Fullan, 2012; Fullan, 2011; Sahlberg, 2011). Professional educators would corroborate Levin's observation. Over 40 per cent of teachers and 35 per cent of leaders feel that their governments' policies do not 'support quality education for all children'; over 55 per cent of teachers in our study believe that their government does not hold quality teaching as a high priority, and 66 per cent do not believe their systems actively promote their professional capacity. Similarly, over half of the school leaders in our sample indicated that they did not consider that their school systems were committed to quality leadership, 57 per cent did not feel valued by their systems, and, not surprisingly, 72 per cent felt their school systems were not prepared to pay for quality leadership. Both groups seemed to find their professional lives increasingly determined by the latest policy whims of governments and by the reactions and responses to these decisions by teachers' unions.

Unions

Teacher unions have historically played an important part in educational policy and practice in Canada. They have traditionally held the image of themselves as professional organizations similar to the governing bodies of doctors' and engineers' professional practice, charged with upholding the highest standards of professional practice, rather than viewing themselves as akin to a traditional trade union with a limited focus on salary and working conditions. These two images have however always wrestled, sometimes uneasily, within teachers' unions. While calling themselves associations in New Brunswick and federations in both Ontario and British Columbia, they have increasingly become more 'trade-union' oriented in the past 15 years, working in defence of teachers' salaries and working conditions, and arguably becoming much more militant in response to centralized government control and policy making. Governments' periodic negotiations with provincial teachers' unions appear to leave principals, district officials, and even local school boards caught uncomfortably between two powerful contending forces and left to clean up the fallout at the local school and district levels. Some have suggested that by removing principals from unions in British Columbia and Ontario, for example, governments have eliminated a more moderate and reflective element from unions, with the result that unions have adopted a very narrow image of professionalism focused on teacher autonomy and resistance to change. Even in New Brunswick, where principals remain included in unions, there is some unease. As a New Brunswick principal explained, 'Once a teacher put in a grievance, there is no guarantee that I would get representation; one official would represent both of us with a bias in favour of the teacher'.

We asked both principals and teachers whether they felt unions should be an 'agency for school improvement in school systems and schools'. This was our way of finding out whether educators saw unions as professional organizations concerned with professional image or more narrowly as trade unions. Both principals and teachers were quite divided as to the role that unions should play in school improvement, although 70 per cent of teachers saw unions as agencies for school improvement, and therefore professional in orientation, compared to only 37 per cent of the principals. A very experienced elementary principal didn't see 'improvement' as part of the union's mandate at all:

> I think they negatively impact education. They promote mediocrity! It's the lowest common denominator. Trade unions by law bargain for salary and working conditions. They don't care about kids. They're not supposed to care about kids. So all their decisions are based around what's best for the employees' work environment which is at times contrary to what's best for kids. But that's their job. I can't blame them for it.
>
> (Elementary school principal)

Almost 60 per cent of both the principals and teachers agreed that unions should protect all teachers, regardless of competence, and over 75 per cent of principals agreed that unions were in fact supporting all teachers regardless of competence compared to 65 per cent of teachers. This probably accounts for the previously described discrepancy between principals' and teachers' perceptions of school leaders' attentiveness to teacher incompetence.

A young secondary teacher declared:

> ... [the union] supports weak and incompetent teachers and threatens and challenges any administrators who treat their individual staff members according to their skill level and dedication. The union erroneously supports a system where all are expected to work to the lowest common denominator and persecutes any leader who challenges that thinking.
>
> (Secondary school teacher)

Disaggregated data on unions revealed that in New Brunswick, where principals remain in the teachers' union, 37 per cent of principals had a positive perception of unions and 36 per cent negative, with the remainder unsure, whereas in both Ontario and British Columbia – where principals are outside of the union – 82 per cent and 80 per cent respectively held decidedly low trust, high distrust views of their provinces' unions' purposes and practices. It would appear that trusting relationships may exist within schools among school leaders and teachers, but there has developed a very 'calculative' and even security-based trust relationship between principals and teachers' unions at district and provincial levels. An experienced elementary principal described how he dealt with a militant union representative:

> We had a very young union rep who was new to our school. She came to me insisting that we adhere to the letter of the collective agreement. I said, 'you and I can work really well together but we're both bound by the collective agreement and I promise you if we go to the letter of that agreement it's going to hurt you and your colleagues more than it hurts me because I have more teachers who are late for their duty, who want to leave the building on their prep periods and do those kinds of things. This staff works professionally and I trust them so if a teacher says "Sam can I go get a coffee on my prep?", "Of course you can", because I know you stay three hours after school closing coaching teams. I'm not going to nickel and dime your time.' She came in hardnosed and she held a union meeting with staff, the staff revolted against her to the point where she had to step down. They said, 'they (the principal and vice principal) did these things for us, we felt trusted'.
>
> (Elementary school principal)

It is at the local level where people can engage face to face, and trust can be built and maintained.

Our survey results tend to reflect teacher and principals' concerns over 'one size fits all' government and union policies. Teachers and principals who are not directly involved at the highest levels usually learn to trust external institutions through intermediary agencies and agents in the same way as most people learn to trust or distrust governments, corporations and public institutions through their engagements with the media, occupational organizations or just word of mouth. Since most 'big' issues are now resolved at the highest levels, educators at local levels really feel they are at the mercy of unknown and somewhat unknowable forces.

The audit society

Some teachers and principals in our research felt actively distrusted because of the increased use of what they considered unnecessary resource audits at the provincial and district levels, media criticism from politicians looking for political advantage by 'teacher bashing', and a naïve public focus on test scores and simplistic and decontextualized measures of educational excellence. As a teacher explained, 'when the system fails it is never the government's fault that introduces it, but rather the teachers that failed to implement it with little or no professional development'. A recurrent theme in our research from teachers in particular is that governmental and district officials who have never worked in a school or are long removed from their school experience constantly judge their work even though they have limited and often erroneous understandings of the challenges of contemporary schooling. As a result, teachers and other district employees instinctively adopt a low-trust, high-distrust, security-based initial stance against even well thought out and beneficial policies originating externally to the school (Starr, 2014). For example the district attendance management policy in Ontario, which we previously saw a teacher describing as something that her principal had used coercively against her, was actually well intended and financed. A principal who took the time to carefully understand and interpret the policy to his staff explains it this way:

> One of the biggest issues right now in our District is the attendance management policy. I see it from a different perspective and again I've shared the rationale behind it with staff. Once they understand that, it's been fine, but I think staff originally saw it as a punitive and monitoring kind of system. I guess trust for me is a very personal, human characteristic and a system or organization can't have those human qualities. The District instituted the attendance management system because some staff habitually called in sick when they weren't sick. Also we have a number of employees in

our district that have been very sick with cancer and other very serious illnesses for extended periods of time. Depression is huge, anxiety is huge; it's probably the fastest growing disability. I'd say at least 80 percent of the situations I have had to deal with have been mental health. So now the District has supported the attendance management system by purchasing the services of a company that gives all sorts of support to staff members. They don't get penalized. In the past you got 20 days sick days and then you were docked pay; now you get 11 sick days and everything after that up to 200 days is at 97 percent pay. Not a bad deal, but grossly misunderstood and misinterpreted.

(School principal, Ontario)

A number of principals complained about their district's external and internal financial auditing processes, which were designed to ensure that school personnel used taxpayers' money appropriately. Many principals objected to accountants making decisions about what schools needed and how they should operate. At the same time, some principals who took the time to build relationships and colonize the process viewed the audits as helpful to themselves and their school. A secondary principal explained:

I wasn't aware, as a vice principal, how much time I was going to have to spend learning finance. But from an audit point of view right now, schools do not have a legitimate way to count money, to protect money, and therefore across the province schools lose money. I get what they're saying and I get the frustration from principals because audits aren't supposed to be fair. I mean they're supposed to be honest and correct. The issue is the management of the school may not have as much direct daily work in education and so principals must learn to segment parts of their brain. Trust means for me as principal, that I have to trust that the managers at the district office and the facilities people all have the best interest of kids even though the guy who's doing the building renovations wouldn't know the name of a single child. The Purchasing Department is there to be my wise friend and sometimes your wise friend says look you dumb ass you shouldn't have spent money on that. That's a healthy friendship. I think that there are some principals who do not understand that it's their responsibility to understand the thinking of the various people with whom they work and work with them.

(Secondary school principal)

What principals do object to is what one principal called 'stupid audits' from people with no knowledge and understanding of how schools function. An elementary principal told a story of how she was criticized in writing by an external accountant from a large international accounting firm because her secretary left a small amount of money unattended on her desk while she dealt with a child who was bleeding profusely.

Our research suggests that principals and teachers are not inherently opposed to increasing calls for accountability. When asked if the public deserved independent information on the successes and failures of school, only 18 per cent of the principals and 20 per cent of teachers disagreed, although 37 per cent of teachers were unsure. Principals in all regions, though, complained about the intensity of requests from 'on high' for more and more information, and tended to distrust the process more than the motives. Many felt that their time was being eroded by a 'paper blizzard' that tied them to their desks filling in forms rather than engaging in meaningful accountability that opens doors to school improvement. Peter, who has been a principal for 21 years, summarizes the accountability pressures this way:

> Over the past 15 years our work has become very pragmatic and directly linked to accomplishing things on paper. I don't have a problem with doing certain types of paper, but the paper has to mean something for my kids and our school and community. As long as they (the district office) get the paper they're happy. It should be much more than that. In the past a visit from senior administration meant deep discussions, shared plans, and you could sense the ownership from both parties. Senior leaders have so much to do complying with provincial demands for 'paper' that they're collecting or collating that they don't have the time for school visits and dialogue. So we'll schedule our year end visit and my superintendent will come in, I get an hour and half, and it is all product checklist as opposed to process and conversation. We also have different departments sending out surveys and information requests but no one's making connections between them. This is the biggest thing that pulls me away from visiting classrooms, from spending more time with kids and teachers.
>
> (School principal)

While principals and teachers appreciate the need for public information, they are wary of the overuse and misuse of standardized tests. An Ontario principal complained that 'all my superintendent is interested in are my school's scores on EQAO [a provincial testing system].[8] He asks about nothing else. If for some reason like an influx of special education students my scores are down I am told "get them up", if they are at or above the board's average he wants them higher. Absolutely nothing else matters.' The principal added that this narrow focus on literacy and numeracy in EQAO has tended to downgrade the importance of other subject areas in the curriculum. Having begun as a useful and trusted curriculum and programming strategy, EQAO has morphed into a school rating device, and educators see teacher and principal rankings like those in the US on the horizon.

In spite of these irritants, the principals and teachers in our sample, in the words of one New Brunswick principal, 'love the profession and try to live it'. The interview data is infused with this sense of optimism in the face of adversity and a dedication to the wellbeing of children. This 'indomitable sense of purpose' and belief that teaching and leading were indeed public services, not commodities to be bought and sold, still motivates and energizes the profession in Canada.

Self-trust

While relational and institutional forms of trust have a profound bearing on teachers' and leaders' efficacy, it is self-trust, the capacity of teachers and leaders to trust their own judgements, abilities, and professionalism, that makes a difference for students once the doors of classrooms are closed. In spite of new technology and alternative staffing patterns, teaching still remains a solitary, very private activity in most places. Our survey data identifies a serious erosion of teachers' trust in their own professionalism in all three regions of Canada surveyed, and a profound distrust of policy makers at the district and provincial levels. The following comments added spontaneously to our survey speak to a crisis of self-trust among Canadian teachers.

- 'Learning can optimally take place within an environment where people feel "safe". We don't feel safe.'
- 'I love my job and the students I work with but I am incredibly discouraged. I am glad my career is winding down. It is a very difficult climate to enter as a new teacher and a testimonial to the dedication, commitment and character of those in the profession who work tirelessly to support their students. I believe that the Ministry and boards have little trust in teachers.'
- 'At the school, the board and Ministry levels, I believe that only teachers care about students and education. No one seems to have a clue what is actually going on in classrooms and with students despite all their fancy talk of being '"educators".'

- 'There is too much rhetoric and not enough honesty.'
- 'The employees on the ground, teachers, are rarely given a voice. If trust is important then grand goals need to coincide with real action. There seems to be too much game playing, politics so to speak. Walking the talk matters.'
- 'The government leaders of the department of education look down on teachers as less than the professionals; they are constantly changing the system, leaving the teachers to determine how to make the new system work and pick up the pieces.'
- 'Trust in leaders in the school level is more common. Trust in leaders at the district level is minimal.'

While it may be argued that only dissidents add comments to surveys, the negativity of virtually every teacher's comment speaks to a worrying dissonance within the Canadian teaching profession. While it would appear that the levels of distrust grow as one moves from the east coast to the west coast in Canada, from the dislocation caused by reorganization in New Brunswick to the insecurity about what comes next in Ontario to the fallout of a bitter teachers' strike in British Columbia, our evidence suggests that teachers in all three regions feel left out of decision-making when it comes to policies that affect their lives. Since these policies are usually worked out by centralized governments and centralized unions, teachers and leaders reported a significant communications gap between and among policy makers and policy implementers at all levels of the system.

School-level leaders however seemed somewhat more confident in and more trusting about the future. Those who seemed to trust themselves and their abilities had a clear focus on an educational mission that influenced all their decisions and actions. An elementary principal described how she and her staff came through a teachers' job action unscathed:

> I think leading them through a difficult time in the Province last year that I've come through with my staff trusting that I'm making decisions that are based on kids and that I care about them and their professional growth and development and also who they are as people and understanding their needs as educators and professionals particularly through a challenging time.
>
> (Female elementary school principal)

The leaders with self-trust were problem seekers who anticipated events and took steps to deal with issues before they became serious problems. Another principal who had experienced teacher job actions in the past as an assistant principal explained how he dealt with the problem:

> It was clear that a job action was coming so I did some preemptive things. I had meetings with staff right at the very beginning and I said we are going to be going through some difficult times together I want us to focus on how we're going to be when we get through these difficult times, because we will.
>
> (Male principal)

Rosabeth Moss Kanter in her 2004 book *Confidence* suggests that the key to staying grounded in the midst of adversity is to work hard, gather support, and focus on those things that you can control (pp. 357–67). A teaching principal in New Brunswick explained:

> I definitely feel trusted as a professional. I am in a small school. I am thankful to work with a very dedicated, professional staff. Our staff is also very small so we know each other well and are able to make time for discussion with both teaching and non-teaching staff when there are decisions to be made. As with any school in the year 2015, there is always a need to be open-minded to 'change'. I believe the fact that we have built trust with each other facilitates trusting and being open to change which certainly has positive impact on student achievement. I also have a very strong community of parents.
>
> (Principal/teacher, New Brunswick)

A principal in a secondary school felt her personal integrity was an important ingredient in her confidence as a leader.

> I think I've gained trust because I've never asked people to do something I'm not prepared to do myself and so they'll see me literally in the trenches doing things that. The secretaries in particular have said I've never worked for a principal that's willing to do those types of things. I say well the job has to be done so we'll step up.
>
> (Female secondary school principal)

Her personal self-trust enabled her to win staff support through her transparency around decisions. 'I don't play games with decisions,' she said. 'I'm very transparent in my processes and share them with the entire school and the Board and the Superintendent.'

Like this principal, experienced teachers and principals in our New Brunswick sample who have lived through good times and bad times in their schools and districts seem to look to the future with guarded confidence that principals and teachers will work their way through reorganizational difficulties as they always have. Ontario principals and teachers tend to be more reflective. They have a 'wait and see' attitude. They have high trust in their own competence and ability to respond to change because they have been doing it for 20 years, but they are also somewhat wary, low trust, after having put so much trust in 'the education premier' who many believe subsequently betrayed them. Our British Columbia data suggests that insecurity, low trust, and high distrust characterizes the prevailing mood among principals and teachers in that province. There appears to be pervasive low trust that the future will get much better, and high distrust in the provincial government and its ideology and policies. The strength of the Canadian school system remains, however, as it always has, in the highly qualified and for the most part capable professional staff, and in the ability of local districts to mitigate the excesses of big governments and big unions.

Conclusion

It is difficult to assess the connection between trust levels and the Canadian educational system in the same way one might describe the British educational system or even the American system, where states are increasingly beholden to the federal government, because education in Canada is divided among 13 quite autonomous educational jurisdictions. For example, one might conclude from raw data that Canada has significantly less income disparity than comparable nations, and that its public is therefore more trusting than those in the United States or the United Kingdom (Wilkinson and Pickett, 2009), yet the levels of inequality in both Ontario and British Columbia are comparable to the US and UK. To extrapolate therefore and say that Canada is more of a high trust country than either the US or UK is only partly true. It is for this reason that that we can only draw our Canadian conclusions with the broadest of brush strokes and recognize that one or more of the 13 jurisdictions might be an exception.

The most obvious trend we find is the tension within Canadian education between the perspectives of the professional and production models on the purposes, practices, and potential of education. This contest has resulted in an increased centralization of educational policies and procedures as provincial governments attempt, to a greater or lesser degree, to make the educational sector more measurably productive, cost-effective, and accountable. These efforts have come at a cost to teachers and principals' autonomy, workload, and sense of professionalism. In response teacher unions have centralized their efforts, becoming much more politically driven and arguably more militant and aggressive in defining teachers' autonomy. Clearly, teachers and principals vacillate between calculative and security-based trust in dealing with these two powerful forces – big government and big unions. Their interactions often leave principals and district officials and school boards to work out compromises at the local level, where face-to-face dealings have a better chance of building bonds of trust. But even here accountability pressures, assertive parents, cost cutting, changing demographics, and other local issues appear to strain relationships between and among educators at the school and district levels. Policies that potentially benefit students, like inclusion in New Brunswick, and procedures that can protect principals, such as financial audits and attendance procedures in Ontario that actually support teachers, are often misinterpreted and misrepresented. Our interviews revealed numerous situations where people of goodwill who made the effort to understand the issues and the views of 'the other' and build bonds of trust were able to ameliorate potentially divisive policies and practices within large school districts.

As one of our New Brunswick respondents exclaimed, 'big is not better'. The move toward large school districts with extensive bureaucratic structures creates barriers to identification trust and leads teachers, principals, and district officials to operate from a low trust, high distrust stance. The anonymity of district people burdened by accountability demands and the facelessness of district officials charged with human resources, purchasing, maintenance, and finance make trust a property that is present only sometimes. Interestingly, when asked on our survey whether schools should control these kinds of issues, principals and teachers responded overwhelmingly in the negative. District officials need to get out of their offices and spend time in schools to understand the reality of why schools exist. Similarly, school people need to understand the pressures and challenges that district officials confront as intermediaries between increasingly activist provincial education departments and unions on the one hand and schools on the other. Canada is at a tipping point. Will it buy into the American and British production models, or stay with its historical and largely successful professional model of educating its young? Can provincial governments respect the professionalism of their teachers and principals while responding sensibly to demands for accountability, financial restraint, and easily understood 'results'? Will unions recognize government's needs for financial discipline in a struggling economy and reconnect to their professional roots, or remain confrontational and militant? There is a saying, apocryphally of ancient Chinese origin: 'may you live in interesting times'. For Canadians involved or interested in education, the next few years will certainly be 'interesting times'.

Notes

[1] Acadians are the descendants of French colonists who settled large sections of the present-day Maritime provinces as well as the US state of Maine. Between 1755 and 1764, the British government with the support of New England colonists sent 11,500 Acadians to what is now the state of Louisiana. The term 'Cajun' is derived from 'Acadian'. Many returned in time to their former homeland but were specifically denied claims to previous land holdings.

[2] It has been argued passionately that there is a fifth major theme, namely Canada's relationship with its aboriginal people. For an explication of this theme see Saul (2014). Since the education of aboriginal people is a trust story like no other and deserving of a chapter unto itself, I have chosen to direct you to Saul's work rather than delve into it in this text.

[3] Canada rates among the most highly trusted countries in the world. On the 2010 Corruption Perceptions Index, Canada scored 8.9, whereas the United Kingdom scored 7.8 and the US 7.1 (Transparency International, 2010).

[4] The three provinces' respective Gini coefficients (a measure of income inequality) are 0.397 for New Brunswick, 04.34 for Ontario, and 04.36 for British Columbia. British Columbia and Ontario are the most inequitable provinces in Canada and their Gini scores are comparable to those of more inequitable societies like Hong Kong and the United States (Tencer, 2011).

[5] See my extensive discussion of succession policies and particularly the benefits and detriments of hiring to a school or a district in Fink (2010).

[6] I'm grateful to my longtime friend and colleague Rod Campbell for his ongoing advice on educational policy and practices in his beloved New Brunswick.

[7] Canada is among the world's leaders in terms of its ability to integrate newcomers into the mainstream. OECD's report on the equity in learning outcomes as measured by the 2009 PISA exercise states, 'In Canada, where almost 25% of students have an immigrant background, these students perform as well as students without an immigrant background' (OECD, 2010: 71).

[8] Education Quality and Accountability Office (EQAO) is a testing system that is generally well accepted in Ontario because it is directly connected to the provincial curriculum. It is, however, limited to literacy and numeracy at four grade levels. The problems are not necessarily with the test, but the misuse to which it is put.

References

Conference Board of Canada (2014) 'Education: Provincial rankings: How Canada performs'. Online. http://conferenceboard.ca/hcp/provincial/education.aspx, (accessed 5 July 2014).

Day, C., and Schmidt, M. (2007) 'Sustaining resilience'. In B. Davis (ed.), *Developing Sustainable Leadership*. London: Paul Chapman/Sage, 100–32.

Delhey, J., and Newton, K. (2005) 'Predicting cross-national levels of social trust: Global pattern or Nordic exceptionalism?' *European Sociological Review*, 21 (4), 311–27.

Fink, D. (2010) *The Succession Challenge: Building and sustaining leadership capacity though succession management*. London: Sage.

Fullan, M. (2011) 'Choosing the wrong drivers for whole system reform'. Centre for Strategic Education Seminar Series 204. Melbourne, Australia: Centre for Strategic Education.

Hargreaves, A., and Fullan, M. (2012) *Professional Capital: Transforming teaching in every school*. New York: Teachers College Press.

Hargreaves, A., and Shirley, D. (2012) *The Global Fourth Way: The quest for educational excellence*. Thousand Oaks, CA: Corwin.

Levin, B. (2010) 'Governments and education reform: Some lessons from the last 50 years', *Journal of Education Policy*, 25 (6), 739–47.

Levin, B., Glaze, A., and Fullan, M. (2008) 'Results without rancor or ranking: Ontario's success story'. *Phi Delta Kappan*, 90 (4), 273–80.

Mehta, J., and Schwartz, R.B. (2011) 'Canada: Looks a lot like us but gets much better results'. In Tucker, M.S. (ed.) *Surpassing Shanghai: An agenda for American education built on the world's leading systems*. Cambridge, MA: Harvard University Press.

Moss Kanter, R. (2004) *Confidence: How winning streaks begin and end*. New York: Crown Business.

OECD (2010) *PISA 2009 Results: Overcoming social background*. Vol. 2 of *PISA 2009 Results*. 6 vols. 2010. Paris: OECD Publishing. Online. www.oecd.org/pisa/pisaproducts/48852584.pdf (accessed 20 July 2014).

Reeves, D. (2011) *Finding Your Leadership Focus: What matters most for student results*. New York: Teachers College Press.

Sahlberg, P. (2011) *Finnish Lessons: What can the world learn from educational change in Finland?* New York: Teachers College Press.

Saul, J.R. (2014) *The Comeback: How Aboriginals are reclaiming power and influence*. Toronto: Viking.

Schmidt, M. (2010) 'The new facts of life: Leading the British Columbia school system into the context of globalization, marketization, and accountability'. In Anderson, K. (ed.) *The Leadership Compendium: Emerging scholars of Canadian educational leadership*. Fredericton, NB: The Atlantic Centre for Educational Administration and Leadership (ACEAL), 10–32.

Starr, K. (2014) 'Principals' perceptions about resistance to implementation'. In Chitpin, S. and Evers, C. (eds) *Decision-making in Educational Leadership: Principles, policies and practices*. New York: Routledge, 127–47.

Statistics Canada (2001) 'Trends in the use of private education'. *The Daily*, 4 July. Online. www.statcan.gc.ca/daily-quotidien/010704/dq010704b-eng.htm (accessed 4 April 2014).

Tencer, D. (2011) 'Canada Income Inequality: Which provinces have the widest income gap?' *Huffington Post Canada*, 5 December. www.huffingtonpost.ca/2011/12/05/canada-income-inequality-by-province_n_1129729.html (accessed 31 January 2016).

Transparency International (2010) 'Corruption Perceptions Index: 2010 results'. Online. www.transparency.org/cpi2010/results (accessed 31 January 2016).

Tucker, M. (ed.) (2011) *Surpassing Shanghai: An agenda for American education built on the world's leading systems*. Cambridge: Harvard University Press.

Wilkinson, R., and Pickett, K. (2009) *The Spirit Level: Why more equal societies almost always do better*. London: Allen Lane.

Chapter 5

Finland: Trust under pressure

Petri Salo and Torbjörn Sandén

Finland's population at the end of February 2015 was close to 5.5 million (Statistics Finland, 2015). About 5 per cent of the population was born in another country. Populations originating in Russia, Estonia, and Sweden form the three largest immigrant groups. In 2013 Finnish citizenship was granted to about 9,000 foreign citizens permanently resident in Finland. Among these, 2,500 were under the age of 15. Current expenditure on regular education in Finland is 6.5 per cent of GNP, which is slightly more than the OECD average of 6.1 per cent. Teachers' salaries too are slightly above the OECD average (OECD, 2014).

The history of Finnish education is in many ways the story of the evolution of our national identity. In 1809, as a result of a war between Sweden and Russia, and following 600 years in which the country was a part of the Swedish Kingdom, Finland became a semi-autonomous Grand Duchy within the Russian Empire. During the period of the Grand Duchy, nationalist Finnish ideals and ideas started to evolve as the Finnish language and culture coexisted with the entrenched Swedish language and culture. Church schools, in particular, functioned as important cultural institutions in the formation of this Finnish folk identity. An early sign of trust in education as a vehicle for cultural and national awakening was the creation of one of the world's oldest chairs in education (pedagogics) at the University of Helsinki in 1852. Teacher education was this chair's main responsibility. A significant step towards a national school system occurred in 1866, when secular authorities initiated a primary school system that replaced the church's responsibility for basic education. Three years later the educational component of a Finnish nation state and a civil society was significantly advanced when a National Board of Education was established (Uljens and Nyman, 2013: 35). The influences for the reform and the educational ideals by which it was realized had strong German origins. As a nation under construction Finland put its trust into *Bildung*, a German concept difficult to translate into English, but referring simultaneously to enlightenment, civilization, culture, and human processes of formation. This complex concept refers to the potential of and a confidence in human growth, the development of the nation, and humanity at large. It reflects a trust in education as an end in itself. Johan Vilhelm Snellman, an important Finnish philosopher of that time, captured the spirit of this nationalist trust in education with the following statement, which is still part of the collective Finnish memory at the beginning of twenty-first century: 'The safety of small nations is grounded on *Bildung*' (Antikainen, 2013: 205–6). If children were to learn to read their Finnish mother tongue then schools would have to become leading institutions in Finnish society. The ideal of *Bildung*, when combined with the cultural and political struggles to establish a language of one's own as a crucial building-block for nation building, helps to explain why Finns still highly value education, schools, and the teaching profession.

Following the Russian revolution and the outbreak of civil war, Finland declared its independence in 1917. As a newborn independent nation one of its important nation-building actions was to initiate a Compulsory School Attendance Act in 1921, which guaranteed equal basic education for all children. On the matter of school provision, the act stipulated that no child ought to have a longer journey to school than 5 km. As a result of this, Finland is still a country of small schools. Geographical proximity to schools, in a vast country with many remote areas, explains the fact that the proportion of children between the ages of seven and thirteen attending the *kansakoulu* ('folk school', as primary schools were then called) was already high (about 90 per cent) before the Second World War. Post-war birth rates resulted in a dramatic increase in pupil numbers, and the government established new schools all over Finland. Primary schooling was lengthened to encompass the ages 7 to 15 by the end of the 1950s. This extension of the comprehensiveness of schooling also led to discussion of a future nine-year comprehensive school (Uljens and Nyman, 2013: 36–7).

Despite the establishment of such nine-year schooling and the ambition of having a school close to every child, the range of public education in Finland during the 1950s and early 1960s was still quite limited, and the level of students' educational attainment remained relatively low. Only a few students completed more than nine years of basic education, and the achievement of a university degree was uncommon. Education in Finland lagged at that time far behind the country's closest neighbour, Sweden. The period 1960–70 was in many ways a watershed in education policy thinking in Finland. Schools abandoned the established 'parallel system', an internationally widespread pedagogical idea that young people had inherently differing abilities to acquire knowledge and should thus be sorted into separate groups for schooling. Inspired by Sweden, Finland acquired a new awareness grounded in the conviction that all should have equality and that education should be a fundamental right for all children and adolescents. This resulted in a new solution: comprehensive school. During the period 1972–7 the publicly funded comprehensive school gradually replaced the old school system founded in 1866. Part of the strategy was to spread and maintain the school network so that pupils had a school close to their home whenever possible, and in other cases to provide free transportation. Instructional efforts to minimize low achievement were a pedagogical focal area from the beginning. Since the introduction of the comprehensive school, Finland has slowly but systematically implemented an educational policy which includes several components designed to provide for coherent and complementary systematic teacher and principal development, and to support good results in each school. The most pervasive reform has been that every teacher must earn a master's degree in education, which in practice means that they have to undertake research and complete a master's thesis on a pedagogical problem (Simola, 2007).

A unifying characteristic for most reforms implemented after 1970 is that trust and confidence are strong building elements. Instead of control and inspections, selection, tracking, or streaming students during their common basic education, the system has relied on its professionals: not only the teachers and principals, but also the municipalities. Starting early in the 1980s the national government further decentralized school governance, allowing municipalities to attend to local needs and conditions. The Finnish National Board of Education (FNBE) had strong confidence in municipalities' ability to make considered decisions and to come to sensible conclusions. The municipalities were early on authorized to decide how resources could be utilized most efficiently. Government acknowledged teachers' and principals' professionalism by giving them a broad mandate to decide on the teaching methods and learning materials that would most successfully promote learning among their students. According to Sahlberg (2007: 156–7) this new trust gave rise not only to school improvement, but to greater diversity.

Finland in the context of the Nordic countries

Despite certain historical differences from its Nordic neighbours, Finland (a young republic surrounded by four kingdoms) shares geography and history as well as political–societal ideas and models with Iceland, Norway, Denmark, and Sweden. The Nordic welfare state model is mainly a result of the struggles undertaken by late-nineteenth-century social movements for political rights and acceptable working conditions and education. Access to vocational training and informal lifelong learning were on their agenda from the very beginning. Later on, in the 1960s, these countries established similar welfare systems, based on extensive public services, and a free comprehensive nine-year compulsory education system aimed at democracy, equal opportunities, and social justice. The curricula focused on establishing active citizenship anchored in a recognizable national identity (Antikainen, 2006; Frímannsson, 2006). Antikainen (2013: 217) summarized the four cornerstones of the Nordic welfare state as follows:

- equal social rights for all citizens (universalism)
- responsibility of the public authority (state) for the welfare of all citizens
- striving to narrow differences in income and gender equality
- striving towards full employment.

By demanding equity standards, integration, and inclusion, high levels of participation in and completion of basic education, comprehensive education has been an integral component in realizing the welfare state ideology. The Nordic education systems seems to have succeeded in combining international conditions and influences with local values and practices (Antikainen, 2006: 230; Rubenson, 2006: 333–9). Finnish historian and philosopher of education Pauli Siljander (2007: 79) identified four principles characteristic of the Nordic countries' educational systems as established in the 1960s and 1970s:

- the overall goal of furthering equality, to be reached by raising the educational level of the whole population
- unified comprehensive education for all as a basis for both specialization and continuing education
- a structure of the education system enabling a smooth progression from one level to another
- on each educational level, pupils and students with learning difficulties to be given extra attention.

When studied from the outside (e.g. Dupriez and Dumay, 2006: 244–50), the Nordic countries still appear to constitute an identifiable case of their own, with their low levels of differentiation and grade retention, refusal to separate pupils on the basis of their school performance, and comprehensive education for all. Low levels of inequality of opportunity in school seem to correlate with low levels of social inequality within society at large. Antikainen (2013: 218) notes that even today, despite the effects of restructuring and competitiveness, Nordic countries stand out for their educational performances. The equality and transparency characteristic of the Nordic education systems and societies at large promote social capital and trust, resulting in innovations and competitiveness.

Yet, from the 1990s onwards it has become obvious that the Nordic neighbours have grown apart to some degree. This development became apparent with the publishing of the first set of OECD PISA test results. Finland stood out as the top performer, while the rest found themselves merely good performers. While Finland's Nordic neighbours, especially Sweden, have largely adapted to the so-called Global Educational Reform Movement, with its themes of strict standards, testing, accountability, privatization, and marketization, Finland has chosen a policy and education strategy based on gradual, steady, even somewhat slow progress. Finland seems to have remained in the era of professional accountability, whereas Sweden has joined the global reform movement focusing on leadership effectiveness and performance accountability. Somehow, Finland seems to have combined democracy and equality with a purposeful progressivism and pragmatism that enables local values and practices to interact with global conditions and influences. Unlike its Nordic neighbours, however, Finland is a highly homogeneous society. Even if the number of immigrants and foreigners has increased quite rapidly since the 1980s, the proportion of foreign-born residents is still under 3 per cent (Antikainen, 2006: 229–31; Sahlberg, 2007, 2011)

Peculiarities and paradoxes of the Finnish success formula

There is of course no simple accounting for the rapid change and resultant improvement in Finland, but the principle of implementing few reforms and maintaining educational conservatism seems to be a successful concept. The Finnish education system has so far remained quite unreceptive to global influences like standardization, accountability systems, national tests, and privatization (Sahlberg, 2007, 2011). The educational culture has been identified as one relying on a trinity of trust, cooperation, and responsibility (Hargreaves *et al.*, 2007). One of the basic principles of Finnish education is, as mentioned, that all people must have equal access to high-quality education and training. The same opportunities for education should be available to all citizens irrespective of their ethnic origin, age, or wealth. Another cornerstone of Finnish education policy is to have excellent teachers and teaching. Teaching is a popular profession in Finland. The applicant numbers are many times higher than the intake to teacher education programmes. Teachers are trusted, well-prepared professionals, receiving respect and status in society. They operate with significant autonomy, deciding on the teaching methods and teaching materials to be used as well as selecting strategies for pupil and student assessment. Instead of test-based accountability, the system relies on the professional accountability of teachers. Consequential accountability, in which pupils are regularly tested and teachers inspected, has in Finland been replaced by an intelligent accountability based on trust-based professionalism. The examination at the end of upper secondary school (*gymnasium*) is the only standardized national test. Pupils, however, are assessed and graded in various forms from the very beginning of primary school, but the information from these teacher-made tests is used primarily for communication and interaction with the parents (Sahlberg, 2007: 152–7; Simola, 2007: 458–61; Uljens, 2009: 56).

In a world of globalization of educational policies and reforms, Finland has, at least so far, remained a peculiar outlier. Educational policy in Finland has been built on flexibility and loose standards (e.g. schools-based curricula and setting of learning targets) rather than standardized performances, detailed quality systems, control, and auditing. Instead of defining literacy and numeracy as the prime targets of educational reform, the focus has been on learning furthering creativity and personal fulfilment. The paradox is that it is possible to get the top scores in PISA by being reluctant and old-fashioned. A historical and sociological analysis of the Finnish educational system presented by Simola concluded:

> First, the model pupil depicted in the strongly future-oriented PISA 2000 study seems to lean largely in the past, or at least the passing world, on the agrarian and pre-industrialized society, on the ethos of obedience and subjection.
>
> The second paradox is that the politically and pedagogically progressive comprehensive school reform is apparently being implemented in Finland by politically and pedagogically rather conservative teachers.
>
> (Simola, 2007: 467)

The conservative and old-fashioned character of educational practices in Finnish schools became apparent in the mid-1990s when the National Board of Education engaged an international panel of educational experts to evaluate the comprehensive curriculum reform realized in 1994 (Norris *et al.*, 1996). Educators in a nation that had barely recovered from a harsh economic depression at the beginning of the 1990s and who were striving to build a school for the future received with rather mixed feelings reports that the panel had seen, for example:

> ... whole classes following line by line what is written in the textbook, at a pace determined by the teacher. Rows and rows of children all doing the same thing in the same way whether it be art, mathematics or geography. We have moved from school to school and seen almost identical lessons, you could have swapped the teachers over and the children would never have noticed the difference. [...], we did not see much evidence of, for example, student-centered learning or independent learning.
>
> (Norris *et al.*, 1996: 29)

On the other side of this Finnish educational coin, the panel could also identify schools and classrooms as sites of security, concern, respect, confidence, and trust:

> Without exception the schools appeared as calm, secure places for pupils to work. Finnish pupils seemed generally well behaved; problems of order and discipline were few and confined to individuals or small groups. There appeared to be concern for others, and respect for property. Teachers' relationships with pupils generally demonstrated caring and mutual respect, and there was little sense of teachers needing to exercise strict discipline or authority.
>
> (Norris *et al.*, 1996: 39).

Besides being slow and steady, even conservative when it comes to educational reforms, school development, and the transformation of classroom and teaching practices, Finland's education policy, at both national and local levels, is built on the premise that 'less is more'. One-third of Finnish comprehensive schools are still small and have fewer than 50 pupils. The average class size is under 20 pupils. The expenditure per pupil in primary education is about $6,200 USD (OECD average $6,700 USD). Teachers' salaries are slightly above the OECD average. The number of intended hours of instruction in schools is among the lowest in the OECD (OECD 2010a). The amount of homework is fairly low: studying and learning is concentrated within the hours spent in school. Teachers represent a knowledge authority, which results, as noted above, in rather traditional teaching arrangements, and restraint when it comes to individualizing practices, student-centredness, and different forms of group work. The level of discipline and the agreed order is high (Carlgren *et al.*, 2006: 313–14).

Again, an international study aimed at improving school leadership in Finland referred to a visit to a Finnish school as follows:

> However, we did observe group work of a different kind – in a middle school lesson where student groups were quietly and gently cooperating on researching and producing reports on different Finnish towns and regions in an informal manner. Thus even cooperative work seems to be quietly conservative rather than technically complex or dramatic.
>
> (Hargreaves *et al.*, 2007: 15)

This traditional, knowledge-centred school, with teacher-centred practices and classroom culture, appears to adequately prepare Finnish children for the individualized and cognitively oriented problem-solving tasks in the PISA tests. In addition, teachers have a great influence over internal matters in schools such as timetables, curriculum content, and teaching materials, as well as internal policies related to school rules and evaluation (Välijärvi, 2005: 112–13). Success in the PISA tests is dependent on various forms of literacy. As we noted previously, primary schools were first established in Finland in order to acclimate children to their mother tongue, a crucial component of the construction of Finnish national identity. Still these days the vast majority of the Finns are deeply socialized into a culture of reading. The number of different kinds of libraries, including school libraries, is very high. Children simply learn to borrow books at an early age from school. On average, every Finn borrows about twenty books from public libraries every year. Finland is amongst the highest-ranked countries in the world when it comes to the number of books and journals published per capita per year. Eighty-five per cent of Finnish families subscribe to a daily newspaper, and newspapers are read both at home and at school. Importantly, all foreign programmes on television are subtitled in Finnish, rather than dubbed. Children learn to read while watching television (Halinen *et al.*, 2005).

Finally there is one further paradox regarding the Finnish success. Even if youngsters in Finland perform well – by doing as their teachers tell them – they do not enjoy school much. For example, the percentage of Finnish students reporting high or medium interest in various science topics in PISA is without exception below OECD average (OECD, n.d.). Results in the International Civic and Citizenship Education Study (Schulz *et al.*, 2010) capture this Finnish paradox in a nutshell. Youngsters in Finland are the top performers, actually the best, when it comes to civic knowledge, but when it comes to actual engagement in civic life, such as interest in social and political issues or participation in civic activities organized by NGOs,

Finnish youngsters are at the very bottom of the list. Even if they do not identify politically themselves, or relate to political parties, they still vote in the elections, just as their grandparents do and tell them to do.

Due to historical, geographical, and political exigencies throughout the centuries, Finns seem to have developed a mentality that could be described as authoritarian, obedient, collectivist, and consensus-oriented. The nation's trust in education and enlightenment derives from the late nineteenth century and has its roots in Finland's emergence as an independent nation with its own national identity. A stable political environment is also crucial. Educational reforms here have been evolutionary rather than revolutionary. Finland has succeeded in creating sustainable leadership and educational reforms because policies have been based on firm, long-term vision and respect for the professionals whose knowledge and understanding ultimately yield the best solutions and decisions (Aho *et al.*, 2006; Sahlberg, 2007: 153).

Institutional and relational trust in Finland

In Finland, institutional trust – that is, the expectation of appropriate behaviour based on the norms of a school as an institution (Louis, 2007: 3) – coincides largely with certain aspects and outcomes of professional trust. Further, the three structural conditions furthering and strengthening relational trust in schools – small school size, stability of the school community, and voluntary association, as identified in the US by Bryk and Schneider (2003: 44) – all apply to Finnish schools at large. As Sahlberg (2007: 151–3) notes, educational policies in Finland have since the 1980s built on and furthered flexibility and loose standards, and thereby enabled broad learning combined with creativity. Professionalism within education is trust-based. It relies on intelligent accountability, and allows teachers and principals to make professional judgements in their pupils' best interests.

As a result of trust-based professionalism and school culture, teachers and principals in Finland exercise high degrees of professional discretion and autonomy. Supervision of schools, oversight of the work of teachers and principals, and monitoring of results are almost non-existent by international standards. All traditional techniques for controlling teachers' work have disappeared from Finland since the beginning of the 1990s (Simola, 2007: 464–5). The national curriculum functions as an overall framework, open for professional interpretation in municipalities, schools, and individual classrooms, rather than a strict guideline for professional actions. Teachers are given substantial professional freedom to choose their textbooks, instructional materials, and methods of teaching. Above all, assessment is the professional responsibility of the teacher, an ongoing activity that takes place in classrooms, between teachers and pupils, on a basis of respectful interactions that constitutes a micro-level form of relational trust (OECD, 2010b: 123). The Finnish trust formula is somewhat self-evident and highly simple: '... that education authorities and political leaders believe that teachers, together with principals, parents and their communities, know how to provide the best possible education for the children and youth' (Sahlberg, 2007: 157).

Consequently, Finnish teachers, principals, and schools as such are rarely criticized or questioned in the media or by the public. The recurring public debate on schools deals almost exclusively with the amount or proportion of certain subjects in the curriculum, and is maintained largely by teachers. The teachers' union is highly regarded, and has a strong position in the public debate and on the labour market. Teachers in comprehensive schools identify themselves as upper middle class (Simola, 2007: 461), and as a professional interest group they are over-represented in public decision-making at both municipal and national levels. Unlike their colleagues internationally, Finnish teachers are loyal to their profession, with only a small proportion of teachers considering leaving their jobs (Martin and Pennanen, 2015: 40)

Probably due to the fact that Finland is regarded as trustworthy society, meaning that the level of general trust is very high, academic research on trust is quite rare (Laine, 2008: 11). Within the field of education, studies on trust are very few. Raatikainen (2011) studied experiences of trust and distrust among ninth graders, and found that students' trust for their teachers was related both to professional trust (addressing teachers' professional roles and competencies as a teacher) and to relational trust (concerning the extent to which teachers acted as caring human beings open to dialogue). Besides being dependent on a school culture that is committed to furthering institutional trust, trust in schools is built on relational aspects, particularly the collaboration and communication by which students and teachers get to know each other. In Liusvaaras's dissertation on pedagogical wellbeing among teachers (2014: 142–3), trustful relationships between teachers and principals are described as being built on circles of interaction and communication, in which principals' professional competencies (knowledge and acts) reciprocate with a feeling of the principal being present and expressing support. Time given to interactions is of importance, as trustful relationships deepen over time.

The Finnish trust survey

The Finnish trust data consists of responses gathered from 674 teachers and 192 principals. The data was gathered during autumn 2013, through paper questionnaires distributed during mandatory in-service training days, and in early 2014, via a web questionnaire circulated via the Association of Finnish Principals. As the authors work at a Finnish university serving the Swedish-speaking minority their primary interest was to focus on Swedish-speaking teachers and principals. Therefore 77 per cent (525) of the teachers and 43 per cent (83) of the principals in the Finnish data belong to the Swedish-speaking minority. Some 74 per cent of the teachers and 54 per cent of the principals in the data are female. A clear majority of teachers (71 per cent) and principals (81 per cent) work with grades 1–9 in comprehensive schools, with 45 per cent of teachers and 46 per cent of principals work within primary school (grades 1–6). The average age of the principals, at 52 years, is five years higher than the average age for the teachers, 47 years. Three in every four of the principals represented are older than 45 years, whereas slightly over half of the teachers are older than 45 years. The proportion of deputy principals in the data is small, at only 8 per cent. Half of the principals (51 per cent) have over ten years of school leadership experience, and one-third of the principals (36 per cent) have worked for longer than ten years in their current school. When it comes to the teachers, half of them (51 per cent) have been working for 16 years or longer, and 47 per cent have worked for over 10 years in their current school. As noted earlier, Finnish schools are often small. The proportion of teachers and principals working in schools of various sizes is shown in Table 5.1 below.

Table 5.1 Distribution of Finnish survey respondents by school size

	School size		
	Up to 130 pupils	130 to 299 pupils	Over 300 pupils
Teachers	25 %	34 %	39 %
Principals	27 %	31 %	42 %

Principals' institutional trust

The three highest-ranked survey statements concerning institutional trust, as assessed by principals, all had a mean agreement score exceeding 4 (on a scale from 1–5). Eighty-eight to 92 per cent of the principals agreed with each of the following three statements:

- Trustworthy leaders at all levels say what they mean and mean what they say (mean agreement score 4.4; 92 per cent agree).
- Quality leadership is one of the educational system's highest priorities (mean 4.3; 90 per cent agree).
- Government policies support quality public education for all, regardless of family income (mean 4.2; 88 per cent agree).

This indicates that Finnish principals have a strong trust in the educational system, and they express an appreciation of school leadership and belief that trustworthy leaders can make a difference. A trustworthy principal not only has the capacity to influence the learning environment but has a (shared) obligation to do so. Principals' involvement in the school community and their supportive interactions within it seem to enhance trustful–professional leadership (Sandén, 2007). There seems to be a solid collective sense of responsibility in the educational community, with deeply embedded elements such as shared values, dialogue, and a sense of care for every pupil regardless of socio-economic background. The results also support the interpretation that Finland has not joined the global accountability movement in education that assumes that making schools, principals, and teachers accountable for their performances is the key to improve student achievement. On the contrary, the education authorities and political leaders in Finland are held accountable to schools for making expected outcomes possible, which preserves and enhances trust among principals and teachers.

The two lowest-ranked statements about institutional trust (as rated by principals) have mean agreement scores below 3, placing them on the 'distrust' side of the scale. Only about one-fifth of the principals agree that leadership development is strongly supported by the government and that the educational system is prepared to pay for quality leadership. The first of the statements, the one on admitting mistakes, is in the middle of the scale, with 36 per cent of principals agreeing with it.

- Board and school leaders admit mistakes openly and promptly (mean 3.0; 36 per cent agree).
- Leadership development has strong support from higher levels of government (mean 2.6; 22 per cent agree).
- The educational system is prepared to pay for quality leadership (mean 2.4; 22 per cent agree).

Interestingly, the results above indicate that board and school leaders infrequently admit their mistakes, that principals experience a lack of support for leadership development from their superiors, and that there exists a professional feeling that the educational system is not prepared to pay for quality leadership. What does this mean? How can this expression of distrust be understood in relation to the results above? A possible explanation is that there is a trust gap between the principal, the superintendent, and politicians at the municipality level. Although Finnish society in general is school-oriented and supportive, principals apparently lack professional backup within the municipality and from their superiors. Superintendents might be more anxious about keeping politicians satisfied than about guiding principals in their daily work. However, the principals expect more supportive behaviour from their superintendents and wish to share with them leadership responsibilities. As noted by Tarter *et al.* (1989), trust can be built indirectly by supportive behaviour.

Principals' relational trust

In the domain of relational trust, principals gave the highest mean level of agreement to the three following statements, with which almost all of the principals in the Finnish sample agreed:

- Working in a 'high-trust' environment makes a teacher a more effective professional in promoting student learning (mean 4.7; 97 per cent agree).
- Schools operate most effectively on behalf of children within a culture of trust (mean 4.6; 95 per cent agree).
- School leaders place the welfare of their students above all (mean 4.3; 90 per cent agree).

Principals in the Finnish sample strongly agree that high-trust schools exhibit a more effective and creative learning environment. Students' wellbeing and comfort are put into focus. The results indicate that principals who believe in the importance of good relations also believe that the learning needs of students are more resilient in an atmosphere of trust.

The lowest-ranked relational trust items when the survey was administered to principals fell somewhat on the distrust side of the scale.

- School leaders' trust of teachers should be conditional on their teaching performance and results (mean 2.7; 33 per cent agree).
- School leaders act with confidence and authority in their dealings with students and parents (mean 3.3; 48 per cent agree).

- It is best to trust the leadership of those in charge by going along with what they want (mean 2.9; 33 per cent agree).

This seems to accord with the results above that gave high rankings to statements implying a high-trust professional environment. School leaders' trust in teachers is not dependent on the latter's teaching performance and results. Trust doesn't seem to be dependent upon or an outcome of measurements and results.

Secondly, the relationship between schools and parents always seem to arouse tensions. This study is not an exception. It points to the important but sensible question of school and professional autonomy: to what degree should parents be directly engaged in their children's education? The results reveal some degree of uncertainty among principals when it comes to handling contact with parents. They also point toward certain complications when it comes to the relationship between principals and their professional superiors. A majority of principals do not get along smoothly with their superiors.

As the table below indicates, the biggest differences that principals perceive between the real and ideal situation in terms of trust are related to institutional trust.

Table 5.2 Differences between real and ideal aspects of trust as perceived by Finnish principals

Statement	Real		Ideal		Trust dimension
	Mean	Agree	Mean	Agree	
The educational system is prepared to pay for quality leadership	2.4	22%	4.6	90%	Institutional
Leadership development has strong support from higher levels of government	2.6	22%	4.5	89%	Institutional
Board and school leaders admit mistakes openly and promptly	3.0	36%	4.5	90%	Institutional

The table points out a feeling among principals that they are not professionally supported or appreciated in terms of salary and leadership development. As noted earlier there also seem to be signs of professional distrust between principals and their superiors.

Teachers' institutional trust

The three highest-ranked statements pertaining to institutional trust as rated by teachers have to do with support for public education and prioritizing quality teaching. The role of the teachers' union is highlighted.

- Government policies support quality public education for all, regardless of family income (mean 4.0; 79 per cent agree).
- Quality teaching is one of the educational system's highest priorities (mean 3.9; 74 per cent agree).
- Teacher unions are an agency for school improvement in the school system and schools (mean 3.6; 60 per cent agree).

Teachers experience support and perceive there to be trust in the notion of democratic schooling with equal opportunities for all regardless of socio-economic backgrounds. Further, they look at the educational system and the teachers' union as guarantees of quality teaching and school improvement.

This result exposes the union's strong position, as well as evidencing teachers' trust in their union. It is reasonable to assume that the role and function of the union is accentuated in a time of change, economic recession, and several substantial education reforms.

As the means below indicate, the lowest rankings given by teachers to statements about institutional trust still fall in the very middle of the scale.

- The educational system backs its teachers when their professionalism is questioned by the press and other media sources (mean 3.1; 32 per cent agree).
- Schools need complete autonomy to pursue a school improvement agenda (mean 2.9; 32 per cent agree).
- The educational system is prepared to pay for quality teaching (mean 2.8; 32 per cent agree).

The results above indicate at least a slight hesitation as to whether the educational system will back teachers when their professionalism is questioned. It remains to be seen whether signs of growing distrust among teachers for media sources is a result of an increased focus on efficiency and productivity, or of loss of professional autonomy. On the other hand, teachers do not necessarily expect full autonomy to pursue school improvement. They seem to accept that education authorities and political leaders may express their opinions on educational policies as long as regions, municipalities, and schools are treated equally. Probably due to the strained overall economic situation since 2008, Finnish teachers do not express continuous trust that there will be investment in the quality of teaching.

Teachers' relational trust

The highest rankings given by teacher respondents to statements about relational trust concern the effectiveness of high-trust environments and principals' leadership competence as the basis for trustful relationships within the school community.

- Working in a 'high-trust' environment makes a teacher a more effective professional in promoting student learning (mean 4.3; 86 per cent agree).
- Teachers' trust of their leaders is conditional on the leader's competence (mean 4.2; 85 per cent agree).
- School improvement depends on school leaders' ability to build trusting relationships with all staff members (mean 4.0; 80 per cent agree).

There is consensus among teachers (86 per cent) and principals (97 per cent) that a high-trust environment has the greatest impact on student achievement. Leadership patterns, principal–teacher and teacher–teacher relationships are also seen as levers to promote quality teaching and learning outcomes. Teachers acting in high-trust settings, and who believe in their own professional abilities, are probably more resilient when it comes to challenging situations, and they derive greater satisfaction from their work.

The lowest rankings concerning relational trust among teachers fall at the very middle of the scale:

- Teachers' assessment includes more than just test scores (mean 3.0; 39 per cent agree).
- Students' views on teachers' performance is part of teachers' performance review (mean 3.0; 39 per cent agree).
- School leaders must act as gatekeepers to protect teachers and children from the negative effects of some government and/or district policies (mean 2.9; 31 per cent agree).
- Teachers have the time and space to work collaboratively (mean 2.7; 37 per cent agree).

The responses above from Finnish teachers demonstrate some of the aspects of the professional culture in Finnish schools. Assessment of student learning is based on face-to-face interaction in the classroom, and on tests constructed and developed by teachers themselves, not national or external standardized tests. Finnish teachers are highly trusted and autonomous professionals when it comes to the evaluation of student outcomes. Still, autonomous professional practices in the classroom have a downside, collaborative professional work not being a component of the Finnish school culture. As Finland is in the process of instituting curriculum reform, on quite a radical scale – scrapping traditional 'teaching by subject' in favour of 'teaching by topic' – the independence of teachers' work in classrooms is likely to be challenged. If this is to be successful, use ought to be made of the reservoirs of professional trust.

The biggest differences that teachers perceived between real and ideal aspects of trust related to relational dimensions (see Table 5.3).

Table 5.3 Differences between real and ideal aspects of trust as perceived by Finnish teachers

Statement	Real		Ideal		Trust dimension
	Mean	Agree	Mean	Agree	
School leaders must act as gate-keepers to protect teachers and children from the negative effects of some government and/or district policies	2.9	31%	4.6	89%	Relational
Teachers have the time and space to work collaboratively	2.7	37%	4.6	92%	Relational
School leaders are knowledgeable about effective teaching practices and contemporary learning theories	3.4	53%	4.6	92%	Institutional

Teachers (with 89 per cent agreeing) decidedly express a need for their principal to act as a gatekeeper. It is obvious that teachers wish for a less hectic and more manageable workday. For this they need a gatekeeper with the courage to protect teachers from disruptions, such as reforms, overwhelming demands, unrealistic requirements, and unmet expectations. Remarkably only one-third agree with the statement that school leaders actually act as gatekeepers. Teachers' strong support (92 per cent) for a collaborative professional practice can also be seen as an expression of a desire for ways or methods to cope with change.

Interestingly, teachers also express some doubts about their principals' professionalism, when it comes to their insights into learning theories and teaching practices. This is unexpected since principals in Finland are all qualified teachers and most of them have an assigned teaching responsibility.

Comparing principals' and teachers' trust

When the two groups of professionals within education are compared, the Finnish data shows that the highest accordance between principals and teachers for the following statements:

- Government policies support quality public education for all, regardless of family income (difference 0.1).
- Schools need complete autonomy to pursue a school improvement agenda (difference 0.1).
- The educational system backs its teachers when their professionalism is questioned by the press and other media sources (difference 0.0).
- Teacher unions protect all teachers regardless of their competence (difference 0.1).
- In difficult situations teachers support their school leaders (difference 0.1).

The main aim of the Finnish Comprehensive Reform of the 1970s was to make public educational opportunities accessible for all. According to the trust data available this principle is still essential to Finnish teachers and principals. The results imply that municipalities still act autonomously even if the possibilities and space for pedagogical development have declined due to stronger governmental steering. Yet, and in keeping with the strong overall institutional trust that applies in the field, this trend is accepted by principals and teachers. Further, both principals and teachers are doubtful as to whether the system as such is prepared to defend their professionalism if it is questioned. But they seem to have a mutual respect and care for one another in professionally difficult and challenging situations.

The biggest differences between principals and teachers were found for the following statements:

- School leaders maintain trust by addressing poor teacher practice promptly and effectively (difference 0.8).

- Trustworthy leaders at all levels say what they mean and mean what they say (difference 0.7).
- School leaders act with integrity; they 'walk their talk' (difference 0.6).

Principals' senses of self-efficacy and professional performance do not seem to coincide with teachers' understanding of the same. Good performance and success reinforces the conceptions of one's own ability and effectiveness to lead and enhance a school. Therefore, it is not unthinkable that Finnish principals, due to high levels of achievement, have adopted a strong professional belief in their own professional capacity. Sandén (2007: 220) refers to how Finnish principals in interviews frequently used the word 'I' when reporting how projects have been successfully carried out. This highlights ambitions, confirming principals' confidence in their own effectiveness and expectations of achieving good results. The expectation that one will do well and experience success is strong, even so strong that their perception of real and ideal situations is somewhat distorted.

Ideal scenarios versus real scenarios – principals and teachers

For two-thirds of the statements, principals rated the ideal scenario considerably more highly than the situation in reality. But, interestingly, for one-third of the statements the difference between the ideal situation and reality was almost non-existent (that is, ranged from 0.1 to 0.2). Three of the statements where respondents' level of agreement differed little when considering real and ideal situations were about institutional trust.

- Schools need complete autonomy to pursue a school improvement agenda (difference 0.2).
- Leaders at all levels need to know and show concern for staff members' personal circumstances (difference 0.2).
- School leaders must act as a gatekeeper to protect teachers and children from the negative effects of some government and/or district policies (difference 0.2).

Yet, a majority of the statements where real and ideal scores matched closely were related to relational trust.

- School improvement depends on school leaders' ability to build trusting relationships with all staff members (difference 0.1).

- School leaders' trust of teachers should be conditional on their teaching performance and results (difference 0.2).
- School leaders need to be in charge of all aspects of the school's operation (maintenance, construction, transportation as well as the learning programme) to ensure effective teaching and learning in schools (difference 0.2).
- Schools operate most effectively on behalf of children within a culture of trust (difference 0.2).
- School leaders act with confidence and authority in their dealings with students and parents (difference 0.2).
- Teachers can be candid with their school leaders (difference 0.1).
- It is best to trust the leadership of those in charge by going along with what they want (difference 0.1).

When it comes to teachers the correspondence between the reality and the ideal situation was far less close. Teachers mostly rated statements much more highly as descriptions of the ideal situation than of the reality. However, there are some exceptions. The first one is that 'Schools need complete autonomy to pursue a school improvement agenda' (difference 0.2). Second, 'Teachers' assessment includes more than just test scores' (difference 0.1). Third, 'It is best to trust the leadership of those in charge by going along with what they want' (difference 0.1).

In a general sense, it is not surprising or unexpected that there is a gulf between perceptions of reality and of the ideal situation among both principals and teachers. In a context of high expectations, combined with strong institutional trust in the school community and several large and ongoing education reforms, the pressure on both principals and teachers is high. This pressure is somehow to be combined with, or related to, principals' and teachers' need and wish for continuous professional development. Nevertheless, an interesting observation can be drawn: autonomy seems to be an appreciated and contributing factor in school improvement among both school leaders and teachers.

The average ratings that principals and teachers give to statements concerning institutional trust and relational trust are demonstrated in Figure 5.1. As can be noted, there are some differences in how principals and teachers perceive the real scenario as compared to the ideal scenario.

When it comes to institutional trust both Finnish principals' and teachers' experience is that the difference between reality and the ideal situation is remarkable (the mean difference being 0.9). A corresponding but smaller difference can be identified in principals' real and ideal perceptions concerning relational trust (0.4). On the another hand, teachers seem to experience a greater relational trust difference (0.9) between the ideal scenario and the reality. Teachers' concern for stronger relational trust is in some way unexpected and quite difficult to interpret. The data at hand cannot disclose whether the teachers are primarily concerned with principal–teacher or teacher–teacher relations. Based on the results presented above we can assume that the discussion about teachers' autonomy versus a need for broader collective responsibility may be of importance.

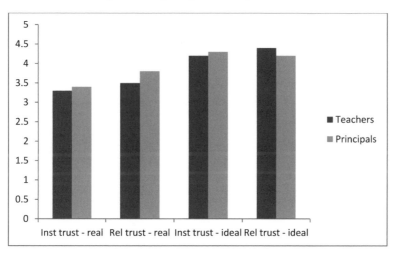

Figure 5.1: Institutional and relational trust statements: mean agreement scores in real and ideal scenarios from teachers and principals in Finland

Expressions of trust as formulated by principals

In the following we aim at illuminating aspects of institutional, professional, and relational trust as formulated by a group of Finnish principals. They participated in an action research project, *Local Leadership Praxis*, in the region of Ostrobothnia during the years 2012 and 2014. The project involved 12 principals, organized into four professional study circles, who met regularly over a two-year period to discuss and reflect on their professional tasks, and to support each other professionally in developing their leadership practices and the professional school community. The first section provides an account from one study circle comprising two experienced secondary school principals, Pernilla and Pauline, and Carl, a relatively new principal in a primary school.

The first quote below illuminates an understanding of professional trust as strongly related to handling matters, new forms to be used, or feelings of being overworked, based on a factual style of self-expression. Expressing strong feelings or exaggerating undermines professional trust. Asked in what ways teachers show trust to their principals, Pernilla said:

> When the principal, for example on a staff meeting, introduces a new kind of form, instead of arguing or protesting, you have faith in that the principal's talking about the right kind of things and that he will strive to arrange everything to its best. Or if the teacher's letting the principal know that she's overworked, she doesn't exaggerate or diminish the whole thing, but puts everything the way it is, not just something like 'I'm so terribly tired'; the exaggerating diminishes trust.
>
> (Pernilla, secondary school principal, Finland)

Involving and expressing feelings seems to consume professional trust, and can be understood in terms of professional downgrading. Being professionally honest is related to decisiveness. It opens up possibilities for collaborative and collegial actions. Respect as an aspect of relational trust seems to be related to regard and integrity that is professional rather than personal (Bryk and Schneider, 2003). When asked what her trust in teachers consisted of, Pernilla responded:

> I trust in a teacher, who does not exaggerate; who doesn't involve personal feelings in such a way that it would underestimate me, when sharing something about the pupils. If the teacher bases her acting on feelings it won't be right, neither if she approaches her workload according to how it feels and not according to what she gets paid for. If one says that I work immensely hard, it will consume trust, but if you're honest about it and say that for these hours I get paid, I'll try to do my best, that's enough. I trust a teacher who says that this is tricky – but could we try to figure out how to handle it – together?
>
> (Pernilla, secondary school principal, Finland)

Pernilla's reflections on trust between principals and teachers have to be related to and contextualized within a Finnish mentality and communication culture that is based on taciturnity, absolute responsibility, and a straightforward honesty, and which seldom includes spontaneous positive feedback.

> Pernilla: Saying out loud everything that's good, doing that's pretty tough for us, Finnish people. You have to consider, if you dare, or if one gets too proud.

Carl: But when you've really worked hard with yourself, it even feels quite easy. Saying it to a single teacher or to the whole group of teachers, to boast, but it sure has taken its time.

Pernilla: Just the word 'to boast' has a bit of negativity ...

Carl: Hmmm, perhaps, but should we say 'positive feedback'?

Pernilla: But 'to thank'!

Researcher: But what about that lecturer that you had engaged, didn't he say that negative feedback ...

Carl: ... is of no use

Pernilla: ... will become a hindrance.

(Pernilla, secondary school principal,
and Carl, primary school principal, Finland)

The aspects of professional and relational trust as expressed above apply also to the relationship between principal and vice principal. Pernilla introduces the concept of 'absolute trust'. It refers firstly to unambiguous professional agreements, secondly to an understanding of the principal as the bearer of final responsibility, and thirdly to keeping personal issues off the professional agenda.

Pauline: The relationship between principal and vice principal is a challenging one, it is like bad cop, good cop.

Carl: My vice principal, when he began, we made a deal that before staff meetings or meetings with our headteachers, we discuss the matters on the agenda beforehand, so we would more or less agree on things.

Pernilla: It requires an absolute trust. Some time ago I just happened to hear, nothing earth-shattering, but about something my vice principal had agreed on with one of the teachers. And I told her this. Her first reaction was to blame it on someone else. But the next morning she came and asked to be forgiven, and said also that she understands that our relationship requires an absolute confidence. We handle and agree on our work together. Trust is essential in all human relationships, but when you work together, it has to cover, at least all of your work duties.

Researcher: What is trust based on? Which are the premises for an absolute trust?

Pernilla: Openness, you agree on the work matters together, in a manner that the principal remembers that the final responsibility is always on you, principal hits always the last nail, or otherwise …

Pauline: Is it possible that the vice principal and principal's relationship is based only on work, or do you have to deal also with personal and private issues?

Researcher: What do you mean?

Pernilla: Teacher is tired and …

Pauline: Are we discussing work matters or do we let feelings go into an avalanche or a rough-and-tumble? I know, as I have been a vice principal, that it is mind-easing when a teacher comes to you to confide, and simultaneously to criticize the principal a bit. This awakens the question, are we discussing work or something else? Things can be handled in many ways, in a straightforward manner, by direct orders, but also constructively by discussing, pondering options, without letting the personality romp about, and mixing feelings into everything.

(Pauline and Pernilla, secondary school principals, and Carl, primary school principal, Finland)

As a contrast to trust as some kind of absolute entity, as presented above, Martin, an experienced principal with 25 years of insights into school, shares his way of enhancing trust among pupils in the following manner. He couples this with his understanding of the role of school in these times.

And as for trust, when it comes to my pupils I stick to a very plain method, as soon as there's even a slightest opening to boast about them – I do. They're truly adaptive and they embrace the positive words and get as soft as butter in sunshine. Such a plain little thing (in our school) works perfectly. If you're able to find even a slightest opening to lift them up, you do. Essentially they're amiable as well as open for school and appreciative of it.

There's one aspect when it comes to this. In this our turbulent world of today, with the homes gliding back and forth, so to speak, school represents security, firmness, routines, and the predictability that cannot be found at home. And I believe that this has led to school receiving more of an important position. There's a greater understanding for school than there was 25 years ago.

(Martin, school principal, Finland)

When it comes to teachers, Martin is similarly aware of the need for boasting and giving positive responses, building up relational trust. Still, he seems to be doubtful as to whether he acts on the basis of this professional insight. It seems as if the excellence and autonomy of the teachers form sort of hindrance.

> The same applies for the teachers; I don't know if I'm any good at it? Once in a while it strikes me that this should be done to also the teachers, the lifting. Someone once said: are we truly aware of how good we are? That's a good question, we do work well and teachers are engaged 'above their ears' with work.

> I try to do it, if only I remember it, to give them the same positive feedback as I give to the pupils. And they do get softer. If you want something done the key is to first tell them something they can be proud of, after that they will do the things you want them to. They're able to handle every single classroom-situation, but even though they're excellent, they need that little moment of pride, because they do a good job, and the more you boast about them – the better they get.

(Martin, school principal, Finland)

Trust under pressure in Finland: Summary and implications

The latest PISA results indicate declining learning outcomes among Finnish students, especially in mathematics. The lifestyle of young people is changing, and various activities beyond the school and classrooms compete for their attention. National initiatives have been taken to meet and respond to the requirements that nascent working life and social life are assigning in the twenty-first century. When it comes to school, the current period of school reform in Finland is characterized by increasing outside pressures on principals and teachers.

This trust survey confirms the fact that institutional trust, based on and related to professional trust, forms the basis for the culture and practices within comprehensive schools in Finland. Teachers and principals have a strong sense of self-efficacy. Schools as organizations and institutions, the educational system as such, are highly valued and regarded. This enables teachers and principals to act autonomously and professionally, for the best of the children, on the basis of their educational qualifications and experience-based convictions. The trust is based on a collective sense of professional responsibility, and could be described as an intra-organizational and intra-institutional trust based on the 'professional sovereignty' of teachers and principals. It is dependent on competence as realized and observed in professional actions. This sovereignty closely resembles the characteristics of teaching culture, individualism, presentism, and conservatism, as identified by Lortie (1975) already in the mid-1970s. The teachers unions further maintain it. Interestingly, it seems that this intra-organizational professional sovereignty is not fully applicable or a resource available when it comes to, for example, the relationship and communication with parents. Even if both teachers and principals look at themselves as fully-fledged professionals, they express certain dissatisfaction with the way in which their professional effort is rewarded, in terms of salary or care for the quality within teaching or school leadership.

On the other hand, the Finnish trust data indicates some weaknesses or challenges when it comes to relational trust, between teachers and principals as well as between principals and their superiors. Somehow, strong professional autonomy and consequent self-efficacy give rise if not quite to a relational distrust then at least to a certain professional distance and respect, allowing or forcing teachers and principals to act individually and autonomously. The latest TALIS study (Taajamo *et al.*, 2014) discloses, firstly, a fading interest among teachers in engaging themselves in professional development. Secondly, the study indicates deficiencies when it comes to collegiality, professional feedback and support for teachers' work in classrooms, interactivity, openness, and shared leadership. A recent Finnish study on teacher mobility and transition (Martin and Pennanen, 2015: 42) concludes that teaching is becoming a multifaceted pedagogical profession, which calls for strong collegial support and collaboration within multidisciplinary groups. The times of 'lonely riders' are gone. The strong institutional trust built on autonomous professionalism has to be completed with relational trust.

Implications for principals

A growing body of research on Finnish school leadership (Salo, 2007; Sandén, 2007; Vuohijoki, 2006) has reported on the vulnerable state and complexity of the principal's task. Discussions among school leaders indicate that the job proves increasingly laborious. This study reveals signs of professional distrust, or professional distance, between principals and their superiors. Principals don't seem to get the endorsement and support they expect from their superiors. The relationship between principals and superintendents needs more attention. Thus, could it be that what is expressed in this survey as institutional distrust could in fact be a sign of relational distrust? Relational experiences evidently shape institutional expectations. Principals wish for a more supportive, strategic, and coaching leadership from their superiors and from higher administrative district levels. The data also support the notion that principals need more confidence in their cooperation with parents. In-service training and education programmes for principals ought to pay more attention to the influential role that principals play in the parent–school relation. The findings also highlight the importance of reconsidering principals' roles as gatekeepers and inspirers. Slow change and a certain lack of receptiveness to global trends (Sahlberg, 2007) seem to be appreciated by both teachers and principals, and form a sustainable base for school improvement.

Implications for teachers

Even though all Finnish principals are qualified as teachers, the relationship between teachers and principals seems to be characterized by a certain professional distance, or relational distrust. It appears that teachers are unconvinced about what principals know about effective teaching and contemporary learning theories. Their observation relates as well to the statement that teachers urgently need gatekeepers. The claim illuminates the demanding balancing act that must be undertaken to reconcile active instructional leadership styles with professional teacher autonomy. The study reveals the importance of clarifying what kind of leadership style patterns teachers long for and consider to be part of instructional leadership. But, at the same time, it is equally important to define the content and essence of the concept and practice of teacher autonomy. It highlights the need for professional investments in time, space, and practices for furthering collaborative work, teachers' professional team spirit, and social cohesion. Interpersonal interactions have always been a central determinant of relational trust. The data also supports the widespread Finnish perception that investment in equal, high-quality public education for all contributes to high-trust communities.

This study and data account for how teachers and principals experience trust in a time of change, on the basis of two trust dimensions: institutional and relational trust. The distinction and relationship between these two dimensions of trust is complex. In spite of this, the results from

Finland are well in line with, and can be made comprehensible in relation to, other studies on the Finnish educational system and the professional culture within it. The study also strongly supports the literature that identifies trust as a core resource for school culture and improvement (Bryk and Schneider, 2003; Hargreaves *et al.*, 2007; Sahlberg, 2007; Louis, 2007).

References

Aho, E., Pitkänen, K., and Sahlberg, P. (2006) 'Policy development and reform principles of basic and secondary education in Finland since 1968'.World Bank Educational Working Paper Series, no. 2. Online. http://siteresources.worldbank. org/EDUCATION/Resources/278200-1099079877269/547664-1099079967208/ Education_in_Finland_May06.pdf (accessed 1 February 2016)

Antikainen, A. (2006) 'In search of the Nordic model in education'. *Scandinavian Journal of Educational Research*, 50 (3), 229–43.

— (2013) 'Remarks on the Nordic model and the Finnish pattern of education'. In Braches-Chyrek, R., Nelles, D., Oelerich, G., and Schaarschuch, A. (eds) *Bildung, Gesellschaftstheorie und Soziale Arbeit* (pp. 205–13). Opladen/Berlin/ Toronto: Verlag Barbara Budrich.

Bryk, A.S., and Schneider, B. (2003) 'Trust in schools: A core resource for school reform'. *Creating Caring Schools,* 60 (6), 40–5.

Carlgren, I., Kirsti, K., Myrdal, S., Schnack, K., and Simola, H. (2006) 'Changes in Nordic Teaching Practices: From individualised teaching to the teaching of individuals.' *Scandinavian Journal of Educational Research*, 50 (3), 301–326.

Dupriez, V., and Dumay, X. (2006) 'Inequalities in school systems: Effect of school structure or of society structure?' *Comparative Education*, 42 (2), 243–60.

Frímannsson, G.H. (2006) 'Introduction: Is there a Nordic model in education?' *Scandinavian Journal of Educational Research,* 50 (3), 223–8.

Halinen, I., Sinko, P., and Laukkanen, R. (2005) 'A land of readers'. *Educational Leadership*, 63 (2), 72–5.

Hargreaves, A., Halász, G., and Pont, B. (2007) *School leadership for systemic improvement in Finland. A case study report for the OECD activity Improving school leadership.* Working paper. Paris: OECD Publishing. Online. www. bestlibrary.org/files/school-leadership-for-systematic-improvement-in-finland.pdf (accessed 3 January 2012).

Laine, N. (2008) 'Trust in Superior–Subordinate Relationship: An empirical study in the context of learning'. Ph.D. diss., University of Tampere.

Liusvaara, L. (2014) 'Kun vaan rehtori on korvat auki. Koulun kehittämisellä pedagogista hyvinvointia [If only the principal has the ears open – Pedagogical wellbeing through school development]'. Ph.D. diss., University of Turku.

Lortie, D.C. (1975) *Schoolteacher: A sociological study.* Chicago/London: University of Chicago Press.

Louis, K.S. (2007) 'Trust and improvement in schools'. *Journal of Educational Change*, 8 (1), 1–24.

Martin, A., and Pennanen, M. (2015) *Mobility and transition of pedagogical expertise in Finland.* Finnish Institute for Educational Research Reports, no. 51. Jyväskylä: Finnish Institute for Educational Research.

Norris, N., Asplund, R., MacDonald, B., Schostak, J., and Zamorski, B. (1996) *An independent evaluation of comprehensive curriculum reform in Finland.* Helsinki: National Board of Education.

OECD (n.d.) 'PISA country profiles'. Online. http://pisacountry.acer.edu.au/ (accessed 13 October 2010).

— (2010a) *Education at a Glance. OECD Indicators.* Paris: OECD Publishing. Online. www.oecd.org/document/52/0,3343,en_2649_39263238_45897844_1_1_1_1,00. html (accessed 13 October 2010).

— (2010b) 'Finland: Slow and steady reform for consistently high results'. In OECD, *Strong Performers And Successful Reformers In Education: Lessons from PISA for the United States.* Paris: OECD Publishing, 117–35. Online. www.oecd.org/pisa/pisaproducts/46581035.pdf (accessed 1 February 2016).

— (2014) *Education at a Glance 2014: OECD Indicators.* OECD Publishing. http://dx.doi.org/10.1787/eag-2014-en (accessed 4 April 2016).

Raatikainen, E. (2011) 'Luottamus koulussa. Tutkimus yhdeksännen luokan oppilaiden luottamus- ja epäluottamuskertomuksista ja niiden merkityksestä koulun arjessa [Trust in school. An examination of 9th grade students' writings about trust and mistrust at school – meanings and implications]'. Ph.D. diss., Helsingfors universitet.

Rubenson, K. (2006) 'The Nordic model of lifelong learning'. *Compare: A Journal of Comparative and International Education,* 36 (3), 327–41.

Sahlberg, P. (2007) 'Education policies for raising student learning: The Finnish approach'. *Journal of Education Policy,* 22 (2), 147–71.

— (2011) *Finnish Lessons: What can the world learn from educational change in Finland?* New York: Teachers College Press.

Salo, P. (2007) *Skolans sociala arkitektur* [The social architecture of school]. Åbo: Åbo Akademis förlag.

Sandén, T. (2007) 'Lust att leda i lust och leda. Om rektorers arbete under en tid av förändring [Desire and Disillusion in School Leadership. Head teachers and their work at a time of change]'. Ph.D. diss., Åbo Akademi University.

Schulz, W., Ainley, J., Fraillon, J., Kerr, D., and Losito, S. (2010) *Initial findings from the IEA International Civic and Citizenship Education Study.* Amsterdam: International Association for the Evaluation of Educational Achievement.

Siljander, P. (2007) 'Education and 'Bildung' in modern society: Developmental trends of Finnish educational and sociocultural processes'. In Jakku-Sihvonen, R., and Niemi, H. (eds) *Education as a Societal Contributor: Reflections by Finnish educationalists.* Frankfurt am Main: Peter Lang, 71–89.

Simola, H. (2007) 'The Finnish miracle of PISA: Historical and sociological remarks on teaching and teacher education'. *Comparative Education,* 41 (4), 455–70.

Statistics Finland (2015) 'Preliminary population statistics'. Online. www.stat.fi/ til/vamuu/2015/11/vamuu_2015_11_2015-12-17_tie_001_en.html (accessed 10 February 2016).

Taajamo, M., Puhakka, E., and Välijärvi, J. (2014) 'Opetuksen ja oppimisen kansainvälinen tutkimus TALIS 2013. Yläkoulun ensituloksia [The international survey on Teaching and learning TALIS 2013. First results for secondary schools]'. Helsinki: Opetus- ja kulttuuriministeriö.

Tarter, C.J., Bliss, J.R., and Hoy, W.K. (1989) 'School characteristics and faculty trust in secondary schools'. *Educational Administration Quarterly*, 25 (3), 294–308.

Uljens, M. (2009) '21 Förklaringar till finländska ungdomars framgångar I PISA [21 Explanations for the success of the Finnish youngsters in PISA]'. In Uljens, M. (ed.) *PISA, pedagogik och politik*. Rapport nr 25/2009. Vasa: Pedagogiska fakulteten vid Åbo Akademi, 53–66.

Uljens, M., and Nyman, C. (2013) 'Educational leadership in Finland or building a nation with *Bildung*'. In Moos, L. (ed.) *Transnational influences on values and practices in Nordic educational leadership: Is there a Nordic model?* Springer: Dordrecht, 31–48.

Välijärvi, J. (2005) 'Muutoksen kohtaaminen opettajan työssä [Facing change in teaching]'. In Luukkainen, O., and Valli, R. (eds) *Kaksitoista teesiä opettajalle*. Keuruu: PS-kustannus, 105–120.

Vuohijoki, T. (2006) *Pitää vain selviytyä. Tutkimus rehtorin työstä ja työssä jaksamisesta sukupuolen ja virka-aseman suhteen tarkasteltuna* [You just have to cope: the work and professional well-being of principals work researched in relation to their sex and official position of authority]. Turku: Turun yliopiston julkaisuja. Annales universitatis turkuensis, sarja-ser. C. 250.

Chapter 6

Lithuania: Faster than history but slower than a lifetime?

Eglė Pranckūnienė and Jonas Ruškus

Singing Revolution and social transformations

Lithuania is a country of deep and continuing societal transformations. Situated between Western Europe and Russia, Lithuania, like the other Baltic states (Latvia and Estonia), has experienced significant highs and profound lows in her history both ancient and recent. The glory days of the Grand Duchy of Lithuania, between the twelfth and eighteenth centuries, were followed by 120 years of Russian Tsarist rule. In 1918, Lithuania gained independence but was then occupied by the Soviets from 1940 to 1990, including a period under the brutal Nazi regime from 1941–4, finally regaining independence in 1990. The country joined the European Union in 2004 and the eurozone in 2015. Each of these dramatic political changes was accompanied by societal collapses, when social structures – value-normative, economic, cultural systems – transformed, taking on an entirely new frame and substance.

Lithuania clearly expressed its will to adhere to democratic European values through the 'Baltic Chain', an event held on 23 August 1989 whereby approximately two million people joined hands to form a human chain spanning 6,755 km across Estonia, Latvia, and Lithuania. The Baltic chain was an instance of an overwhelming civic movement known as the Singing Revolution, which took place in the Baltic states and sought to create new, independent states. 'The victory of the Singing Revolution of the Baltics was not predetermined by history but by the common understanding of the region's *telos* – self-mastery' (Kavaliauskas, 2014: 21).

Despite the energy associated with self-mastery, the transition from a Soviet to a democratic regime has been neither simple nor linear. Lithuanian sociologist Norkus argues that the post-communist epoch in Lithuania finished when Lithuania adopted the Anglo-Saxon neo-liberal mode of exit from communism, and was formally terminated in 2004 when the country joined the EU: 'Observation of the ongoing reform process in Lithuania during the last decades shows an unambiguous trend leading in the direction of the more consequent liberal market economy system' (Norkus, 2008: 735). We have to conceive neo-liberal reforms in these countries as a part of a global 'wholesale expansion of a market society', but also as reflecting an aspiration of these countries to escape the communist past and to embrace the utopian idea of western welfare (Giddens, 1997: 29). Another Lithuanian scholar, Kavaliauskas (2012: 334), contradicts Norkus, stating that 'the post-communist transition is not linear, because spiral, circular or even regressive transformations are following'.

Reflecting on the nation's multidimensional experiences of rapid change, philosopher Leonidas Donskis states:

> Lithuania and other Baltic states have become laboratories in which the speed of social change and cultural transformation is measured and tested ... these societies have developed 'faster than history' – faster than history but slower than a lifetime. People often complain that their lives and careers have been ruined by the rapid social transformation. They take it as a tragedy, arguing (not unreasonably) that their lives, energies and careers have been wasted, if not completely spoiled. A human lifetime proves to witness the sweeping change of a society.
>
> (Donskis, 2005: 27)

To develop 'faster than history' means to go through ups and downs, from euphoria to reality shock, from opening new possibilities to living in insecurity and risk.

Education reform was one of the driving forces for the quest for independence in Lithuania. The vision of the 'National school' was developed in 1988 on the eve of independence. The initial idea of reform was idealistic, based on the vision of an egalitarian and democratic society, on national aspirations and humanistic values. After the fall of the Iron Curtain, the formation of educational policies and trends fell under the influence of the Global Education Reform Movement (Sahlberg, 2006), as well as national political and economic shifts and interests. It led to some contradictions between the movement for emancipation from the Soviet system, the effort to restore national values, and the pressure of global organizations like OECD, George Soros's Open Society foundation, the World Bank, and the European Union (Želvys, 2009: 13–23). These agencies were offering 'blueprints' of educational policies and practices, which would purportedly lead (if implemented properly) to increased educational opportunities and improved educational quality through the 'coercive spread of (neo)liberal education reforms such as standardization of curricula, decentralization and privatization of schools, or the introduction of national educational assessment and international testing' (Silova and Brehm, 2013: 55–6). Paraphrasing Norkus (2008: 568) we could say that we in the former Soviet republics were building capitalism not on the ruins of socialism, but from the ruins of socialism and Soviet quasi-globalization; therefore western globalization, standardization, marketization, and internationalization in these post-communist societies formed peculiar and unique patterns. The post-Soviet mentality has and will have an influence on political decisions (sometimes at an unconscious level), so we cannot avoid the post-Soviet heritage in trying to understand current educational processes (Želvys, 2009: 13–23).

Summarizing the overview of social transformation in Lithuania, we assume that trust can be considered a transversal variable able to enlighten the essence of educational reform in the context of societal transformations. In this chapter we aim to reveal how agents of educational reforms – teachers and school leaders – are experiencing the phenomena of trust in the context of dramatic societal transformation and when the educational systems have developed from Soviet to neo-liberal approaches in 25 years.

Trajectories of educational change since 1990

Western countries tried several educational reform methods following the Second World War. Hargreaves and Shirley have termed these respectively the 'First Way' of innovation and inconsistency, the 'Second Way' of markets and standardization, and the 'Third Way' of performance and partnership (Hargreaves and Shirley, 2009). An overview of these 'three ways' of reform in Western countries shows the effects of political ideologies on the development of education. In terms of trust, it is clear that the transfer of neo-liberal values into the education system created an exceptionally distrusting environment. In Western countries, neo-liberal politics replaced either liberal or social-democratic politics, which exhibited much higher levels of trust in professionals and featured less significant and extensive accountability measures.

The Lithuanian education community made a rapid leap from a distrusting Soviet environment with extensive control measures to one that was on the opposite end of the spectrum. According to Silova, policy makers in most post-communist Eastern European countries have embraced (neo) liberal education reform 'packages' to pursue an allegedly linear transition from communism to democracy (Silova and Brehm, 2013: 5).

Education reform was initiated through the development of the concept of the National School, in 1988 and of the general concept of education in Lithuania (1992). A strong and charismatic leader, Professor Meilė Lukšienė, managed to form a movement of intellectuals to create a vision of Lithuanian education. This was an effort to demolish the Soviet school and to build a new school based on humanistic and democratic values:

> ... at the core of a nation's independent and full life is the individual, who is ... mature and dedicated to the new historic period of national development, is aware, makes decisions independently, is active in society, bases his worldview on national and basic human values, is able to competently and responsibly participate in the creation and development of a democratic society and state.
>
> (Ministry of Education and Culture, 1992: 5)

The reformers (the first author of this article was one of them) had a lot of enthusiasm but did not have sufficient experience to achieve political agreement and gain wider support from the educational community. Gradually, their systemic and holistic vision started breaking into smaller pieces. In the later stages of this process, the education system was shaped by the influence of economic, political, and global trends that tried to accommodate conflicting principles, values, and fashions, e.g. competition-based quality management versus the notion of education for all. This process can be illustrated by an insight from Arnove: 'The previous dominant themes of education for the formation of participatory citizens and national unity ... are barely mentioned or given secondary consideration in policy reforms/deforms which have tended to focus on the excellence or quality of an educational system, rather than its provisions of equitable access, participation, and attainment' (Arnove, 2005: 81).

Vaiva Vaicekauskienė, reflecting on the reform of the education system in post-communist Lithuania (Vaicekauskienė, 2013), notes three separate periods:

I. 1990–7: aiming for humanization, democratization, and modernization;
II. 1998–2002: aiming for continuity and accessibility of education;
III. 2003–12: aiming for cost-effectiveness, quality, and data-driven management.

Table 6.1 Stages of education reform in Lithuania

Stage I: 1990–7	Stage II: 1998–2002	Stage III: 2003–2012
Aiming for humanization, democratization, and modernization	Aiming for access (education for all) and continuity	Economy of education, quality, and data-driven management
Main events		
• De-Sovietization: total reform of curriculum and textbooks • Accreditation of school heads and teachers based on new demands • Structures of school self-governance, autonomy of universities • More choice in public education: different types of programmes and schools • First private and alternative schools • Beginning to integrate children with special needs • Beginnings of a counselling system for students with special needs, their parents, and teachers	• Reform of comprehensive school, expanding from nine grades to ten • Introduction of centralized *matura* examination at national examination centre • Uniform system for university entry • Introduction of universal pre-school education • Profiling at secondary level • Decentralization and liberalization of textbook publishing • Decentralization of professional development • Introduction of colleges (non-university higher education) • New model of school financing – 'student's basket' (per capita)	• Restructuring of school network due to demographic changes • Personalized approach at secondary level – more choices for students • Launching of education management information system • Growing system of policy analyses, data, research • Introduction of obligatory school self-evaluation and external evaluation • Access to EU funds for innovations in education • Projects as tools for change • Reform of higher education relating financing to students' choices

A powerful creative energy surrounded the very first stage of educational reforms in Lithuania together with an inspiring vision, high hopes, and firm conceptual foundations. Those who believed in the vision felt that they were:

> ... uniting to start working creatively and the non-believers are watching from afar and have to be encouraged by urging, certifying and reorganising institutions and by other means ... the goals, plans and tasks are becoming more and more menial and move further from that initial grand vision, it is becoming more and more difficult to reconcile the two which is why contradictory decisions are being made.
>
> (Vaicekauskienė, 2013)

There still has been no research into what educators experienced when transitioning from the Soviet system to Lithuania's newly created one, but – speaking from experience – it seems that for some it was a time of joy, while for others a time of great turmoil. A shift needed to be made from an ideologized and standardized curriculum to humanistic education and a curriculum grounded in democratic values. How could pupils' trust be retained when, right before their eyes, their teachers were undergoing an ideological transformation? How could teachers remove the mask of the disseminator of Soviet ideology? Colleagues who started work in the final years of Soviet occupation and who later joined together to enact educational reforms say that they felt the greatest creative freedom and professional autonomy between 1991 and 1997, when Soviet ideology was shaken off and the nationwide bureaucratic education management model had not yet come into effect. Pioneers in this age had the same ideal conditions in which to perform as did Western educators during the heyday of the 'First Way' (although those in post-Soviet Lithuania had nowhere near the same resources), but it was also possible to do nothing at all by sabotaging the ideals of reform. The 'First Way' came to Lithuania about thirty years late, and in some ways is still continuing. Fragmented and inconsistent implementation of reforms is especially pronounced in contemporary Lithuanian educational politics. An example could be the use of the European Union's structural funds to enact educational renewal. A desire to 'hoard' this aid instead of moving in the right direction to enact change has created a situation of 'hasty adoption of migrating ideas' (Bulajeva and Duoblienė, 2009: 256), where there are many valuable initiatives but they are not necessarily sustainable or adaptable on a wider level.

The second and third stages of education reform in Lithuania reflect indecisive 'to-ing and fro-ing' between the social-democratic principles of 'education for all' and neo-liberal approaches, all the while combining this into the rhetoric of New Public Management. According to Vaicekauskienė, in these stages 'governments changed and the education system lived according to its own rhythm, and the greatest effect on it was had by the number of strong personalities, ideas, relationships and the culture created by them together with the Ministers for Education' (Vaicekauskienė, 2013). The directions for change were determined by the prevailing conditions and the economic situation of the time. Between 1998 and 2002, nine-year comprehensive education was replaced by ten-year education, and universal pre-school education was introduced: this reflects the social-democratic goal of involving everyone in education. At the same time, elements of marketization started to appear too. These included centralized *matura* exams, used to rate schools, the 'student basket' principle which encourages competition between schools, and the development of a textbook and educational content publishing market that created the conditions for an education business. Many of these political decisions played a positive role in changing education but, over time, they were the cause of increased differences between schools and in students' outcomes. The 2012 PISA study shows more clearly than ever the effect of social inequality on the success of students (Dukynaitė and Stundža, 2013).

The marketization of education in countries where the market economy and democratic governance models are still being created has a different effect than in countries with longer histories of free market operations. Marketization is often taken to be a value and innovation coming from the West that should increase quality by encouraging competition. However, in the hands of politicians, instead of a tool for increasing quality, it becomes a tool for saving money, actually at the cost of increasing quality (Želvys, 2009: 26). This became especially relevant between 2003 and 2012, when a demographic crisis emerged and schools started being rapidly and drastically reformed on economic and political grounds. The political decisions made regarding education during this time were also tinged with the rhetoric of the Third Way, or New Public Management: external evaluation of schools comes into force, as does deployment of educational innovations by means of projects and EU funds, the introduction of an information management system for education, and the ever-increasing importance of standardized tests. These are all taken to be modern instruments for management and control that are intended to increase quality. This rhetoric is heard all the more often in the National Development Strategy 'Lithuania – 2030' when discussing an active, unified, learning society that needs an education system oriented towards revealing the talents, creativity, and public spirit of each learner, ensuring lifelong learning. Concepts such as professional communities, the learning society, school networks, and data-driven management have become everyday terms in educational discourse, although they play only a very small part in practice.

An eclectic mix of doctrines and ideologies is thus reflected in Lithuanian societal and educational development. The authors of the study *Transformations of Lithuania's Education Policy* note that education policy here is characterized by controversial trajectories based on confused political ideologies, and often imitates the educational processes of other countries (Balujeva and Duoblienė, 2009: 253–66). In terms of the three different 'ways' of reform, it appears that Lithuanian education reform is meandering down all the different ways at once but is most likely stuck between the First Way (innovations and inconsistency) and the Second (standardization and markets).

This brief overview of educational change in Lithuania, which has highlighted only a few aspects, shows that, in comparison to Western democracies, Lithuanian society and public education have experienced an especially rapid and contradictory ideological, social, and political transformation, related to the creation of an independent state, the rapid overhaul of the national political structure, and the consequences of global influence. Dean Fink's questions – 'What kind of educational policy decisions reflect a high or low level of trust in the education system? Are the mechanisms for inspection and control a result of distrust?' – are not, it must be said, being asked in Lithuania. Political decisions do not strongly reflect either trust or a lack of trust, but rather vacillation between migrating ideas and political indecisiveness over the direction in which education should be heading, just as there is indecisiveness over the direction in which the nation should be heading. As a school leader interviewed for this chapter says:

> We need stable agreements, and while they may not be the best agreements, we at least need to agree on how long they will be valid. Then we can assess what worked and what did not instead of changing everything each year. Everything is coming from the top down, decisions are being made by those at the top instead of those who are closest to the children. Of course, there also needs to be a state-wide approach but it should not be happening so quickly. It should not be a case of one minister saying that we are now going to be encouraging leadership and giving you more autonomy and then a year later another minister coming in and

saying that there was too much trust, is now a mess and we need to re-establish school inspection and more strict control. That shows that there is not enough stability, there is too much going back and forth, we do not have a common goal and vision. What we should care about is the success of every child. The strategy 'Lithuania 2030' appears to be a very inspiring slogan but we are getting side-tracked, we are starting to get stuck on the minute details and losing sight of the main goal made by those at the top instead of those who are closest to the children. Of course, there also needs to be a state-wide approach but it should not be happening so quickly. It should not be a case of one minister saying that we are now going to be encouraging leadership and giving you more autonomy and then a year later another minister coming in.

(School leader, Lithuania)

Silova and Brehm describe educators who have experienced rapid reforms in post-communist countries as follows:

Directly affected by the 'touch down' of global educational flows—whether education privatization, decentralization, or child-centered learning—school teachers have been affected the most. In the public eye, teachers embodied the success (or failure) that the post-socialist education transitions set out to achieve. Teachers were thus expected to reject 'old' teaching practices (generally associated with teacher-centered approaches prevalent in the socialist past) and instead embrace 'new' Western teaching methodologies and classroom management techniques that focused on child-centered learning. They became subject to a multitude of new policies and the accompanying national and international in-service trainings and professional development activities. Their professional lives no longer belonged to them, but were rather governed by globally circulating 'norms' about curricula, textbooks, tests, and teaching methods.

(Silova and Brehm, 2013: 3)

Trust in Lithuanian society

In his book *Trust*, American philosopher and traveller Alphonso Lingis, who is of Lithuanian descent, speaks about the power, energy, and excitement of trusting somebody and being trusted:

> The act of trust is a leap into the unknown. It is not an
> effect of ideological, cultural, historical, social, economic, or
> ethnobiological determinisms. But trust is everywhere – in the
> pacts and contracts, in institutions, in forms of discourse taken
> to be revealing or veridical, in the empirical sciences and in
> mathematical systems. Everywhere a human turns in the web of
> human activities, he touches upon solicitations to trust.
>
> (Lingis, 2004: 9)

In previous decades, Lithuanian society made a huge 'leap into the unknown'.
In the preface of this book Lithuania is presented as a 'post-Soviet society
that has rather shallow democratic roots and is working valiantly to establish
democratic institutions, a western style economy, and a quality educational
system within a generally low trust society inherited from its Soviet past'
(ibid.) What, then, is the state of trust in current Lithuanian society?

Political scientists Žiliukaitė and Ramonaitė regularly investigate
the status of trust in Lithuania. The level of generalized trust is especially
important for the former authoritarian states, in which people tend to
trust only those whom they know. Generalized trust speaks about trusting
strangers and others who are different from you. It is manifested by social
interactions and interpersonal contacts, and by the cooperation of people
for mutual benefit. High levels of generalized trust support tolerance. They
help in recognizing cultural and political differences and solving social
conflicts. Generalized and political trust form social capital, which is the
essence of cooperation between citizens and the government and the basis
for the health of civic society. If policy makers are not trusted, they do not
have the social capital necessary to act freely (Žiliukaitė, 2006: 8). And
vice versa – if citizens are not trusted they do not have enough freedom
to act. 'People who are systematically not trusted will eventually become
untrustworthy' (Hazeldine, 1998: 216, quoted in Olssen *et al.*, 2004).

Lithuania is no different from other Eastern and Central European
countries in terms of the low levels of trust among the public. Data from
the 2009–12 European Social Survey shows that Lithuania remains a
distrusting society, although there is some progress being made. The reason
is not only the reduced levels of trust during totalitarian rule but also rapid
social change and still-inchoate democratic institutions. If the level of public
trust in western nations is fairly stable, then in post-communist nations it
can shift very rapidly. This is influenced by the slow increase in economic
prosperity, along with the historical context determined by a turbulent past.
A lack of public trust is especially affected by a lack of social stability:

social routines that are not sufficiently stable, inconsistencies in laws and regulations, as well as a lack of transparency and openness (Žiliukaitė *et al.*, 2006: 224–7; Žiliukaitė, 2006: 219–23). Researchers of social services (Mažeikienė *et al.*, 2014) draw attention to the strain being experienced by citizens of Lithuania when they are forced to choose between the demands of neo-liberal politics, being self-sufficient and responsible, and the expectation – left over from the Soviet era – that the state will take care of everything.

There are other possible, subjective explanations for the relatively low levels of trust in Lithuanian society:

- *A deficit in the sense of well-being among the population.* This is manifested by high levels of emigration and pessimistic views of the future. In education we can sense quite a low level of self-esteem among practitioners, feelings of helplessness and insecurity, and a lack of a sense of empowerment in making changes.
- *Weak integration of citizens into informal social networks.* In education we still lack strong professional associations; there is too little professional solidarity and support, caused by strong competition among schools and teachers.
- *The dominant negative assessment of societal conditions in the country.* In education such insecurity is caused by the inconsistency of educational reforms and policies, by a lack of professional autonomy, and by rising rates of unemployment among teachers.

Robert Putnam reminds us that for political stability and economic growth social capital is more important than physical and human capital (Putnam, 2004: 241). Social capital in Lithuanian society needs to be fostered and developed, even more so than do other forms of capital: economy, culture, and education are all important catalysts creating social networks and social competences. The trust survey results help to reveal the complexity of trust in the educational context.

The Lithuanian trust survey

The sample

Data for the study was gathered by presenting the 30-item Trust Questionnaire, developed by Dean Fink (see Chapter 2), to teachers and school leaders. The questions asked of teachers and leaders were similar but not identical. Respondents were asked to answer each question in two parts, evaluating the current situation regarding trust and the ideal state, i.e. the situation as they would like it to be. The reality and the ideal state were evaluated on an ordinal scale ranging from 1 (completely disagree) to 5 (completely agree). In order to analyse the data and abstract it as much as possible, the questions were grouped according to their content under the headings 'relational trust' and 'institutional trust'.

Two hundred and thirty-eight teachers and 130 school leaders from 15 different municipalities took part in the survey. Fifty-nine per cent of the participants work in secondary schools and over 38 per cent have been working as teachers for over 21 years, spending the majority of their careers in the same municipality and school. Out of the administrators, 31 per cent are headteachers and the rest are deputy heads. Forty-eight per cent of the headteachers are headteachers of gymnasiums, with various levels of experience – from 1 to over 21 years. Fifty-seven per cent of those who have been working for over 21 years have stayed in the same municipality throughout their careers, and 33 per cent have worked exclusively in a single school. Analysis of the data showed that demographic parameters did not have a statistically significant effect on the results of the survey.

In order to explain, clarify, and delve deeper into the results of this quantitative trial, additional interviews involving one teacher and one leader (both having significant experience and varying roles in the education field) were conducted. Together with the interview, questions about relational and institutional trust were raised during various group discussions, so we can state that our insights reflect the broader experience of practitioners.

The need for an additional – qualitative – interview stage was also made evident by the fact that the aforementioned questionnaire is a product of a different educational culture, in which the issue of trust has received a significant amount of awareness. Respondents did not always identify with the items in the questionnaire. This can be demonstrated by the relatively high levels of agreement with statements in the questionnaire that did not cause the Lithuanian respondents to reflect on the situation in their context. Therefore, it would seem that the respondents did not have an opportunity to clearly state their position in favour of one side or the other, and that they simply agreed a priori with affirmative items. Several respondents stated that the questions appeared to be too general and so they found it difficult to present a summarized opinion. In addition, during analysis of certain answers, we noticed that many statements were marked as 'not certain' and 'agree'; this also confirms that the respondents were not especially sensitized to the topic of trust.

High levels of trust, or a laissez-faire approach?

Looking at the results of the survey, at first glance it appears that that both teachers and leaders rate the levels of relational and institutional trust, both real and ideal (Figure 6.1), relatively highly. Both teachers and administrators rate relational trust items (both real and ideal) very similarly. But there is a big difference in teachers' and leaders' representations of trust. Teachers emphasize institutional trust higher than relational in both real and ideal evaluations. It means that teachers have more trust in administrative and policy measures than in interpersonal exchanges. Leaders, on the contrary, emphasize relational trust with regard to institutional trust, also in both real and ideal evaluations. All differences between teachers and administrators are statistically significant, $p<0.05$ according to the Wilcoxon signed rank test.

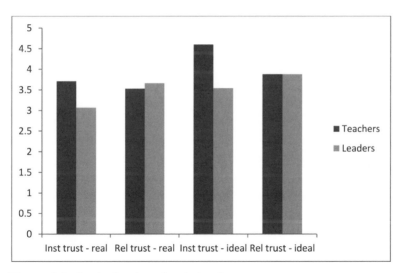

Figure 6.1: Institutional and relational trust statements: mean agreement scores in real and ideal scenarios from teachers and principals in Lithuania

The results of the interviews were more contradictory. The results of both the interviews and the survey show that the respondents rate the levels of relational trust more highly than those of institutional trust. This is an area for which the educators take responsibility, due to their values, professionalism, and attitude to their work.

One teacher offered the following opinion on how she experiences trust in her as a professional:

> I feel that I am trusted by the pupils, their parents and my colleagues, too. This is something you feel when you receive meaningful tasks, are offered to join workgroups or when you feel that your opinion is important.
>
> (Teacher, Lithuania)

This teacher also emphasized the idea that the trust placed by school leaders in teachers is determined by teachers' professionalism, the quality of their work, and their relationship with the pupils: 'School administrators notice good teachers. I never had any difficulties with them. They saw what I was capable of straight away.' It is not easy for teachers to acquire professional standing, as is evidenced by the fact that relational trust is not always present and neither are mechanisms for mutual professional support:

> I know of many teachers who stopped working in school because they did not receive the recognition they were looking for. Teachers don't receive suitable recognition for their efforts. It's especially difficult for young people in schools to gain authority.
>
> (Teacher, Lithuania)

It is very important for teachers to work in an environment in which they are trusted and one in which they feel they have the support of leaders: 'Being in an environment in which I was trusted gave me a lot. If I constantly felt I was being criticized, I would find it far more difficult as I am very sensitive to criticism.' The trust placed in teachers by leaders is reflected in their relationships with pupils: 'Students can see that you have the support of the leaders and you feel they are behind you.'

For his part, the school leader interviewed for this chapter emphasized the values that determine interpersonal trust: 'I think people trust me more as a person, and some trust me as a professional while others don't; some would come to me for help and others wouldn't and that is due to their values.' He noted how difficult it is to retain the trust of teachers when you have to criticize their work and warn them about performing poorly:

> It's very difficult to do that and retain their trust. Again, it's about values. I try to help whenever I can if the person wants to be helped. If they don't, or don't know how to, usually it's a case of mismatched personal values and then you just have to let it go ... I don't think that teacher trusts me more because of that but then the trust comes from the children, when they're happier.
>
> (School leader, Lithuania)

How is a trust-based environment fostered in schools? The leader believes that you need to spend as much time talking as possible, and share both the positives and things to be improved:

> I spend a lot of time talking, whenever the children tell me what is upsetting them or what's hurting them, I see that as a sign of trust. I try to foster trust by asking why instead of trying to scare people off. You need to talk, talk as much as possible; you need to provide parents with as much information as possible.
>
> (School leader, Lithuania)

During the interviews, the more problematic aspects of relational trust became clear. First of all, the interviews indicate a lack of openness, a fear of opening up and sharing experiences in schools. The school leader interviewed gave the following account of how teachers are afraid of speaking openly to parents:

> We need to invite the community into school as much as possible. Teachers don't want that, they feel unsafe, they're scared, but we need to become more open. Some ask: 'why did you inform parents about how you spent the aid they provided? You'd be better off asking them for more aid.' I think a trusting and knowing culture helps create good ideas. Whenever you let yourself be openly accountable that helps in a wider sense, too.
>
> (School leader, Lithuania)

The teacher we interviewed noted that there are varying levels of trust between colleagues:

> Sometimes they reject your idea; they don't want to work together, they say – what, you have nothing better to do? How can there be trust with situations like that? I trust the pupils, especially the little ones, but it's sometimes more difficult with the adults.
>
> (Teacher, Lithuania)

To summarize, it could be stated that relational trust in schools is contextual and determined by individuals, situations, and the organizational culture in schools: but all of this is in the hands of the educators themselves. They have the power to enact change. Committed professionals who believe in the power of trusting others try to foster a trusting culture, but they come up against challenges: varying attitudes to the mission of schools and teachers, competition between schools (and teachers), and the closed-doors nature of the education system.

Figure 6.1 above shows that the level of institutional trust is relatively high, and here the more significant differences between the reality and the ideal state are clearly visible. In our opinion, the relatively high level of institutional trust reported is determined by a certain fatigue felt by educators, due to the constant changes taking place in education in Lithuania. The answers thus reflect a laissez-faire approach whereby it is easier to dissociate oneself from what is occurring on the political level.

Another possible reason for such a positive rating for institutional statements is that the questionnaire items reflect a more western socio-cultural and political context. The respondents rated the statements fairly superficially, as they were quite remote from their reality. Furthermore, analysis of separate statements shows that many items were marked as 'not certain' and 'agree'. The answers provided should thus be treated as revealing certain tendencies in terms of trust in Lithuanian schools, but the socio-cultural aspects affecting the results should also be taken into account.

During the interview stage, a much more contradictory and painful attitude to institutional trust came to the fore. Both leaders and teachers view the extensive regulation of their work as a sign of a lack of trust. Disappointment is expressed that knowing minute details about procedures and regulations is taken to be a sign of real professionalism:

> Many people think that everything should be regulated and knowing the regulations is most important. People who believe that don't trust me. Those who are more interested in throwing around blame don't trust me, while those who try to look for answers together do. Another is example is the centralized accountancy to which you have to copy and send all your documents ..., you need to fix minute details, you cannot make any mistakes, in a way, it's a case of shared responsibility but on the other hand the system is so bureaucratic that it seems that we're working for pieces of paper rather than for a better future for our children.
>
> (School leader, Lithuania)

The lack of trust is mutual, because educators don't trust decision-makers who work only on introducing regulations:

> I don't trust bureaucrats who spend their time simply copying papers. There is too much red tape. Bureaucrats don't care about the actual work that teacher and school do, that's where there is a lack of trust and indifference.
>
> (Teacher, Lithuania)

Another sign of a lack of trust can be found in the fact that the opinions of teachers are often ignored: their views are not taken into account when important decisions are made.

> For example, the mayor of the city decides to make school start at 9 am when the community had already decided to do it differently, but that's up to schools, they should be the ones to make these decisions. That shows that they don't really care about what schools think, schools just get orders from above without any discussion.
>
> (School leader, Lithuania)

> Everything comes from above, decisions aren't made by those who are closest to the children.
>
> (School leader, Lithuania)

> I trust those who believe in teachers and schools and those who believe that there can be a positive relationship between them. It's unfortunate that such voices don't get heard.
>
> (Teacher, Lithuania)

The ever-increasing divide between politics and practice is also emphasized, along with politicians' indifference to real problems in education:

> There is a significant gap between politics and the reality. Of course, everything comes down to a lack of trust. We still have that legacy, ... the desire to show off our government, to be members of a hierarchical system.
>
> (Teacher, Lithuania)

The ill-conceived and poorly planned changes introduced in education, together with the lack of agreements and stability, are singled out as the most important cause of the lack of institutional trust:

> As soon as there is a change of government, the decisions made previously are immediately reversed, as if they were bad to begin with, for example the way school leaders are selected. Now they're saying that you don't need community representatives during the selection process. That didn't even last one year. They could at least leave it for a few years, then we could come to a conclusion, what worked well, what needs to be improved and then we could change it.
>
> (School leader, Lithuania)

The biggest difference between leaders and teachers is in their attitudes to institutional trust. The difficulties teachers experience with reference to institutional trust, both real and idea, are made more explicit than is the case with leaders, who rate institutional trust less highly (although still relatively positively). This is confirmed by an interview given by a teacher, where she spoke about how teachers rarely take an interest in more general discussions about education:

> There are many questions that teachers don't discuss, for example the issue of school autonomy. Teachers feel they are not competent to discuss these topics. General educational topics are not discussed in schools. ... Usually, the administration chooses what they need to be informed about and what need to be discussed and everyone can't wait until it's all over.
>
> (Teacher, Lithuania)

Leaders are more critical with regard to institutional trust. Their more careful attitude is determined by the fact that they act as the intermediaries between the political (macro) and relational (micro) levels. Who, if not them, knows best that trust can be negatively affected by rapid societal and political changes, placing people and institutions at risk? Leaders are responsible for the safety of school so, in supporting relational trust, they (like teachers) are more careful about institutional trust. This position clearly reflects certain positions of institutional alienation, 'rational trust' (Cardinal *et al.*, 1997), or simply the perception of a need to 'trust and verify'.

Expectations for trust

Both teachers and leaders clearly highlight institutional trust as problematic. A need and hope for institutional trust is much more pronounced than is the case for relational trust. To refine our analysis, we introduce a dimension measuring lack of trust, considering that the difference between real and ideal can be interpreted as an indicator of a lack of trust. Figure 6.2 presents the difference between real and ideal, or problematization, of relational and institutional trust. Analysis shows that teachers consider institutional trust to be the most challenging area, while leaders' problematization of institutional trust is slight but higher than teachers' and leaders' relational trust. Lack of institutional trust, especially among the population of teachers, appears as a main issue of trust at school level in Lithuania.

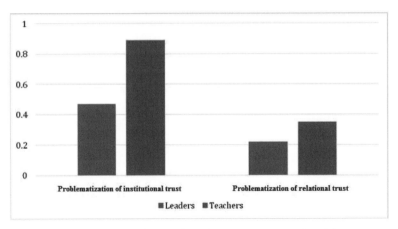

Figure 6.2: Lithuanian leaders' and teachers' perceptions of problems with institutional and relational trust

We believe that this result reveals that teachers and leaders show a desire for more stability and peace on the political level, an appetite for more stable and predictable social and educational directions that would protect schools from regular turmoil. The explicit expectation for institutional trust reflects a certain conflict between the micro (relational) and macro (political) levels, with the institutional (mezzo) level acting as the buffer or intermediary. It could be said that Lithuanian teachers and leaders would rather have 'high trust/low distrust' as opposed to 'trust but verify' or 'high trust/high distrust'; that is, they would prefer a more trusting, human, and respectful relationship on both the relational and institutional levels.

From 'trust and verify' to 'high trust/low distrust'

The development of Lithuanian education reflects both universal tendencies and unique configurations born of geopolitical and historical context. Looking at the reforms in Lithuanian education in the last 25 years, we can state that, compared to Western countries, Lithuanian society and the education system experienced much more rapid and contradictory ideological, social, and political change. This was determined by the fact that the foundations of the new independent state were built on the ruins of a Soviet legacy; it was also affected by social transformations, and by global economic, political, and cultural influences. All of this is reflected in the opposing forces that championed on the one hand the social-democratic aspiration to 'education for all' and on the other the goal of neo-liberal access, and in the combination of the two to conform to the rhetoric of New Public Management. It is seen too in the shifting of educational goals from sociocultural to economic and instrumental terms (referring to the model suggested by Paulston and LeRoy and adapted by Arnove, 2005: 81).

The rapid and fundamental changes in both social and educational values determined the unique changes in the dynamics of trust. During periods of especially rapid reforms, educators and schools are usually seen as 'objects' of global politics and change as opposed to conscious and creative individual. The question of trust in terms of objects is not discussed, various methods of control and regulation are created in order to control 'objects', with an increasing top-down imposition (Arnove, 2005: 81).

Results from our study show that teachers and school leaders feel alienated from the macro level of educational policies. Teachers and leaders note there is an ever-increasing divide between education practice and policy, and that politicians are indifferent to the real issues. A lack of trust at the macro level is explicit. According to teachers and leaders, a sign of the lack of trust is the extensive regulation of schools. Rapid, ill-advised, and poorly planned changes are taken to be the reason for the lack of institutional trust, along with a deficiency of common understanding and stability. Furthermore, interview respondents also noted that the opinions of educators are often ignored and they are not involved in decision-making process. Respondents' explicit expectation for institutional trust reflects a certain conflict between the micro (relational) and macro (political) levels with the institutional (mezzo) level acting as the buffer. On the other hand, fairly explicit relational trust was noted, as when teachers and leaders believe in the power of trust and try to create a culture based on trust in spite of difficulties. The relatively high levels of relational trust show the potential for a bottom-up movement whereby teachers and leaders continue working in the name of pupils, preserving their professional dignity despite external pressures.

The likely direction of the change needed in Lithuanian education is highlighted by the differences in the educational systems and ideologies of Lithuania and Finland, where Finland values and fosters professional capital, which creates conditions in which education professionals can undertake their noble mission in a trust-based environment, thus strengthening their social capital (Hargreaves and Shirley, 2012: 49). Lithuanian education reformer Meilė Lukšienė has stated on many occasions that significant changes will not take place until schools move from being an object under constant regulation to being an autonomous and responsible agent of reform (Lukšienė, 2014).

The exclusion of policy and practice has been highlighted in educators' public forums. Four main issues were highlighted during the 2013 National

Leadership Forum (attended by over 600 education professionals): the inertia of the education system and its unsuitability to meet the needs of learners; contradictory national education policy; the prevailing economic attitude to education and the diminishing of a value-based approach; and lastly the lack of dialogue in education in order to promote trust. Attendees invited everyone with an interest in education to continue the dialogue, which spread to various districts in Lithuania.

To conclude, we can state that the question of trust in Lithuanian education (especially institutional trust) is yet not a subject of public discourse. Hargreaves and Shirley's typology of educational reforms reveals that education professionals in the West experienced a crisis of trust once governments introduced neo-liberal policies in education. Such tendencies of marketization and standardization are taken to be progressive directions in education in Lithuania, and the lack of trust regarding them has not been subject to sufficient analysis and public debate. There needs to be more serious reflection on the processes, louder voices from educators, and braver aspirations for deep learning and professionalism. We believe in the potential for education in Lithuania and feel that the time will come for Lithuania to move toward a Fourth Way, where education is no longer a political hostage but develops in accordance with inspiring moral goals and with trusting communities of practice for the success of every learner.

References

Arnove, R.F. (2005) 'To what ends: Educational reform around the world'. *Indiana Journal of Global Legal Studies*, 12 (1), 79–95.

Bulajeva, T., and Doublienė, L. (eds) (2009) *Lietuvos švietimo politikos transformacijos*. Vilnius: VU leidykla.

Cardinal, L.G., Guyonne, J.F., and Pouzoullic, B. (1997) *La dynamique de la confiance : Construire la coopération dans les projets complexes*. Paris: Éditions Dunod.

Donskis, L. (2005) 'The unbearable lightness of change'. In Samalavičius, A. (ed.) *Forms of Freedom: Lithuanian culture and Europe after 1990*. Vilnius: Kultūros barai.

Dukynaitė, R., and Stundžia, M. (2013) 'OECD PISA 2012 metų pristatymas'. Online. www.smm.lt/uploads/lawacts/docs/686_f51836d864358476c32d0a3923e6be58.pdf (accessed 1 January 2015).

Giddens, A. (1997) *Jenseits von Links und Rechts: Die Zukunft radikaler Demokratie*. Trans. Schulte, J. Frankfurt am Main: Suhrkamp.

Hargreaves, A., and Shirley, D. (2009) *The Fourth Way*. Thousand Oaks, CA: Corwin Press.

— (2012) *The Global Fourth Way*. Thousand Oaks, CA: Corwin Press.

Hazeldine, T. (1998) *Taking New Zealand Seriously*. Auckland: HarperCollins.

Kavaliauskas, T. (2012) 'Apie Zenono Norkaus teleologinį mąstymą klausiant: ar vidurio Europoje pokomunistinė transformacija jau užbaigta?' *Darbai ir dienos*, 58, 323–34.

— (2014) *Transformations in Central Europe between 1989 and 2012: Geopolitical, cultural, and socioeconomic shifts.* Lanham, MD: Lexington Books.

Lingis, A. (2004) *Trust.* Minneapolis/London: University of Minnesota Press.

Lukšienė, M. (2014) *Educating for Freedom.* Vilnius: Alma Littera.

Mažeikienė, N., Naujaniene, R., and Ruškus, J. (2014) 'What is mixed in welfare mix? Welfare ideologies at stake in the Lithuanian case of social service delivery'. *European Journal of Social Work*, 17 (5), 641–655.

Ministry of Education and Culture (1992) *The General Concept of Education in Lithuania.* Vilnius: Author.

Norkus Z. (2008) *Kokia demokratija, koks kapitalizmas? Pokomunistinė transformacija Lietuvoje lyginamosios istorinės sociologijos požiūriu* [Which Democracy, Which Capitalism? Post-communist transformation in Lithuania from the viewpoint of comparative historical sociology]. Vilnius: Vilnius University Press.

Olssen, M., Codd, J., and O'Neil, A.M. (2004) *Education Policy: Globalization, Citizenship and Democracy.* London: Sage.

Putnam, R.D. (ed.) (2004) *Democracies in Flux: The evolution of social capital in contemporary society.* Oxford: Oxford University Press.

Sahlberg, P. (2006) 'Education reform for raising economic competitiveness'. *Journal of Educational Change*, 7 (4), 259–87.

Silova, I., and Brehm, W.C. (2013) 'The shifting boundaries of teacher professionalism: Education privatization(s) in the post-Socialist education space'. In Seddon, T., and Levin, J. (eds) *Educators, Professionalism and Politics: Global transitions, national spaces, and professional projects.* New York: Routledge, 55–74.

Vaicekauskienė, V. (2013) *Nepriklausomos valstybės švietimo kūrimo pamokos: 1988-2012: Švietimo problemos analizė.* Vilnius: Švietimo aprūpinimo centras.

Želvys, R. (2009) 'Lietuvos švietimo politikos kontekstas'. In Bulajeva,T., and Doublienė, L. (eds) *Lietuvos švietimo politikos transformacijos.* Vilnius: VU leidykla, 13–23.

Žiliukaitė, R. (2006) 'Pasitikėjimas: nuo teorinių įžvalgų empirinės analizės link'. *Kultūrologija*, 13 t., 205–52.

Žiliukaitė, R., Ramonaitė, A., Nevinskaitė, L., Beresnevičiūtė, V., and Vinogradnaitė, I. (2006) *Neatrasta galia: Lietuvos pilietinės visuomenės žemėlapis.*Vilnius: Versus aureus.

Chapter 7

Sweden: 'A postmodern cocktail'

Lars Svedberg

Sweden is the fifth-largest country by area in Europe, with a population of 9.7 million, of whom 15 per cent were born in another country. Spending on education as a function of GNP is around 15 per cent above the PISA average. Teachers' annual working time is 1,767 hours. Of this time, approximately a third is used for direct teaching, with another third used for planning and follow-up. A quarter of the time is at teachers' own disposal, and the remaining one-twelfth is common time for school development, in-service training, and similar aspects.

The first decade and a half of the twenty-first century presents a confusing situation internationally. Trying to improve educational results, some countries have explicitly gradually abandoned the comprehensive school project, whereas other countries remain faithful (at least at the rhetorical level) to the comprehensive tradition. Intertwined with these shifts in policy, we see transnationally the emergence of new forms of governance as a response to changing and often uncertain conditions (Ball and Junemann, 2012; Breakspear, 2012; Meyer and Benavot, 2013; Macpherson *et al.*, 2014). An overview of current research in Sweden shows that school leaders' work is negotiated, conditioned, and categorized in three dimensions: politics and profession, national intentions and local conditions, and education as democracy or education as a commercialized commodity in a market (Johansson, 2011). This means that the relations between the actors in education have changed and are changing, particularly due to the introduction of market forces in education. The ideals of the comprehensive project seem to be fading. The question of 'who you can trust' is particularly topical now in Sweden, where the former citizen of the welfare state has been transformed gradually into a customer in an educational marketplace. The learner is increasingly conceptualized as a consumer and education as a consumer good.

In the name of democracy

After the Second World War, a series of reforms were launched in Sweden with the purpose of developing an educational system worthy of the welfare state. Although Sweden had largely escaped the horrors of the First and Second World Wars, there was a strong determination to prevent the emergence of non-democratic movements. The emerging welfare state, governed by the Social Democrats, was imagined to be characterized by equal opportunities for all citizens regardless of social background and gender. This is typically formulated in a government report from 1946, still frequently cited although it was written in the aftermath of the Second World War: 'Democracy has no use for mass-dependent people. The democratic school's task is thus to develop free human beings for whom cooperation is a need and a joy' (National Board of Education, 1946; my translation).

The definition of a comprehensive project was formulated in the period after the Second World War, and equality debates brought into conflict arguments in support of the older separationist (elite/mass) educational system and arguments for a fundamental change in education. The new democratic education project was justified by framing the common good in terms of equal opportunities. After more than a decade of preparations, the new comprehensive 'School for All' was introduced in 1962. Under this new system all children, regardless of social capital, were brought together to be educated in the same classroom, rather than in two separate educational systems as before. Since this period, all Swedish national curricula have begun with similar key statements to that in the quote above about the moral purposes and values of education. From a historical perspective, this is the very beginning of the modern Swedish school project – an inclusive project that was very successful for several decades and a model that inspired several other countries (not least our neighbour Finland).

A market-friendly agenda

Up until 1990, Sweden did very well on international comparisons. However, the way education was governed started to be criticized in the late 1980s for being too centralized, rigid, and bureaucratic. The educational success story had gradually lost its appeal, and the old public administration (OPA) was questioned by new public management (NPM) ideals. In the early 1990s, the responsibility for education was further devolved to local authorities, and a new system of governance was introduced where teachers' employment was delegated from the state to local municipalities. The introduction of 'management by objectives' in Sweden during this period was a major institutional reform that significantly changed the prerequisites for political actors and their relationship to professionals (Jarl and Rönnberg, 2010). The basic idea appears to have been to govern *less,* through municipalization, delegation, and decentralization, and at the same time to govern *more,* through goals, inspection, and evaluation. Since then, more than 55 reforms have been introduced in education. This constantly changing (and nervous) educational governance system presents a number of challenges for principals as well as for teachers. A consequence of this market-friendly approach during the last two decades is that today, about 15 per cent of all Swedish children from pre-school to upper secondary school get their education in independent schools. The family of independent schools has considerable internal differences: some are small co-operatives run by parents or staff, whereas others are parts of large, listed companies owned by venture capitalists (which in many cases make a considerable profit). Particularly in the bigger cities, the competition is keen between independent and municipal schools. Those in favour of independent schools emphasize the advantage that parents can choose between different school offerings and pick a school they regard as suitable for their child. Those opposed to independent schools emphasize the downside of this system, and point to an increased segregation, arguing that such a system hampers transparency over how public money is spent and that these schools can go bankrupt and close down like any business organization (which has happened and continues to do so). Education has become a sector that is increasingly being opened up to profit-making and trade, and to agenda-setting by private, commercial interests.

Given this short background, Sweden is an interesting case for our times. On the one hand, Sweden's standing in international comparisons like PISA and TIMMS has dropped, but on the other, the country still performs very well in civic/democratic comparisons like *The Economist*'s (2015) Democracy Index. Today, media are generally busy pointing out problems and scapegoating, but rarely pay attention to positive results and outcomes. However, educational politics is now more cautious concerning market issues. Verification and control strategies such as increased and centralized policies, standardized tests, and tighter audits and inspections are now more and more in demand. Given this context, a relevant question concerns what happens to principals' and teachers' trust and to trust in principals and teachers when results drop in international comparisons, and when politicians are eager to provide quick fixes and show disrespect by telling teachers what to do in the classroom.

Relational trust and institutional trust

Trust has increasingly become a theme for research during the last ten or fifteen years. Trust is often considered a subset of social capital, but at other times the term 'trust' is used as a straightforward synonym of 'social capital'. Bourdieu (1986) and Coleman (1988) introduced the term 'social capital', and argue that trust should be understood as the density of networks and as something that is born and sustained only by the networks' existence. Putnam (1993) defines social capital, for example, as a phenomenon that consists of individuals' participation in formal and informal networks, principles of reciprocity, and degrees of interpersonal trust. Many people nowadays love to use the term 'trust', which produces a dilemma – trust can mean everything and nothing. A starting point, anyway, is that trust is a relational phenomenon close to social capital. In this vein, trust can be seen at once as a psychological, organizational, and sociological phenomenon. From a psychological perspective, trust is an essential quality, a 'hard currency' in human relationships between parents and children, between teachers and students, and between employees and managers. From an organizational perspective, it is a tendency of the various parts and levels of an organization to pull in the same direction, and from a sociological perspective, trust is the glue that holds together a society and a democracy – the capacity to be able to trust people you do not know. From this trust perspective, management's perhaps essential task is to be exemplary in terms of cultivating a respectful dialogue in the interfaces between organizational domains and creating trust in a unifying idea rather than listening to politically correct educational gurus. Trust is an indispensable currency, particularly in education (Hargreaves and Fullan, 2012).

For the empirical purposes of this study, we employ Fink's two categories of trust (see Chapter 2): *relational trust* between leaders and colleagues, and *institutional trust* among schools, districts, and their communities. In this section, the three highest- and the three lowest-rated statements from a survey given to Swedish principals and teachers are accounted for as they relate to institutional trust and relational trust, and we set out how the respondents perceive 'the real scenario'. These lowest and highest levels of trust will together provide indicators relevant for the wider system. In conclusion, the findings are summarized and responses in relation to 'the ideal scenario' are also reported.

The Swedish trust survey

The sample

The Swedish version of the web questionnaire upon which this chapter draws was answered by 224 principals and 96 teachers in 2014. The principals in the survey were taking part in the National Programme for School Leaders; a number of them asked teachers in their schools to answer the survey. Of the principals, 30 per cent are male and 70 per cent female, and they are fairly evenly distributed between primary, secondary, and upper secondary education; a third are deputy principals, and two-thirds are principals; their average age is 47 years, and they have on average 5 years of experience. This means that the principals in the sample are in an early stage of their careers and younger than the average principal. The proportion of principals from independent schools in the sample is high compared to the entire population.

Of the teachers, 26 per cent are male and 74 per cent are female, and they are fairly evenly distributed between primary, secondary, and upper secondary education; their average age is 46 years, and they have on average 13 years of experience. This means that the teachers in the sample are fairly experienced; they have a similar distribution of gender, and their average ages are more or less the same as is the case for the principals. The proportion of teachers from independent schools in the sample is also high compared to the entire population of Swedish teachers.

Further data is drawn from two focus-group interviews with principals and two focus-group interviews with teachers. The heterogeneously composed focus groups were invited to comment upon the three highest- and three lowest-rated questionnaire items relating to principals' and teachers' institutional trust and relational trust.

Principals' institutional trust

The three highest-ranked questionnaire items relating to principals' institutional trust are as follows, in descending order. Bearing in mind that the scale of responses ranges from 1–5, where 1 = 'strongly disagree' and 5 = 'strongly agree', these highest-ranked statements, with mean scores ranging from 3.78 to 3.86, are all below 4, which points towards a modest average agreement in relation to trust.

- School leaders are knowledgeable about effective teaching practices and contemporary learning theories.
- Trustworthy leaders at all levels say what they mean and mean what they say.

- The public and policy makers deserve independent information on the successes and failures of each school.

Among the principals, there is a modest agreement that there exists a good standard of knowledge among colleagues. Thus, principals' image of their own profession appears to be positive, both in terms of knowledge and sincerity: they 'walk the talk'. There is also a belief that the transparency of each school's successes and failures is fairly good when independent information is available (and then probably not in the sense of 'naming and blaming').

The three lowest rankings given by principals to questionnaire items concerning institutional trust are as follows (all on the 'disagree' side of the scale, with mean scores for agreement below 3):

- Teacher unions protect all teachers regardless of their competence.
- The provincial educational system is prepared to pay for quality leadership.
- The government backs its teachers when their professionalism is questioned by the press and other media sources.

The items whose rankings indicate the lowest levels of agreement concern three fairly separate aspects of trust. First, teacher unions are perceived as protecting their members, regardless of their competence, and as unhelpful when it comes to acting as an agency for school improvement. Secondly, principals are not pleased with their salaries. Thirdly, and with by far the lowest rating, the local politicians and the school board are not perceived to back their teachers when they are questioned. The role of unions, unreliable school boards, and a system not prepared to pay for quality leadership thus appear to be the three lowest-rated institutional aspects of trust.

Principals' relational trust

The three highest-ranked items pertaining to relational trust as rated by the cohort of principals are as follows. With mean agreement scores from 4.23–4.3 per cent, these attracted relatively higher levels of agreement than those pertaining to institutional trust.

- School improvement depends on school leaders' ability to build trusting relationships with all staff members.
- School leaders place the welfare of their students above all other stakeholders (government, teachers, unions, and even parents).
- Working in a 'high-trust' environment makes a teacher a more effective professional in promoting student learning.

Principals value relational trust for at least two reasons: school improvement depends on leaders' ability to build trusting relationships, and a high-trust environment enables teachers to promote better student learning. Along with this, student welfare is also said to be a high priority among principals.

The three lowest rankings given by principals to questionnaire items concerning relational trust are as follows. With means from 2.92–3.62, the first two items listed below fall on the 'agree' side and the third statement on the 'disagree' side of the scale.

- School leaders feel valued by senior levels of the government.
- Teachers rally behind their school leaders during difficult situations.
- It is best to trust the leadership of those in charge by going along with what they want.

The first two relational trust items attracting relatively low levels of agreement are about the principals' hierarchical position. It appears that a bit more appreciation from their superiors is in demand. Also, though they perceive teachers to rally behind them in tough situations, principals would like to see more of this. By far, the lowest agreement was given to the item concerning blind trust and passively following superiors.

Teachers' institutional trust

The three highest ranked items concerning institutional trust as rated by teachers are as follows. With means from 3.24–3.35, it should be pointed out that even these highest ratings fall into the zone of uncertainty between disagreement and agreement.

- Quality teaching is one of the educational system's highest priorities.
- Teachers' unions protect all teachers regardless of their competence.
- The public and policy makers deserve independent information on the successes and failures of each school.

Among teachers, there is modest agreement that the system prioritizes quality teaching. As in the case of principals, there is also a belief that transparency about the successes and failures of each school is fairly good when independent information is available. Teachers moderately agree that unions protect teachers regardless of their competence. (Principals rated this in the opposite way, as a cause for low trust.) However, we do not know whether all teachers perceive this as a good thing or not.

The three *lowest* rankings given by teachers to institutional trust-related items are as follows (means 1.93–2.35).

- The educational system backs its teachers when their professionalism is questioned by the press and other media sources.
- The educational system is prepared to pay for quality teaching.
- District and school leaders admit mistakes openly and promptly.

The fairly strong disagreements with these statements illustrate a low-trust system. The system is in this case reported to fail to stand behind its teachers when they are questioned, and teachers' superiors are not that frank; they do not openly and promptly admit mistakes. Additionally, teachers say that the educational system is not prepared to pay for quality teaching, despite the fact this is one of the educational system's highest priorities (according to what the same teachers rated as high institutional trust). Here, principals and teachers both feel poorly backed and poorly paid.

Teachers' relational trust

The three highest rankings given by teachers to items concerning relational trust are as follows (means 3.93–4.31):

- Teachers' assessment includes more than just test scores.
- Teachers' trust of their leaders is conditional on the leader's competence.
- Teachers' willingness to support each other's teaching is crucial to school improvement.

Teachers say they see beyond test scores when they assess students, which probably is possible only in a context of functional relationships. Furthermore, teachers' trust in their leaders is conditional, and trust is earned by showing competence. It is also crucial for school improvement that the teaching culture is perceived as being supportive.

The three lowest rankings given by teachers to items concerning relational trust are as follows (means 2.44–3.08):

- It is best to trust the leadership of those in charge by going along with what they want.
- School leaders maintain trust by addressing poor teacher practices promptly and effectively.
- Teachers have the time and space to work collaboratively.

As with principals, teachers express their professional independence and reject a passive followership. Teachers describing the ideal situation also felt that it was less than impressive for principals to address poor teacher practice promptly: this kind of intervention is not a way to maintain trust. The esprit de corps is obviously rather vulnerable regarding this matter.

Since a collaborative teaching culture is highly ranked, the perceived lack of time and space to work collaboratively is by far ranked the lowest.

Comparing teachers' and principals' trust

The highest accordance between teachers' and principals' ratings is found in the statements below.

- In difficult situations, teachers support their school leaders.
- The educational system backs its teachers when their professionalism is questioned by the press and other media sources.
- It is best to trust the leadership of those in charge by going along with what they want.

Teachers and principals share the same ratings and mildly agree that teachers support principals in difficult situations. They also share the opinion that the system hardly backs its teachers when media question them. Neither teachers nor principals are in favour of following leaders without good reasons.

The lowest accordance between teachers' and principals' ratings was found for the statements below:

- School leaders maintain trust by addressing poor teacher practice promptly and effectively.
- School leaders need to know about and show concern for staff members' personal circumstances.
- District and school leaders admit mistakes openly and promptly.

Principals believe that trust is maintained by addressing poor teacher practices promptly and effectively, but teachers do not agree. Teachers appreciate when school leaders show concern for staff members' personal circumstances, but principals do not give this a high priority. Finally, teachers are more sceptical than principals regarding whether district and school leaders admit mistakes openly and promptly. All these statements concern relational trust.

Ideal scenario and real scenarios

For almost all of the 30 statements, principals clearly rate their 'ideal scenario' higher than the 'real scenario'. However, there are two exceptions: The first is 'Teacher unions should be more discriminative and refrain from protecting teachers regardless of their competencies.' The second is 'Ideally, principals should not have to act as gatekeepers to protect teachers and students from negative effects of political decisions to the extent as they do now.' Both of these statements take a negative stance.

In all of the 30 statements in the questionnaire except for one, teachers also rate the ideal situations more highly than their realities. The only exception is that they feel there should be even less 'trusting the leadership of those in charge by going along with what they want'. The diagram below illustrates the average ratings given by principals and teachers in the real and ideal scenarios to items concerning institutional and relational trust.

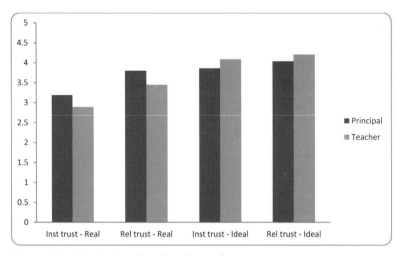

Figure 7.1: Institutional and relational trust statements: mean agreement scores in real and ideal scenarios from teachers and principals in Sweden

Principals' institutional trust levels are much lower than their relational trust levels, and in the case of teachers this pattern is even more pronounced. There is also a considerable discrepancy between how principals and teachers rate real trust and the ideal trust in both categories. Generally it appears that principals' levels of trust are higher than teachers' levels of trust in the real scenario, but the opposite is true in the case of the ideal scenario. What stands out here is the wide gap between teachers' low levels of actual institutional trust and how they would like things to be.

In most aspects, the focus group interviews confirm the results from the survey. It was striking that the more the importance of trust was discussed, the greater the emphasis on it became, as past experiences were recalled to mind. Teachers as well as principals pointed out a strong relationship between trust and results, as illustrated in the two excerpts below:

> It is important that we clarify the expectations we have of each other. Then we can develop a collaborative environment of trust and confidence. If we can do this well, it constitutes an important

breeding ground for teachers to be successful in teaching and for students to realize their potential.

(Teacher, Sweden)

It is important that we develop a culture of trust. Only then we will achieve our goals.

(Principal, Sweden)

The importance of trust was further emphasized in discussion of its absence, i.e. cases when distrust is expressed through naming and shaming:

I have experienced open distrust from my local politicians ... They act like cowards when they blame the principals as being guilty for their unpopular decisions/changes.

(Principal, Sweden)

A noticeable difference between the survey and the focus group interviews concerned the role of teacher unions. Principals and teachers alike said the local union representatives quite often had difficulties in finding a constructive role, and hung on to blind support from their members. It was argued that such strategies are counterproductive in the long run. However, teachers' unions at the regional and national levels were said to be much more constructive.

With these four statements, a summary of the findings from the survey and from the focus group interview is made:

- Principals' *institutional* trust concerns their own profession and the capacity of the system to be transparent about educational outcomes. Trust here is low concerning the moral capacities of the educational institution: they perceive themselves to be working against a backdrop of protectionist trade unions (at the local level), an educational system that lacks the stamina to back its teachers, and a system unwilling to pay for quality leadership.
- Principals' *relational* trust concerns their capacity (and the perceived necessity) to build a high-trust environment with teachers and students. Here, trust is the key to promote effective student learning.
- Teachers' *institutional* trust is generally low. The relatively highest levels of trust are associated with a perception of a system that has high-quality teaching as a high priority, that values transparency over outcomes, and that features trade unions that protect their members through unconditional support. Like principals, teachers are concerned about the moral capacities of the educational institution: teachers do

not feel backed by the system in difficult situations. They believe that district and school leaders do not admit mistakes, and that the system is unwilling to pay for high-quality teaching.

- Teachers' *relational* trust is high in relation to three distinct aspects: they agree that (1) assessment goes beyond test scores, indicating the importance of the qualitative aspects of teaching; that (2) a key to school improvement lies in teachers' willingness to support each other, indicating the importance of the collaborative aspects of teaching; and that (3) trust for leaders is conditional and depends on their levels of competence. Two of the lowest rankings in this aspect concern the relationship between teachers and principals. Principals' legitimacy is to be earned and should not be taken for granted, and interventions with regard to poor teaching are not an obvious way to build trust. Above all, lack of time is a threat to teachers' mutual collaboration.

High trust–High distrust

The answers from the surveys and from the focus group interviews are quite striking: principals' institutional trust is low and relational trust is high, and this is even more the case for teachers. This is further underscored when we take the discrepancy between the real scenario and the ideal scenario into account. It appears that Sweden falls into the high-trust/high-distrust quadrant described in Chapter 2:

> Trust emerges when the trustor perceives that the trustee intends to perform an action that is beneficial. The perceived positive intentions in calculus-based trust derive not only from the existence of deterrence but because of credible information such as certification or references from reliable sources regarding the intentions or competence of another.
>
> (Fink, this volume).

Principals seem to hold their own profession in high esteem when it comes to their knowledge and morals, but feel that the educational system does not back its members or pay for what they say they value, i.e. high-quality leadership. When it comes to their own schools, building a high-trust environment is said to be a condition for success, and, vice versa, the perceived lack of trust from superiors or teachers is a bothersome concern. Could it be that principals seek to compensate for a lack of institutional trust by (over)emphasizing relational trust?

A similar pattern is found among the teachers. They feel that transparency is appreciated and high-quality teaching nominally prioritized, but there is no willingness to pay for this. The protection from teachers' unions is appreciated, especially since teachers' trust in leaders at all levels is conditional. As in the case of principals, to counterbalance this, the trust among colleagues and the willingness to provide collegial support are valued.

Additional perspectives

A biannual survey from the Swedish National Agency for Education regarding parents and teachers' attitudes toward education shows a similar pattern (National Agency for Education, 2013). Parents in particular, but teachers as well, value the quality of secondary and upper secondary education. However, trust in national politicians – and even more so in local politicians – is very low. Schools are rated highly by local parents, who can see what actually takes place in their local school with their own eyes, but in sharp contrast with this nine out of ten teachers and parents say their trust in local and national educational institutions is low or very low. It is to say the least troublesome when parents, and especially teachers, have so little confidence in those who have been elected and who make important decisions about educational resources, organization, and objectives.

Another recent Swedish study has evaluated how principals and superintendents work together. Since research quite consistently shows that principals are important, it is assumed in this study that superintendents in turn are important for principals. Thus, one aspect in this study is the degree of trust between superintendents and principals (Svedberg, 2014). In Figure 7.2 below, trust levels have been exemplified in five statements (from 5 = strongly agree to 1 = strongly disagree).

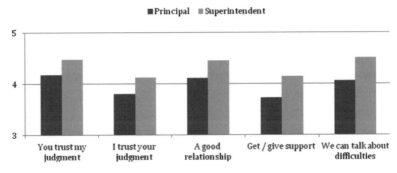

Figure 7.2: Aspects of trust: average ratings in Sweden

The results show that superintendents trust principals slightly more than vice versa. There is also a shared belief that principals/superintendents' own judgement is given greater credence by the opposite party than the reverse.

But, on average relational trust appears to be high between principals and their superintendents.

A conclusion from these studies is that when institutional trust falters, face-to-face contacts appear to become even more important. This proximate interaction takes place simultaneously on several levels – verbal, physical, contextual, intentional, and non-intentional – which are all important for the transmission of qualified knowledge, understanding, and empathy: coordination problems decrease, motivational issues can be dealt with, and verbal messages that are not compatible with body language can be noted. In small networks, there is an opportunity to get to know others and assess their skills: these encounters establish a sense of belonging and are regarded as socializing. It's not just a question of an effective exchange of information; it is, above all, direct participation in a whole world of ideas that increases the quality of organizational life.

A post-modern cocktail

In retrospect, the Swedish educational reforms during the last couple of decades have not lived up to expectations. The reforms have been implemented hastily with scant political support, and often against teachers' will. This has led to a school system that does not create equivalence or make the teaching profession attractive. The 55 reforms, one by one, might each very well in some sense have been well motivated. However, taken together, they have metaphorically speaking reacted with one another in unpredictable and unintended ways, producing a 'cocktail effect' in education. By analogy to medical science, one cannot experimentally evaluate the combined effect of multiple reforms simultaneously. Ultimately, it should be a matter of professional expertise and judgement to determine how much medication the patient can tolerate. When reforms do not produce what is expected, problems tend to be defined as implementation shortcomings or motivational issues rather than structural problems or even failing policies. Thus, many teachers and principals are confused. The symptoms of this cocktail effect include an increased need for information when the system becomes increasingly complex and difficult to decipher. In turn, this uncertainty results in more appointments, meetings, phone calls, plans, emails, and other communication efforts. Moreover, in the name of accountability, an increasing number of documents are in constant demand and need to be produced, discussed, negotiated, and revised.

The trust paradox

A large proportion of Swedish teachers and principals, who by tradition have had high confidence in the welfare state and its institutions, now feel frustrated by all of the reforms that have given rise to a hungry audit apparatus but have had no positive impact in classrooms. This discrepancy between Sweden's general culture of trust and its poor performance on international measures is noticeable and intriguing. Obviously, general trust in institutions is still high and has been so since the introduction of the welfare state half a century ago, and Sweden still does well in surveys like the Democracy Index (*The Economist*, 2015). A reason for the poor performance could very well be that a lack of stability, in combination with the marketization of education, has gradually eroded the sense and degree of professionalism among educators. This can be seen not least by the way in which teachers' status and the profession's attractiveness have fallen precipitately as reforms have progressed. Other professions have probably been shown more respect, and hence have been much less affected by these by these fundamental changes that have had a high impact on education.

According to Power (1997), by definition the 'audit society' is one that has come to understand the solutions to many of its problems in terms of auditing. Undoubtedly, Swedish principals spend more and more time reacting to results from internal and external audits. The audit society is governed by an audit logic, or even audit machinery, for which the value-related and epistemological premises are cloudy. The forms of governance and the ways to respond to these generate a considerable number of documents that are characterized by structural and technocratic logics. In this vein, school leaders get more and more occupied by administrativia and produce strategies, plans, reports, etc. Power (1997) argues that a purpose of audit procedures that should not be neglected is to comfort decision-makers, so that they can feel confident that everything is working well – so well that the auditors are satisfied. These 'rituals of verification', are self-reinforcing: the more we use them, the more need for them we discover. New reasons to distrust schools are found, and, in the long run, a name-and-blame culture is nourished. We have now reached a point where evaluation and review systems have been expanded to such a degree that they themselves generate a time-consuming bureaucracy that introduces new efficiency problems (Meyer and Benavot, 2013).

Similar ideas are presented by Lundquist (2010), who coined the term 'economism' to describe how the ideology of NPM affects the public sector and, not least, the role of civil servants. Lundquist (2010) argues that this economism has broken down the role of civil servants and the public ethos that previously characterized the Swedish public administration. He claims that one reason for this is that economism strengthens efficiency values excessively, at the expense of democratic values. It holds the ambition that one size should fit all, irrespective of context, as predicted by Scott and Meyer two decades ago (1994):

> An older world in which schools were managed by educators, hospitals by doctors, railroads by railroad men now recedes into quaintness. All these things are now seen as organizations and it is this that produces a great expansion, almost everywhere, of management ... A disembodied management, which can be applied in any time and place and activity setting ... One can now discuss what constitutes the proper basis of organization without much mentioning the actual substantive activities that the organization will do.
>
> (Scott and Meyer, 1994: 54)

Similar intrinsic mechanisms of the audit society and the intricate interplay between trust and distrust are well-described by Gustavson and Rothstein as a paradox:

> Audits are a social institution that can be seen as a mechanism in which the opposites trust and distrust are woven together in an intricate interplay. One can express this as a paradox: Audits are an institutionalized form of distrust designed to create trust.
>
> (Gustavson and Rothstein, 2012: 67)

This logic of the audit society is not fully compatible with a logic based on trust in professionals. What is valid and meaningful in audit logic with a market approach is not always valid and meaningful to professionals. However, if these two logics are drawn to their extremes, the consequences are absurd. In contemporary criticism, there is a tendency to sometimes demonize NPM beyond recognition. Management reforms have at least partially improved the cost-effectiveness of public spending and are, to a certain degree, necessary and rejuvenating.

These days, Swedish teachers, as in the survey and focus groups in this chapter, often experience contradictory expectations: teachers are said to be crucial and the key to high results, but, at the same time, there is an organizational quest for a 'teacher-proof system' with guiding concepts such as best practices, inspection, and control. These double messages demonstrate a lack of respect and can be tough to digest. On the one hand, trust is most needed in situations of high uncertainty—i.e., in situations where trust is most difficult to obtain. On the other hand, trust is less needed in the stable situations where it is most easily produced (Yamagishi, 2011). The trust paradox means that principals have to get results out of the audit apparatus as a means to calm and reassure the educational board and, at the same time, to ensure trust and legitimacy from teachers. The inherent distrust of audits and uncertainty produced by the system has to be counterbalanced by trust within personal relations in order to reduce ambivalence.

Leaders need to balance the accountability agenda and the demands of the audit apparatus – what Power (1997) called rituals of verification and symbols of compliance – against the professional agenda, in which education is primarily a moral project with social and emancipatory goals that have the ability to transform lives and futures.

Finally, these communication skills and this balancing act both require personal involvement, emotional work, and emotional labour. Trust is the currency that is required in professional relationships, perhaps to counterbalance the system's uncertainties and incongruences.

References

Ball, S.J., and Junemann, C. (2012) *Networks, New Governance and Education*. Bristol: Policy Press.

Bourdieu, P. (1986) 'The forms of capital'. In Richardson, J.G. (ed.) *Handbook of Theory and Research for the Sociology of Education*. Westport, CT: Greenwood Press.

Breakspear, S. (2012) 'The policy impact of PISA: An exploration of the normative effects of international benchmarking in school system performance'. OECD Education Working Papers, No. 71. Online. http://dx.doi.org/10.1787/5k9fdfqffr28-en (accessed February 2014).

Coleman, J.S. (1988) 'Social capital in the creation of human capital'. *American Journal of Sociology*, 94, S95–S120.

The Economist (2015) 'Democracy Index 2014: Democracy and its discontents. A report from The Economist Intelligence Unit'. Online. www.sudestada.com.uy/Content/Articles/421a313a-d58f-462e-9b24-2504a37f6b56/Democracy-index-2014.pdf (accessed 3 February 2016).

Gustavson, M., and Rothstein, B. (2012) 'Tillit till makten att granska [Trusting the power to review]'. In Reuter, M., Wijkström, F., and Kristensson Uggla, B. (eds) *Vem i hela världen kan man lite på? Förtroende i teori och praktik* [Who on earth can you trust? Trust in theory and practice]. Lund: Studentlitteratur.

Hargreaves, A., and Fullan, M. (2012) *Professional Capital: Transforming teaching in every school*. New York: Teachers College Press.

Jarl, M., and Rönnberg, L. (2010) *Skolpolitik. Från riksdagshus till klassrum* [Educational politics: From parliament to classroom]. Malmö: Liber.

Johansson, O. (ed.) (2011) *Rektor—En forskningsöversikt 2000–2010* [The Principal – A research overview]. Stockholm: Vetenskapsrådet.

Kristensson Uggla, B. (2012) 'Förtroendekapitalets komplexitet och mångdimensionalitet'. In Reuter, M., Wijkström, F., and Kristensson Uggla, B. (eds) *Vem i hela världen kan man lita på? Förtroende i teori och praktik*. Lund: Studentlitteratur.

Lundquist, L. (2010) *Etik i offentlig förvaltning [Ethics in public governance]*. In Rothstein, B. (ed.) *Politics as organisation*. Stockholm: SNS Förlag.

Macpherson, I., Robertson, S., and Walford, G. (eds) (2014) *Education, Privatisation and Social Justice: Case studies from Africa, South Asia and South East Asia*. Oxford: Symposium Books.

Meyer, H.-D., and Benavot, A. (eds) (2013) *PISA, Power and Policy: The emergence of global educational governance*. Oxford: Symposium Books.

National Agency for Education (2013) *Attityder till skolan 2012* [Attitudes to Education 2012]. Report 390. Stockholm: Skolverket.

National Board of Education (1946) *Report of the 1946 National School Commission, including guidelines for development of the Swedish school system*. Swedish Government Official Reports, SOU 1948:27.

Power, M. (1997) *The Audit Society: Rituals of verification*. Oxford: Oxford University Press.

Putnam, R.D. (1993) *Making Democracy Work: Civic traditions in modern Italy*. Princeton, NJ: Princeton University Press.

Scott, W.R., and Meyer, J.W. (eds) (1994) *Institutional Environments and Organizations: Structural complexity and individualism*. London: Sage.

Svedberg, L. (ed.) (2014) *Rektor, skolchefen och resultaten – mellan politik och profession* [The principal, the superintendent and the results – between politics and profession]. Malmö: Gleerups.

Yamagishi, T. (2011) *Trust: The evolutionary game of mind and society*. Tokyo: Springer.

Chapter 8

The English case: Reform in a hurry

Tom Whittingham

The politicization of English education

Over the past 30 years, English educational leaders at all levels have experienced a bewildering plethora of policy changes, as policy makers – both Conservative and Labour – have lurched from one reform panacea to another and from one short-term expedient to another, with little thought given to the implications of these multiple and sometimes contradictory policies for policy implementers at the school level. Secretaries of state for education, each anxious to put a personal stamp on the system, followed one another in rapid order. Targets were set and then arbitrarily moved, money allocated and then reallocated before a project had a chance to show results, and change policies announced with much fanfare and soon forgotten. During the period 1979–97, the UK's Conservative governments initiated the first phase of policy changes to address the alleged underachievement of English students and the perceived widespread failure of British schools to prepare the young for the challenges of the twenty-first century. The 1998 Education Reform Act created a national curriculum for all state-supported schools as well as a national system of student testing and school inspections. The Act was a determined attempt to centralize accountability systems, diminish the power of local education authorities, and devolve resources and responsibility for meeting national standards to individual schools.

One of the most important and lasting changes in the English education reform agenda was the creation of the Office for Standards in Education (Ofsted). In 1992 the Conservative government created Ofsted, through which school inspectors – sometimes from private-sector agencies – would monitor schools every three or four years. Funding was devolved from Local Education Authority (LEA) budgets by the Secretary of State Kenneth Clarke to fuel Ofsted's associated costs. The withdrawal of this element of LEA statutory function was to prove a foretaste of the demise of LEAs' wider educational function. This heralded a totally different approach to verifying school performance from the previous inspection regime, under which well-respected HMI (Her Majesty's Inspectors) not only verified school performance but worked for its improvement. Christopher Woodhead was appointed to the role of Her Majesty's Chief Inspector of Schools in 1994, a post he held until 2000, and introduced a policy that required every school to be inspected every four years. Supposedly expert inspectors would comment on schools' standards in terms of pupils' achievement, the strength of a school's leadership, its use of resources, and the quality of the social, moral, spiritual, and cultural education provided. They would publish a report immediately following the inspection and the failure of underperforming schools was to be made public, a policy referred to as 'naming and shaming'.

Writing in *Education Next* in summer 2004, Woodhead reflected that the 'the unions and the education establishment hated the whole thing. Why, they asked plaintively, did the government want 'to pillory and demoralize' hard-working teachers? They compared school inspections to the Spanish Inquisition. And in the end they won. During the past four years, the inspection process has been softened gradually in response to teachers' criticism' (Woodhead, 2004: n.p.) – or at least it was changed to give the appearance of softening. Woodhead's rather nostalgic look at the institution he headed understates the deep and visceral reaction many educational professionals had towards this 'low trust' change agency. Ofsted inspectors, whom educators generally perceived to be more interested in fault-finding and finger-pointing than in helping to improve the system, acted as monitors for all the hyperactivity of successive governments.

Enter New Labour

When Tony Blair and his Labour Party won the election of 1997, educational professionals looked forward to a more measured, engaging, and thoughtful pace of reform and initially embraced 'New Labour's' vision of transformation, modernization, innovation, enterprise, dynamism, creativity, and competitiveness, all set in the context of a changing global economy. To Blair and his colleagues, educational reform was a prerequisite for economic competitiveness. As he explained, 'Complaining about globalisation is as pointless as trying to turn back the tide. Asian competition can't be shut out; it can only be beaten. And now, by every relative measure of a modern economy, Europe is lagging' (Blair, 2006: n.p.). As recognized by education theorists at this time, to thrive in the global knowledge economy it is going to be important to change the whole education system to ensure a wide base of knowledge workers who understand and use information technology. Thus education is the key, in order to ensure the skills for the knowledge economy exist in abundance (Ball, 2008). Blair pledged to raise standards with a blitz of initiatives and reforms such as national literacy and numeracy strategies, establishing Education Action Zones and funding after-school activity groups. While educators welcomed the Labour Party's considerable investment in education, many worried about the narrowing of educational purposes and the speed at which change continued to occur (Ball, 2008; Burch, 2009; Brown and Lauder, 2001).

New Labour in the first decade of this century decided to keep most of the trappings of the previous Conservative government's 'low trust' approach to schools by maintaining its Ofsted and its widely disliked Chief Inspector. They allowed a scaling up of pressure on schools to raise test scores, intensified target setting and introduced league tables that effectively name and shame underperforming schools, as judged by Ofsted and its much criticized data collection. New Labour set the tone for a period of one initiative and strategy after another, leaving little time to consolidate and grow before schools were asked to 'weigh and measure'. The long term effect was to erode any goodwill and trust by the unremitting drive for change with little time or support for consolidation. This led to system fragmentation and an overemphasis on accountability; change was being seen as 'done to' educational professionals not 'enabled with'.

Re-enter the Conservatives

Britain of course was not alone in its preoccupation with the connection between education and national prosperity in a global economy. The Organization for Economic Co-operation and Development (OECD), of which Britain was an active member, influenced policy via its collection, analysis, and marketing of education policy information. The OECD thus developed an advisory role to policy makers at the highest level. It has exerted widespread influence across education policy making over a number of years, and did so particularly during the 2010–15 Conservative–Liberal Democrat UK coalition government, which replaced the Labour government in 2010. The OECD's mantra is that 'formal education systems will play a crucial role in awakening and sharpening critical intelligence allowing individuals to move far beyond fear and introversion' (OECD, 1998: 117). Perhaps among the most effective of OECD's policy drivers is its three-yearly Programmes for International Student Assessment (PISA). PISA has been a significant influence in countries whose students perform less well on it, and has resulted in critical self-examination that has stimulated significant educational change. Britain's continuing sluggish performance on PISA compared to other nations can in part account for the feverish policy development of successive governments over recent decades. It would appear that, in England at least, PISA skewed the policy agenda pursued by the Coalition to the exclusion of other worthy goals, such as arts education.

Enter Michael Gove: Man on a mission

In 1998 Benjamin Levin and Jonathan Young stated that there was a 'policy epidemic' in education, one resulting in an unstoppable flood of unstable, uneven, and interrelated reform ideas. In 2010, as if to exacerbate this 'epidemic', the Coalition's new Secretary of State for Education, Michael Gove, stepped in. Gove was a man on a mission, quite determined to change the system to match his personal ideology. With little consultation with anyone – Gove notoriously referred to teachers and academics who had the temerity to question some of his reforms as 'The Blob' – Gove launched wave after wave of systemic changes that had the effect of publically denigrating teachers. What emerged from this, in 2010, was a white paper on teaching and learning that in essence told the profession that if they wanted greater autonomy then they should design it. Michael Gove encouraged (some argue coerced) schools to become academies, characterized by freedom from local authority control. He brought in performance-related pay, and introduced unqualified teachers into free schools and academies. The constant overhauling of the system appeared relentless. Yet in 2014 the Conservatives removed him and installed the more conciliatory figure of Nicky Morgan as Secretary of State for Education.

Consistent with past practices, however, the pace of legislation on education under the Coalition was very rapid, with such bills passing more quickly even than did new anti-terrorism laws. All the trappings of a production model of educational reform as described in a previous chapters – targets, accountability, competition, choice, leadership, performance-related pay, and academization, mixed in with advocacy for professionals to collaborate, new models of governance, and a system geared for school-to-school competition – were to become new ways of thinking. Ironically, educational decision-making remained highly centralized, with managerial decisions delegated to school headteachers. The white paper called for a redefinition of the ways of thinking about the 'how' of schooling, the values placed on work, and its core purpose.

Erosion of the middle tier, the local authority

Each part of the United Kingdom (England, Scotland, Wales, and Northern Ireland) operates its own educational system. In England, historically, local authorities through their education committees shared power over education with the central government. This gave the system some cohesion and ensured connection between schools, LEAs, and the central government. From the point of view of central government's reformers in a hurry, these education committees clogged the system, especially if the 'wrong party' controlled the LEA. The 1993 Education Act displaced LEAs as sole providers of state education and, step by step, Conservative and Labour governments took turns weakening the role of LEAs in terms of educational policy making. By 2015 the role of local authorities was almost totally marginalized, though some highly effective local authorities persisted and had formed effective partnerships with schools to address the school improvement agenda. Yet one large question remains after years of furious change: did the reforms lead to increased achievement, or did the old problems still remain – if, indeed, they ever existed?

Once again the education system in England is, in 2016, in the midst of a huge shake-up. The recent Coalition government initiated a very aggressive policy promoting two models of schools, both independent of the local authority: the academy, at both secondary and primary levels; and the free school, established along the lines of the Swedish free schools and American charter schools. Schools that adopt these models are granted increased autonomy, which on the surface looks like the hallmark of a more trusting policy climate, than is given to schools that remain within the local authority, which continues to control the budgets of the schools under its aegis. The intent in promoting these new school models is to break out of traditional staffing patterns, curricula, and leadership structures. Yet despite this overarching statement of choice and invitation to innovate, the central thrust of Coalition education policy was clear: the drive to convert all schools into academies was and is relentless. The Conservative victory in 2015 suggests these policies will continue and even be accelerated in spite of evidence from Sweden that free schools work against equity.

Moreover, the new Ofsted inspection framework introduced in September 2014 could lead to a fivefold increase in the number of schools being told they need to improve. In her 2015 annual conference address to the Association of Teachers and Lecturers (ATL), ATL General Secretary Mary Bousted, 'denouncing the government's record on schools ... said the education system was "being run on a wing and a prayer", with teachers exhausted, stressed and burnt out in a profession that was being "monitored to within an inch of its life"' (Weale, 2015: n.p.). In her furious speech, Bousted commented that 'the schools watchdog, Ofsted, was a weapon of fear and terror, an organisation plagued with quality control problems and a credibility chasm with the teaching profession' (ibid.).

But nothing seems to be slowing the relentless politicization of education. David Cameron, after his re-election as Prime Minister in May 2015, now proposes that when Ofsted first reports that a given school 'requires improvement' (the judgement which has replaced 'satisfactory'), this school must become an academy. In their opening address to parliament in 2015, the newly-elected Conservative majority government stated that they would be addressing 'coasting schools' over the next period in office. Seumas Milne, writing in *The Guardian*, declared that 'Academies are less accountable, less transparent, less locally integrated and less open to parental involvement (governors are appointed, not elected) than local authority schools' (Milne, 2012: n.p.). Local authorities across England now have far less influence and power than once they did. Their traditional role in strategically managing and monitoring educational provision has in many cases migrated directly to academies and free schools.

This legislative change brought about by the Coalition government has effectively stripped out what the McKinsey report 'How the World's Best Performing School Systems Come Out on Top' (2007) refers to as the 'middle tier'. This report demonstrates that successfully developing nations at the forefront of effective educational reform operate with an effective and dynamic middle tier.

Trust research

Against this backdrop of breakneck policy change, evidence about English educators' perceptions concerning trust has been gathered via two methods. The first, the Trust Connection Questionnaire (see also Chapters 3 and 9), an online survey administered internationally, supplied significant responses that we develop below and throughout this chapter. The second method, whereby a small number of selected school leaders were interviewed via email, telephone, and face to face, built on and was informed by the survey responses.

Survey results

A total of 180 English school leaders and teachers responded to the online international Trust Connection Questionnaire, with 120 (66 per cent) of these being school leaders and 60 (33 per cent) being teachers. The respondents covered all phases and types of school settings, including maintained, foundation, independent, academy, and free schools, with 70 per cent of responses coming from staff in the primary phase of education. Eighty per cent of the total responses came from staff in the maintained sector. The questions were identical to those posed to respondents in other countries, a measure designed to standardize the research internationally. To explore the relationship between what leaders and teachers believe should be happening in schools and what is actually happening in schools, the survey sought two responses to each item: the imagined ideal situation (i.e. what should be happening), and the real situation (i.e. what is happening). Following the collection and collation of the survey data, telephone interviews and face-to-face conversations were held with twelve school leaders. Participation was voluntary and anonymity and confidentiality were guaranteed.

Analysis of the trust aspects of the research in England showed that:

- 93 per cent of the respondents agreed that school improvement depends upon and has greater impact where school leaders consciously strive to build trust across their learning communities.
- 96 per cent of the teachers responding trust competent leaders.
- 86 per cent felt that the role of a school leader was as a 'trusted gatekeeper', shielding staff from the endless torrent of policy developments.
- 96 per cent of the respondents felt that effective school improvement requires mutual trust to be built between teachers and parents.
- 83 per cent of teachers felt that a trustworthy leader working in a highly trusting environment could be defined as someone who would 'say what they mean and mean what they say'.

Some particular responses of school leaders are relevant to the question of trust:

- 63 per cent of leaders did not feel valued by the government, despite the latter's strategic statements about 'greater autonomy for schools'.
- 58 per cent did not want greater autonomy; the same percentage felt that the government did not support leaders in ways that made them effective.
- 92 per cent felt that effective school improvement depends on school leaders building and sustaining trusting relationships.
- 93 per cent of school leaders felt that to maintain high levels of trust (credibility and competence) required them to address any poor teaching practice swiftly. Ninety-seven per cent felt that working in a high-trust environment made a teacher more effective.
- 97 per cent of school leaders felt that for all pupils to achieve their maximum potential, a culture of trust must be at the heart of their community; the same percentage felt that trustworthy leaders always 'say what they mean and mean what they say'.

There is clear evidence from the English survey results that trust is vital in and across organizations to underpin and support the agenda of raising school performance. Leaders have a role in modelling and developing consistency in their practice, thus raising their workforce's confidence in them. A majority of survey respondents noted that delivering difficult messages and dealing with school-based issues was more likely to be successful when there was a trusting school environment present. Teachers and heads are highly receptive to change strategies that are implemented in collaborative ways, and strategies that trust professionals to deliver new policies. However, a clear message arises from the survey: leaders do not feel that they are respected by the wider education system. I followed up on a specific survey response with a leader from the South West of England, who had addressed the theme of leaders building credibility and consistency, which he felt were the foundations that built trust in an organization. This primary school headteacher epitomized the interview responses when he indicated that a leader should begin with positives, 'catching' people doing the right thing; that they should acknowledge, verify, and build on strengths.

Interview findings

The spirit or flavour of the interviews is captured in the following quotes. There was little or no evidence that a 'one-size-fits-all' approach to reform implementation works to improve learning for students. Government decisions that emphasize mandating over persuading strategies seems to breed distrust.

> The politics of education and politicisation of the educational agenda – the cronyism and marketization of education under the current government has led to mistrust because there is no evidence base behind the policies that have been adopted. The idea that profit both personal and financial can be made out of playing with children's life chances, is abhorrent ... this flies in the face of evidence and leads to a lack of trust.
>
> (Primary headteacher, East Anglia)

> 'Pressure of Ofsted' was cited in the inquest of the previous Head, who committed suicide on site ... I feel the success of our next Ofsted will be down to confidence, professional development and clear priorities with all stakeholders, especially our pupils – rather than FEAR!
>
> (Primary headteacher, Midlands)

There is no equity and the high stakes nature of inspection ... the consequences of failure are extreme. Leading to high levels of distrust.

(Primary headteacher, East Anglia)

Trust is a fundamental aspect in working successfully as a team. Although I believe in rigorous and fair inspection of all public provision, it has to be seen as uniform.

(School leader, West Midlands)

Building effective working relationships and trust takes time.

(Headteacher, East Anglia)

Sustaining trust comes from investing time in personal relationships, genuinely valuing debate and proving that the reasoned and professionally expressed presentation of views contrary to those held by the leadership does not bring sanction.

(Former headteacher and National Strategy leader)

Many of us feel we are being done to by the Department for Education (DFE), the National curriculum, Ofsted and other top down mandates rather than active participants in a process.

(Primary headteacher, East Anglia)

These summary findings of the survey and interviews seem generically to indicate that both teachers and headteachers highly value trust. However these same teachers and headteachers feel a deep institutional distrust when it comes to dealing with government policy makers, even greater trust is afforded to the policy implementers. A current example of this distrust can be found in the national government's push to establish academy schools.

Academization: A matter of trust

The great financial crash of 2008 had arguably as great an impact on school improvement as it had in many other areas of UK society. Crisis often drives innovation, and the effects of the recent economic disruption in terms of austerity, public service funding, and consequent structural reform have been radical, swift, and far-reaching. Previously introduced reforms, based partly on consensus, have been accelerated with little or no public or professional debate and little recognition of the need to monitor the process, reflect on lessons learnt, or genuinely test these measures against international systems. As a result, in the past five years, well over half of England's secondary schools have moved out of local authority control to become either academies or free schools.[1] During this period, the Coalition government imposed new standards and accountability measures on schools, completely revised the national curriculum with little recognition of or involvement from the profession, and announced plans to reduce school funding in the near future. The undoubted pressures that school leaders face in the context is described in the following response from our online survey: '[L]ack of trust due to much "sitting on the fence" and lack of clear direction. I feel this is where large academies have taken hold/taken over' (Primary headteacher, Midlands).

There appears to be a divergence, therefore, between the policy makers and the policy implementers in this country, resulting in an apparent lack of cooperative effort toward improving learning outcomes for pupils. Another headteacher wrote on the online survey that 'Government needs to work WITH schools not AGAINST and be prepared to listen to school leaders' (Headteacher, southeast England), while another claimed that 'I have been a headteacher for nearly seven years and in that time, I have felt that trust in us has been diminished quite rapidly from Government, Local Authority and from parents' (Headteacher, Cheshire).

The evidence from our research suggests that the fundamental cause of this divergence is a lack of trust. English results from the online survey and from the face-to-face conversations with school leaders revealed that 93 per cent of respondents felt they were not valued by government, with 90 per cent feeling that government did not support school leaders in ways that made them more effective. Eighty-two per cent felt that their leadership development was not adequately supported by the government.

Of the 3,372 secondary schools in England, 60 per cent are now academies, outside of direct local authority control and formally accountable to the Department for Education. Despite this growth in apparent institutional autonomy to deal with managerial issues, the danger is that the overriding focus in our current school system (i.e. the identification and resuscitation of weak schools and incompetent teachers) ignores the reality that most schools and most teachers are not weak.

The Sutton Trust: Big-picture verification

In 2014 the Sutton Trust, together with the Bill and Melinda Gates Foundation, organized a two-day international summit on teacher observation, feedback, and school ethos. An outcome of this summit was the production of a Sutton Trust report, 'What Makes Great Teaching' (2014). This concluded that the ultimate yardstick for great teaching is always the impact that teaching has on student outcomes. A recurring theme in this piece of research and the resultant practical strategies to move forward was the need to create a culture of *trust and challenge* in schools, to enable teachers' professional learning to prosper.

Case studies presented in the report showed that in the most successful schools leaders provide direction and support, but also trust their staff, encouraging creativity and innovation and a degree of calculated risk-taking. A trusted leader also spends a lot of time talking to colleagues. 'A trusted leader is consistent and resolute in maintaining actions in line with the consistently held vision and strategic directions set by the organisation. A trusted leader can hold and maintain the confidences of colleagues', as a former National Strategy leader in our interviews put it. British headteachers who attended the summit argued powerfully that the same conditions were also required for a school system to develop as a whole: that there must be trust between policy makers and policy implementers.

The Sutton Trust further added that, in their experience in schools and classrooms, when trust exists the vast majority of children and adults feel more able and are empowered to learn, develop, and grow. This position aligned with our trust research in England, as evidenced by interview comments such as 'trust is vital for school effectiveness and development' (Headteacher, Lewisham). In fact 93 per cent of respondents to the survey agreed that school improvement depended on school leaders building trusting relationships, and a full 98 per cent felt that 'working in a high trust environment made teachers more effective at promoting student learning to higher levels'.

As Chapter 1 argues, social capital includes not only internal collaboration and support but meaningful engagement on the part of schools and professionals with outside agencies, including governments. Of course, a system needs to have a way of identifying and providing support where there is underachievement and poor performance. Ofsted is often held up as that system of checking, of auditing, but is it the right model? Is the Ofsted model based on a positive view of the potential of our children and adults, constituting a system that trusts professional educators, or does it exist merely to identify failure? The auditing arms of the Coalition and subsequent Conservative governments, Ofsted and Ofqual (Office of Qualifications and Examinations Regulation: the non-ministerial government department that regulates qualifications, examinations, and tests in England), do not appear to understand the concepts of trust and consistency. As a Headteacher from Bolton added in response to our online survey, 'Ofsted places unrealistic expectations on teachers to show outcomes, without any concept of what real progress is; quite frankly it is ludicrous and damaging to both the teacher and the students' self-esteem'.

The Sutton Trust believes that policy makers need to demonstrate genuine trust in schools and in their leaders' ability to lead the system. We have learned from colleagues in high-performing educational systems such as Singapore and Finland that professional trust is the key. In summary, the Sutton Trust (2014) argues that governments that want to improve their schools must increase the professional autonomy of school leaders and teachers and actively encourage their use of creativity to improve standards in their schools. Trust them and support them through failures; do not allow the whole system to be driven on zero tolerance of missteps and failures. You can't create winners by calling people losers. Do our current and future school leaders trust the system enough to make the leaps of progress our system leaders are demanding?

The core issue: Are schools really failing?

In his third annual report (2013–14) the current Chief Inspector, Sir Michael Wilshaw, said that primary school standards are continuing on an impressive upward trajectory, with more than eight out of ten schools now rated as at least 'good' on Ofsted's criteria. Sir Michael noted that the overall rate of improvement in secondary schools, however, had stalled, although a higher proportion of secondary schools than primary schools receive the 'outstanding' grading. Yet 84 per cent of primary schools are now rated as having good or outstanding leadership and management judgement, compared with 77 per cent in secondary schools. The proportion of primary schools in which teaching is good or outstanding has risen markedly, from 71 per cent in 2012 to 82 per cent in 2014.

Two variables

Autonomy and accountability

Our research on trust in England suggests that six intervention strategies are common to schools in all phases of their school improvement journeys: (1) building the instructional skills of teachers and management skills of principals; (2) assessing students; (3) improving data systems; (4) facilitating improvement through the introduction of policy documents and education laws; (5) revising standards and curriculum; and (6) ensuring an appropriate reward and remuneration structure for teachers and principals.

One of the tensions underpinning our national government's drive for school improvement is the difficulty of striking a balance between autonomy and accountability. The justification for the proposed 'transfer of power' from central governments to individual schools or groups of schools is the rapid increase in statutory school accountability measures. The government argues that freedom to innovate at the local level will drive up standards, when it is coupled to central, nationally controlled accountability measures. However, significant reductions to the middle tier now mean that responsibility for improving teacher performance in some countries, England among them, now rests with consortia of schools in the form of trusts, chains, or other emerging associations (such as teaching school alliances).

McKinsey's second major report on school systems, 'How the World's Most Improved School Systems Keep Getting Better' (McKinsey, 2010), observed that 'as the school systems we studied have progressed on their improvement journey, they seem to have increasingly come to rely on a "mediating layer" that acts between the centre and the schools (2010: 73)'. Thus the retention of the 'middle layer' appears to be significant.

The unions

Since 97 per cent of teachers and principals in England belong to a union (with several operative in the country), unions too become important players in all of this upheaval. One large English education trade union declined to publicize the online survey we carried out for this chapter, identifying it as 'another request too far!' (pers. comm.). Although the topic of trust was acknowledged as being essential to the work of school improvement, it was felt that 'members are under so much pressure, that the central office of the union felt it ill advised to issue yet another questionnaire request' (ibid.). Securing a viable sample of respondents for the England trust questionnaire was indeed a challenge, and eventually relied more on personal contacts than on publicity through large national teacher organizations. More than transport, energy, health, or mining, education has the highest level of union membership, according to the most recent government figures. The Easter 2015 round of union conferences threw up discussions of striking, exasperated attacks on education policy, and warnings about increased workloads. In return union leaders were accused of being dinosaurs and of discrediting the profession. So why do teachers join a union? Teachers feel extremely vulnerable, with a distinct distrust of the bodies in charge of education, whether the Department for Education or Ofsted. The last education secretary to address the National Union of Teachers' conference was Labour's Estelle Morris in 2002, who after being heckled said 'If I told them that tomorrow was Sunday, I think they'd say it wasn't and pass a motion against it' (Morris, quoted in Coughlan, 2002: n.p.).

Trust: The way forward

The research and the history of educational reform in England show that standards in school leadership are on an upward trend. It is however clear that the pace of reform has at times been unremitting, radiating a message of a lack of faith in school leadership. Endless government initiatives and strategies will not alone move performance to the next level. Leaders and schools must feel a sense of trust and have faith in the system. Leaders today only too readily acknowledge and understand the consequences of failing to deliver results. Quite rightly, successive governments have made concerted efforts to eliminate elements of poor leadership and teaching, because every child in the system matters. As this chapter identifies, the overarching and vexed question remains: 'why is there such a climate of distrust between policy makers and policy implementers that all change must be forced and verified, thus precluding the slow and often difficult steps required in trust-building?' What is now needed is for that level of trust to be built between the schools and the government (the system) to move to the next level of enhanced performance outcomes.

From the research findings (and from the literature) there is no doubt that trust is the glue that secures effective educational change. What the trust research undertaken in England and presented here clearly shows is that (1) a school learning community works better and achieves better when there is a climate of trust permeating the whole organization; and (2) there is still a passion within our schools to perform, to improve, and to strive to be the best. But trust cannot be commanded; rather it is earned through the respect and authenticity that a leader exudes to those within the system. The apparent paranoia that surrounds Ofsted in England runs the risk of undermining the life-blood of our education system: the teaching force. However, the research clearly shows that in order to move to the next level in effective and sustainable school improvement trust has to be at the heart of every organizational and systemic development.

Thirteen years ago, in her Reith lectures, philosopher Onora O'Neill (BBC Radio 4, 2002) identified a 'crisis of trust' due mainly to the overbearing forms of accountability that were distorting the proper aims of professional practice. Giving time and having trust are at the heart of reform, and for years this has been a constant request from educators to government in England. Without trust being built and sufficient time allocated to reform, we could so easily continue within the dysfunctional 'reform in a hurry' pattern, a feature that has plagued our system for too long.

Richard Branson in 2008 stated that his aim was to establish Virgin as the most respected brand in the world, a brand to be trusted in each and every marketplace. Without internal organizational trust, Branson felt that brands acquire no texture, no character, and therefore no public trust. This research indicates that governmental educational reforms need a little less haste, a little less speed, a little less 'reform in a hurry', a lot more valuing of professional expertise, a lot more genuine consultation, and a lot more mutual respect.

Notes

[1] Free schools are far more autonomous than academies or maintained schools, funded by the government but not run by the local council. They are all-ability schools, so can't use academic selection processes as a grammar school might, but they can set their own pay and conditions for staff, and can change the length of school terms and the school day. They are not obliged to follow the national curriculum. Free schools are run on a not-for-profit basis.

References

Ball, S. (2008) *The Education Debate*. Bristol: Policy Press.

BBC Radio 4 (2002) 'The Reith lectures'. Online. www.bbc.co.uk/radio4/features/the-reith-lectures/transcripts/2000/#y2002 (accessed 27 January 2016).

Blair, T. (2006) 'Europe is falling behind'. *Newsweek,* 29 January. Online. http://web.archive.org/web/20070105082131/http://www.msnbc.msn.com/id/11020913/site/newsweek/ (accessed 27 January 2016).

Brown, P., and Lauder, H. (2001) *Capitalism and Social Progress*. New York: Palgrave.

Burch, P. (2009) *Hidden Markets*. London: Routledge.

Coughlan, S. (2002) 'Angry teachers heckle Morris'. *BBC News*. Online. http://news.bbc.co.uk/1/hi/education/1901531.stm (accessed 27 January 2016).

Levin, B., and Young, J. (1998) 'Reshaping Public Education'. Paper presented at the International Congress on Social Welfare, Jerusalem, July.

McKinsey and Company (2007) 'How the world's best-performing school systems come out on top'. Online. http://mckinseyonsociety.com/downloads/reports/Education/Worlds_School_Systems_Final.pdf (accessed 27 January 2016).

— (2010) 'How the world's most improved school systems keep getting better'. Online. *mckinseyonsociety.com/how-the-worlds-most-improved-school-systems, accessed March2014).*

Milne, S. (2012) 'Crony capitalism feeds the corporate plan for schools'. *The Guardian*, 14 February. Online. www.theguardian.com/commentisfree/2012/feb/14/crony-capitalism-corporate-schools (accessed 27 January 2016).

OECD (1998) 'Education at a glance: OECD indicators'. Centre for Educational Research and Innovation. Online. www.oecd-ilibrary.org/education/education-at-a-glance-1998_eag-1998-en (accessed March 2014).

Office for Standards in Education (2014) *Ofsted Annual Report 2013/14*. Online. www.gov.uk/government/collections/ofsted-annual-report-201314 (accessed 27 January 2016).

Sutton Trust (2014) 'What makes great teaching?' Online. www.suttontrust.com/researcharchive/great-teaching/ (accessed 27 January 2016).

Weale, S. (2015) 'Four in 10 new teachers quit within a year'. *The Guardian*, 31 March. Online. www.theguardian.com/education/2015/mar/31/four-in-10-new-teachers-quit-within-a-year (accessed 27 January 2016).

Woodhead, C. (2004) 'The British experience: School reform, hijacked'. *Education Next*, 4 (3) Online. http://educationnext.org/the-british-experience/ (accessed 27 January 2016).

Chapter 9

United States: And the pendulum swings

Craig Hammonds

The United States has a population that exceeds 308 million people, distributed across 3.8 million square miles. There are 55 million students in grades PK–12, of whom approximately 90 per cent attending public school. Fewer than 5 per cent of students aged 5 to 17 with a grade equivalent of K–12 are schooled at home instead of in a public or private school. More than US\$630 billion is spent each year in public elementary and secondary schools: this equates to nearly US\$13,000 per public school student. Over 21 per cent of children aged 5 to 17 years old speak a language other than English at home. In the United States, there are approximately 3.3 million public school teachers and 0.4 million private school teachers.

Universal education, i.e. education available to all and free at the point of delivery, did not exist in early America. The United States Constitution does not specifically arrogate power over education to the federal government, and the Tenth Amendment to the Constitution declares that all powers not delegated to the federal government are reserved to the states: simply stated, this amendment therefore gives state governments their traditional power over schools. The concept of education for all was not introduced until the early nineteenth century. By 1918, all states had compulsory school laws (Walsh *et al.*, 2014). Religion played an important role in the movement as many viewed the ability to read the Bible as a necessary component of salvation (Travers and Rebore, 2000). As the concept of schooling expanded throughout the country, expectations grew as well. When the Soviet Union launched Sputnik in 1957, the United States recognized they had fallen behind in the space race and viewed better schools as the solution for moving to the front of the race (Urban and Wagoner, 2004). This has contributed to an increasing involvement in education by the federal government.

In 1983, a report issued by a presidential commission entitled *A Nation at Risk* proposed recommendations on school improvement. The need for the report was sparked by the lagging performance of US students on the Second International Mathematics Study (SIMS) in the early 1980s.

Policy makers were alarmed by the indication of the report that the current system was not adequately preparing students in maths and science to compete with students in other nations. This marked the beginning of a national movement toward standards-based reform. The No Child Left Behind Act of 2001 (NCLB) increased federal mandates for results-driven and high-stakes education (Wong and Nicotera, 2007). NCLB specified that all children would be achieving at grade level by the year 2014. Unlike previous federal legislation, NCLB directly tied federal aid for schools to students' academic performance and imposed specific requirements on states to deal with schools in which students consistently performed at low levels. According to Cruickshank *et al.*:

> NCLB was complex and included a number of requirements and consequences for states, districts, and schools associated with student academic performance. Among these were increased standards for the preparation and assignment of teachers, greater state and district flexibility in using federal education funds, and an emphasis on 'scientifically-based research.' However, the aspects of the legislation that most directly impacted teachers and schools were those associated with accountability.
>
> (Cruickshank *et al.*, 2012: 349)

Over the past decade, American education has experienced a fundamental shift to an accountability-driven system (Cosner, 2009). In recent years, President Obama has increased federal involvement in the school reform effort by enacting a new programme, 'Race to the Top'. This competition-based effort was created to spur innovation and reforms in state and local K–12 education. It requires states to adopt and implement new Common Core Standards. Despite early 'buy-in' from a majority of states, the Common Core has recently been the subject of a growing buyer's remorse. The standards were recently scrapped in Indiana and Oklahoma, and other states such as Ohio, Louisiana, North Carolina, South Carolina, and Missouri are considering doing the same. Ironically, in a nation split between the political right and left, opposition to the Common Core has united the extremes. To the people on the left, Common Core undermines the professionalism of teachers and their ability to programme for individual students. To those on the right, it is but another intrusion by the federal government into local issues.

'Trust, but verify' is a term that President Ronald Reagan used frequently when discussing US relations with the Soviet Union. Now, 30 years later, the United States continues to recognize the important need for trust and verification when it comes to foreign policy and relations. 'Trust and verify' is an applicable concept in multiple systems that stretch far beyond foreign policy. Educational systems in the United States are complex, and educational policy in the US has often been compared to a pendulum. For many years the educational policy pendulum has swung toward the verification side of the production model. Perhaps the pendulum has reached its apex. In December of 2015 Congress passed, and President Obama signed, the Every Student Succeeds Act (ESSA), replacing NCLB. It is believed that this rare bipartisan measure will reduce the US Department of Education's authority over state education systems. To what extent trust and authority is returned to the state and district level, only time will tell. Is the United States beginning to move toward the professional model? Will it find an appropriate balance of trust and verification?

Research method and design

The purpose of this study was to determine what aspects of trust make a difference to the efficacy of leaders and teachers and to student achievement in both positive and negative trust environments. This study explored the views of teachers and school administrators on the importance of trust in doing their jobs, as well as inquiring into their perceptions of the trust culture in their working environments.

The primary survey instrument used to collect data for this study was the Trust Connection Questionnaire, developed by Dr Dean Fink as the lead researcher. Fink developed two American versions of the survey, one designed for teachers and another designed for school leaders. The 30-question survey also sought teacher and school leader demographic information. Survey research is a method that involves investigators administering a survey to a sample or to the entire population of people to describe the attitudes, opinions, behaviours, or characteristics of the population (Creswell, 2008). Surveys help to determine individual opinions about policy issues or identify important beliefs and attitudes of individuals.

Surveys were distributed to teachers and principals in five states that reflect the broad regions of the United States: Alabama, Indiana, Texas, Washington State, and West Virginia. This sampling provided data from teachers' union states, non-union states, Race to the Top participants, Race to the Top non-participants, states that have adopted the Common Core and states that did not adopt the Common Core standards. States that are traditionally Democratic, Republican, and swing states were included in the sample. To explore the relationship between what should be happening in schools and what is actually happening in schools, the survey sought two responses to each item: the ideal situation (i.e. what should be happening), and the real situation (i.e. what is happening). The respondents included 115 principals and assistant principals, and 659 teachers. When survey data had been gathered, email interviews were conducted with a select group of leaders and teachers from each of the five states.

Among the 115 school administrators that responded to the survey, 68 per cent were principals and 32 per cent were assistant principals; 66.09 per cent reported being in an elementary or intermediate school, 16.52 per cent in a middle school, and 17.39 per cent in a high school. Respondent ages varied, with 32.43 per cent of school administrator respondents born in the decade 1950–9, 36.04 per cent in 1960–9, 24.32 per cent in 1970–9, and 7.21 per cent in 1980–90. The majority of administrator respondents were female (61.95 per cent). Of the administrator participants, 25.44 per cent had been in a school leadership position for 0–5 years, 31.58 per cent for 6–10 years, 28.07 per cent for 11–15 years, 5.26 per cent for 16–20 years, and 9.65 per cent for 21 years or more. Of these administrator respondents, 1.79 per cent had worked in education for 0–5 years, 11.61 per cent for 6–10 years, 15.18 per cent for 11–15 years, 22.32 per cent for 16–20 years, and 49.11 per cent for 21 years or more. Respondents had in 31.53 per cent of cases worked in their present school district for 0–5 years; 15.32 per cent reported working in their current school district for 6–10 years, 16.22 per cent for 11–15 years, 14.41 per cent for 16–20 years, and 22.52 per cent for 21 years or more. A simple majority (56.64 per cent) had been in a leadership position in their present school for 0–5 years, 23.01 per cent for 6–10 years, 14.16 per cent for 11–15 years, 2.65 per cent for 16–20 years, and 3.54 per cent for 21 years or more.

Among the 659 school teachers that responded to the survey, 36.67 per cent reported teaching in an elementary school, 8.63 per cent in an intermediate school, 27.27 per cent in a middle school, and 27.43 per cent in a high school. Ages ranged, with 25.81 per cent born in the decade 1950–9, 29.52 per cent born in 1960–9, 25.35 per cent born in 1970–9, and 19.32 per cent born in 1980–90. Four in every five (80.12 per cent) teacher participants were female. Among the school teachers that responded to the survey, 19.75 per cent had been in a school teaching position for 0–5 years, 18.07 per cent for 6–10 years, 19.14 per cent for 11–15 years, 13.32 per cent for 16–20 years, and 29.71 per cent for 21 years or more. One-third, 32.87 per cent, had worked in their present school district for 0–5 years, 23.50 per cent for 6–10 years, 16.74 per cent for 11–15 years, 9.06 per cent for 16–20 years, and 17.82 per cent for 21 years or more. The largest group of teachers (42.97 per cent) reported having worked as teachers in their present school for 0–5 years, 26.76 per cent for 6–10 years, 13.46 per cent for 11–15 years, 6.12 per cent for 16–20 years, and 10.70 per cent for 21 years or more. A substantial 82.40 per cent reported having worked with their current principal for 0–5 years, while 14.57 per cent had done so for 6–10 years, 2.28 per cent for 11–15 years, 0.46 per cent for 16–20 years, and only 0.30 per cent for 21 years or more.

Limitations and future research
A limiting factor of this study was the exclusion of data collection regarding the impact of educational unions on trust. Future research should include demographic and research questions regarding educational unions and their impact on trust.

Trust in school systems
Trust has been found to be an important aspect of relationships in many organizations, including schools (Hoy and Miskel, 2013). As previously stated, educational systems in the United States are complex. In order to operate at peak performance, complex systems require collaboration, and collaboration requires trust. Trust in schools is important because it improves student achievement (Goddard *et al.*, 2001), it motivates staff and students (Hammonds *et al.*, 2013; Evertson and Emmer, 2009), it builds organizational capacity (Cosner, 2009), it facilitates collaboration (Tschannen-Moran, 2001), it enhances openness (Hoffman *et al.*, 1994), it promotes group cohesiveness (Mineo, 2014), and it supports professionalism (Tschannen-Moran, 2009). Trust relationships are built upon interdependence; that is, the interests of one cannot be achieved without reliance upon another (Rousseau *et al.*, 1998). Results from this study show an overwhelming majority of leaders and teachers (96 per cent) support the ideal that working in a 'high-trust' environment makes a teacher a more effective professional in promoting student learning (Question 29). Ninety-two per cent of school leaders and 96 per cent of teachers also believe school improvement depends on school leaders' ability to build trusting relationships with all staff members (Ideal, Question 7/6). In order for school systems to operate effectively, they must maintain institutional trust.

According to Covey (2006), trust is equal to confidence and distrust is equal to suspicion. Covey goes on to say trust is a combination of character and competence. Mineo (2014) states that the essence of trust is rooted in honesty, truthfulness, and genuineness. During an interview, one principal from Alabama stated:

> I deeply trust my immediate supervisor, which is my superintendent. She is very honest with me and straightforward. She is very competent, which helps me feel comfortable with her decision-making abilities. My superintendent's competency strengthens the amount of trust I have for her.
>
> (Principal, Alabama)

Confidence, character, competence, honesty, truthfulness, and genuineness are all qualities we want in our teachers, our administrators, our students, and ourselves. We all want to trust others and be trusted. We all want to trust our school systems.

Trust at the local level

The Tenth Amendment to the Constitution gives state governments their traditional power over schools. The structure of school systems suggests that a significant portion of the decision-making power regarding educational systems resides at the local level. Districts in the state of Texas even have the term 'Independent' in their title. The idea of independence was supported by a majority of leaders and teachers in this study. Fifty-eight per cent of leaders and 59 per cent of teachers disagreed with the statement 'it is best to trust the leadership of those in charge by going along with what they want' (Ideal, Question 30). It appears the policy implementers (school leaders and teachers) have low trust in the state's educational agenda and in policy makers. Forty-four per cent of teachers and 58 per cent of school leaders (who are typically better informed on law and policy) take a negative view of the state's educational policies (Real, Question 1). During the interview portion of this study, one educator stated, 'I struggle to trust people who appear to be driven by obtaining power and have lost touch with the true purpose of education'.

A need for balance

The reality is that many educational decisions are made at the state and federal level. No Child Left Behind directly tied federal aid for schools to students' academic performance and imposed specific requirements on states to deal with schools in which students consistently performed at low levels. NCLB required each state to implement 'student academic assessments' yearly for students in grades 3–8 and in high school. NCLB sought to improve students' academic performance, but as Fink points out in his introduction to this book, the challenge for those interested in educational change is to find the right balance between trust and verification – to trust and verify. 'Too much trust leaves policy makers vulnerable politically and professionally, and too much verification strips policy implementers of their autonomy and stifles creativity and innovation' (Fink, Chapter 2, this volume).

A perception of distrust

The challenge of finding the right balance of trust and verification is not always easy. Districts often feel the state and federal governments do not trust enough and require too much verification. This perception also holds true at the local level as teachers begin to distrust their own administration when they believe the reins of control are too tight. Depending upon one's perspective, verification from leadership can be viewed by some as distrust. One Alabama administrator wrote:

> Teachers may have some distrust for me when I am making teacher moves. I cannot always share everything I am doing with moves because they may not go through and the wrong information is disseminated. One must keep the information 'close hold', not to be sneaky, but make sure accurate information is disclosed at the end of the process. At times I must keep programs or district plans 'close hold', not to be dishonest, but because I am told to by my superiors. When teachers find out that I knew about the information and didn't tell them, they may feel betrayed and that I am keeping things from them. It is necessary at times but may very well cause distrust.
>
> (School administrator, Alabama)

One principal from West Virginia added:

> Those who distrust are generally those that want to do as they please without any expectation of a consequence for doing so. When I call them out for inappropriate actions they tend to bite back with negative parking lot conversations rather than discussing their concerns in the proper manner. They feel I am out to get them and therefore distrust my every move when all I am really doing is trying to get them to improve.
>
> (Principal, West Virginia)

Different sources of distrust exist including those from outside of the educational system. One principal from Indiana wrote, 'The current American media continues to paint the educator in a role that breeds distrust. This is the fault of many folks both in and out of education.'

A Texas administrator added:

> As much as I have learned and trust in the benefits of social media for teachers, I also understand how they can distort our educational system. Currently in my district, we have a group on Facebook made up of parents who despise many of the practices and policies we use. The messages put out there are very demeaning and sometimes slanderous to our school community, which builds distrust in those who follow it. Ninety-nine per cent of the time, the messages and information put out there on Facebook are not true. So, I do distrust this particular group and their platform to destroy a good system. This makes me distrust, to a certain extent, social media when it is allowed to be used in this way.
>
> (School administrator, Texas)

By simply holding others accountable, the perception of trust can be damaged. During the interview process of this study, one principal wrote:

> Teachers that are underperforming feel threatened by administration, is that distrust, as if administration were out to get them? Parents that have students who are continuously in trouble or making poor decisions tend to sound-bite they don't trust the school. Wanting someone to blame instead of themselves, sometimes makes the school or administration the target.
>
> (Principal)

The impact of trust on autonomy and motivation

The respondents in this study were asked to comment on the statement 'schools need complete autonomy to pursue a school improvement agenda' (Question 2). In response, 49 per cent of leaders and 54 per cent of teachers supported the ideal that autonomy is needed in order to pursue school improvement. One principal stated:

> As an administrator, I feel very trusted by central office. I am able to make decisions that are supported by my superiors. I have autonomy of directing funds, personnel, and programs. I don't have to check in with my superiors before I make decisions, they trust me to make them without their input.
>
> (School principal)

It is important to note that only 35 per cent of leaders and 45 per cent of teachers responding to our survey believed they have complete autonomy to pursue a school improvement agenda. In response to an interview question regarding distrust, one teacher wrote, 'some micromanaging has occurred on my campus this year and that has made me feel distrusted at times'. Another responded, 'When a principal or staff member encourages my decision-making, congratulates my efforts, or generally allows me to do my job, it helps me to know they trust me.' This evidence suggests both leaders and teachers believe that greater trust leads to autonomy, which is necessary for a school improvement agenda. This also suggests school leaders and teachers distrust the decisions made at the state and federal levels in regards to school improvement.

The findings also raise questions about the lack of autonomy at the local level and its impact on leaders' and teachers' motivation. Research suggests autonomy leads to motivation. In his book *Drive: The Surprising Truth About What Motivates Us*, Daniel Pink (2009) draws from four decades of research on motivation. Pink examines what he calls the three elements of true motivation: autonomy, mastery, and purpose. The feeling of autonomy has a powerful effect on individual performance and attitude (Pink, 2009). Elsewhere in an article entitled 'Motivating Teachers and Meeting Expectations', my colleagues and I state:

> Mandated lessons, common assessments, state standards, and prescribed teaching times are important components of a viable curriculum, but the development of these components is often done without teacher contribution. This results in teachers feeling more like robots and less like professionals. Teachers must feel like origins of their own behavior rather than pawns manipulated from the outside (Sergiovanni, 2007). By building a culture of collaboration through professional learning communities, principals provide a platform for teachers to contribute. Pink reminds us that encouraging autonomy does not mean discouraging accountability; individuals must be accountable for their work. Instead of just letting teachers do whatever they want, school leaders must provide clear guidelines and boundaries (DuFour and Eaker, 1998). Educational leaders must establish clear parameters yet build a community where teachers set goals, select professional development, collaborate with other professionals, develop curriculum, and serve on hiring committees. DuFour and Fullan (2013) stated a school culture can

be 'simultaneously loose and tight'. Leaders need to clearly define expectations and what is non-negotiable within a school culture. When teachers understand their boundaries and parameters, they are empowered to work interdependently within the system. With autonomy, teachers allow their creative juices to flow. They become team players, motivated to contribute their talents and ideas towards the greater purpose of training and equipping our next generation.

(Hammonds et al., 2013: 1)

During the collection of interview responses, one educator wrote about how distrust in district leaders caused her to seek employment elsewhere:

> When asked to participate in district level interviews for our new principal I felt very honored and excited to share the vision and voice of the teachers at our campus. Upon participating in the interviews, district officials asked us to collaborate and provide our top three candidates for the position. After conferring with another teacher chosen and parent representative we felt that only one candidate from the pool provided would be a good fit.
>
> When explaining our reasoning to district personnel we were met with open resistance from a few members of the panel who then tried to sway our thoughts into another chosen candidate. When these events started occurring we then had the perception that this candidate was preselected. Our participation was only to be there to jump on the bandwagon and create a false sense of teacher input. I felt that district no longer valued what we thought nor trusted our judgment.
>
> This event has lead me to question many things in my previous district. Most importantly, how disconnected these top leaders are from the reason we are in our position – the kids. I would only whole heartedly follow one member of the panel who still, even as a district leader, shows true, authentic zest for educating and caring for our future.

(School teacher)

Finding the right balance of trust and verification is an arduous yet necessary task. When state and federal policy makers lack trust in local systems, mandates are implemented that reduce local autonomy. When employees believe they no longer have a voice or that their voice is not respected, trust is diminished. The reduction of trust and local autonomy ultimately reduces the motivation of leaders and teachers, resulting in decreased rather than increased student achievement.

The 'Trust Team'

There is a saying, purportedly an ancient African proverb, that 'it takes a village to raise a child'. If it takes a village to raise a child, what does it take to properly educate the 55 million PK–12 students across the United States? Each year the list of responsibilities educators face grows ever longer. The work is more than any one person can individually accomplish. To be successful, it takes a team, and a big one at that. Hammonds *et al.* (2013) state that, as members of a team working together towards a shared purpose and given autonomy in the decision-making process, educators can approach mastery in their profession. Effective teamwork requires trust and support. Work team trust has been found to be related to several key team variables, including perceived task performance, team satisfaction, and relationship commitment (Costa *et al.*, 2001).

Findings from this study support the idea of the need for a team approach. Ninety-five per cent of teachers who responded to the survey believed school improvement requires mutual trust between teachers and parents (Ideal, Question 17). Ninety-six per cent of teachers agreed with the statement that teachers' willingness to support each other's teaching is crucial to school improvement (Ideal, Question 16). In order for teachers to bond with one another as a team, they need time together. Most districts offer teachers a very limited amount of collaboration time prior to the start of the school year and during the school day. Only 33 per cent of teachers report actually having time and space to work collaboratively (Real, Question 13). As DuFour and Marzano have stated:

> One of the major impediments to providing time for educators to work together is the uniquely American notion that a teacher who is not presenting a lesson in front of a classroom of students is not working. Other nations are not encumbered by this premise. Although the hours in the work week for teachers across countries are comparable, American teachers at all levels spend far more time in the classroom than their international counterparts.
>
> (DuFour and Marzano, 2011: 73)

Limited time together can lead to limited trust, as evidenced by the following statement by a Texas teacher:

> Sometimes being the new person on a team, as I was this year, means that I had little or no credibility compared to others that have been teaching on the grade level for quite some time. There is a certain level of distrust there and I continually have to prove myself and my ideas to others.
>
> (Teacher, Texas)

Teachers can easily feel that their job requires them to meet high expectations yet provides them with limited resources. Only 40 per cent of teachers believe the educational system actually backs its teachers (Real, Question 4). A lack of support from policy makers often leaves teachers with a sense of distrust. A teacher from West Virginia responded to an interview question by writing:

> I wouldn't say I deeply trust anyone. The education system is a game of politics after all. But there is a level of trust. I trust my administration. I trust that they are looking out for me and my students. I have to or I wouldn't be able to come do my job every day. I only distrust the politics at play behind the scenes. Anyone could betray me at any minute if it helped their career. For example, if I did something really terrific in my classroom, they could use it to make themselves look better. They might pump up the small part they played in it or even just claim it as their own.
>
> (Teacher, West Virginia)

Principals were somewhat more optimistic, with 71 per cent reporting teacher support from their district (Real, Question 4). Unfortunately, only 31 per cent of the principals responding to this survey agreed that high-quality leadership is one of the state educational system's highest priorities (Real, Question 12). Seventy-three per cent of school leaders surveyed do not believe the state educational system is prepared to pay for high-quality leadership (Real, Question 13). These findings suggest a strong feeling that true teamwork is lacking in the current system.

Teacher and principals

Given the many changes in education taking place, teachers' trust in their school leaders is more important than ever (Calahan, 2013). However, building trust is not a quick process. In response to an interview question, one teacher wrote 'I do feel trusted as an educator. I believe the administration trusts me to do my job effectively in educating my students. Also, I feel that having almost 10 years of experience has made me be trusted by my peers and administration.' A school leader stated:

> For the most part I do feel trusted. I have not always felt this way. When I began teaching in my district, even with more than 9 years of experience, I felt like an outsider. Due to the small town cliques and a tight knit community, it was not common to have someone new come in ... especially from the big town of Houston. After several years in my current district, I was able to earn the trust of my peers and community members that was deserved. Now, I feel completely trusted and have many who confide in me. The community trusts me with the academic success and the well-being of the children we serve. My peers and colleagues trust me as their leader.
>
> (Principal)

According to Day (2013), successful school leaders recognize that building successful leadership takes time. Day goes on to say that the establishment and maintenance of individual and collective vision, hope and optimism, high expectations, and repeated acts of leadership integrity are required in order to nurture, broaden, and deepen individual, relational, and organizational trust. Time, however, is not something that all teachers have with their principals. Almost 97 per cent of the teachers that participated in this study reported having worked with their current principal for less than 10 years. 82 per cent reported having worked with their current principal for less than 6 years. A lack of bonding time between the teacher and principal can also affect the principal's perception of his or her staff. During an interview, one teacher wrote:

> Principals provide an atmosphere in a school environment that sets the tone for the school. In twelve years of teaching experience, I have worked under five principals. As I anticipate my thirteenth year, which begins shortly, I will work for my sixth principal. With each one, the tide changes, and I wait. I wait to see what is revealed after the 'honeymoon' period. How has the atmosphere changed? What is my new environment in my old school? Is the tone set for trust? The answers to these questions will most certainly impact my classroom over the course of the year.
>
> (Teacher)

A principal added:

> I sometimes distrust the intentions of teachers that have been at the campus for several years. They have seen administrators come and go so they are just waiting for you to go too. They can change the culture of the school by transforming the minds of newer teachers.
>
> (Teacher)

Trustworthiness?

When asked about the integrity of their school leaders, only 60 per cent of teachers said their leaders actually 'walk their talk' (Real, Question 23) and 17 per cent disagreed with the statement 'trustworthy leaders at all levels say what they mean and mean what they say' (Ideal, Question 27). In response to an interview question, one Texas teacher wrote:

> The people I tend to mistrust are some of the grade-level principals. I think this mistrust is a result of not seeing them enforce school policies and discipline equally. As a classroom teacher I believe it is extremely important to know that your Associate Principal will support you. Failing to do so results in trust issues.
>
> (Teacher, Texas)

Another teacher stated:

> [The principal] plays favorites and was a willing and skilled manipulator. The good news for me was that I was on the perceived favored side. For those who weren't, and it was blatantly obvious, life was less than grand. I had been encouraged to lie in circumstances by the principal, which I declined respectfully, and I had witnessed lies told to get desired results. Though I felt I could trust my principal and that [the principal] trusted me, watching the manipulation play out always gave me an uneasy feeling. It was like my trust was just waiting to be destroyed.
>
> (Teacher)

A principal from Washington State supported the need for honesty and follow-through by writing:

> I do feel trusted as a professional educator. For me it is about character and integrity. I am honest and upfront with people and believe I have a sense of how to build relationships with people.

People that know me know that they are getting what they get. I don't beat around the bush, straight forward, and I walk the talk. I have also been able to cultivate these types of relationships with central office personnel. I have not been micro managed in my 14 years as an administrator. I see this as people know I know what I am doing. Thus, trust.

(Principal, Washington State)

Findings from the study show 68 per cent of teachers believe their school leaders are knowledgeable about effective teaching practices and contemporary learning theories (Real, Question 15), yet the overwhelming majority of teachers (92 per cent) believe teachers' trust for their leaders is conditional on the leader's competence (Ideal, Question 6). Having a leadership title alone does not ensure the trust of teachers. The progressive distribution of trust is an active process that must be led and managed, requiring leadership wisdom, discernment, and strategic insight (Day, 2013).

Out of the trenches

Teachers are the heart and soul of our educational system. It is with teachers, in the 'trenches' of the classroom, that instruction and learning take place. Interview responses from this study indicate that teachers' highest levels of trust are with those they know and work with directly. One Washington State teacher stated, 'I trust my teaching partner, coaches, and principal. I distrust to a certain extent decision makers at the district level.' Another Texas teacher stated, 'At times I distrust the downtown administration as I feel they have lost touch with what drives learning. I feel that they have lost sight of what it means to teach and how difficult it can be.'

Distrust appears to strengthen the further you climb up the policy-making ladder, as evidenced by the following interview response:

I do feel trusted as an educator. I believe the administration trusts me to do my job effectively in educating my students. Also, I feel that having almost 10 years of experience has made me be trusted by my peers and administration. I trust my teammates most deeply since I work with them closely on a daily basis. I distrust 'the system' of education and how it functions. I feel we have people making decisions at the higher levels of the state, who have no clue about how kids learn and how educators should be judged, or they've never been in the classroom.

(Teacher)

There is no question that trust and collaboration are necessary ingredients in the recipe for school improvement. According to DuFour and Eaker (1998), the most promising strategy for sustained, substantive school improvement is to develop the ability of school personnel to function collaboratively. Yet collaboration, in its truest form, cannot happen in the absence of trust.

And the pendulum swings

The need for trust and verification exists in all systems. As I write this chapter, the political talk in the United States swirls around emails written by Hillary Clinton while she served as Secretary of State. Some in our nation seek verification of Clinton's knowledge and actions during the attack on the American diplomatic compound in Benghazi, Libya. Others in our nation believe we should trust Clinton's statement that she has turned over all work-related emails. It appears the issue of trust stretches from the classrooms in our local schools to the highest offices in our country.

Like other countries, the United States has an educational system that continues to seek the proper balance between trust and verification. Despite the NCLB requirement that all children should be achieving at grade level by the year 2014, the need for educational improvement remains. NCLB reminds us that a document written by policy makers to increase verification isn't enough to improve schools. It takes a combination of trust and verification. Although most would agree that we are far from finding a perfect balance, results from this study suggest a greater need for transparency, collaboration, integrity, and consistency at all levels. Perhaps the recent transition from NCLB to ESSA is an indicator that the pendulum is beginning to switch direction. Many questions remain: what will become of our verification culture? Maybe most daunting and telling, how will the pendulum of trust sway? Only time will tell.

As stated earlier in this chapter, religion was a catalyst for the early American education system. Today, the national motto 'In God We Trust' can be found printed on all US currency. It stands as a symbol of the need for and importance of trust in our society. Regarding the need for trust in our educational system, one Texas teacher perhaps said it best when she stated:

> The lack of trust in a school creates an environment that is counterproductive. When trust is absent, one is less willing to take risks required to push beyond the norm to reach greater success. Risk, reaching for new heights, requires a safety net of support to be available. Without it, risk becomes too dangerous and the consequences too great. One is then forced to stay where

it is safe, to avoid new methods and ideas that could stir the pot, to be content with mediocrity, to fear the very changes that are often thrust upon educators.

When trust is present potential is optimized. Trust provides a safety net which allows me, as an educator, to push myself and my students to new heights of academic rigor and success. Trust allows me to take risks in the atmosphere of teaching and learning that are otherwise unafforded. Trust does not guarantee that there won't be failure; trust implies that there will be the opportunity to evaluate, adjust, and try again. That opportunity provides for the greatest success.

(Teacher, Texas)

References

Calahan, S. (2013) 'Trust me, I'm your principal'. *Principal Leadership*, (14) 4, 22–6.

Cosner, S. (2009) 'Building organizational capacity through trust'. *Educational Administration Quarterly*, 45, 248–91.

Costa, A., Roe, R., and Taillieu, T. (2001) Trust within teams: The relation with performance effectiveness. *European Journal of Work and Organizational Psychology*, 10 (3), 225–44.

Covey, S. (2006) *The Speed of Trust: The one thing that changes everything*. New York, NY: Free Press.

Creswell, J.W. (2008) *Educational research: Planning, conducting, and evaluating quantitative and qualitative research*. Upper Saddle River, NJ: Pearson Prentice Hall.

Cruickshank, D.R., Jenkins, D.B., and Metcalf, K.K. (2012) *The Act of Teaching*. 6th ed. New York: McGraw-Hill.

Day, C. (2013) 'How to trust others to take the lead'. *School Leadership Today*, (4) 6, 68–76.

DuFour, R., and Eaker, E. (1998) *Professional Learning Communities at Work: Best practices for enhancing student achievement*. Alexandria, VA: Association for Supervision and Curriculum Development.

DuFour, R., and Fullan, M. (2013) *Cultures Built to Last: Systemic PLCs at work*. Bloomington, IN: Solution Tree Press.

DuFour, R., and Marzano, R.J. (2011) *Leaders of Learning: How district, school, and classroom leaders improve student achievement*. Bloomington, IN: Solution Tree Press.

Evertson, C.M., and Emmer, E.T. (2009) *Classroom management for elementary teachers*. Upper Saddle River, NJ: Pearson.

Goddard, R.D., Tschannen-Moran, M., and Hoy, W.K. (2001) 'A multilevel examination of the distribution and effects of teacher trust in students and parents in urban elementary schools'. *Elementary School Journal*, 102 (1), 3–17.

Hammonds, C., Kunders, T., and Galow, T. (2013) 'Motivating teachers and meeting expectations'. *Instructional Leader*, 26 (6), 1–2. Online. http://c. ymcdn.com/sites/www.tepsa.org/resource/resmgr/imported/InstructionalLeader/ hammondsil.pdf (accessed 4 February 2016).

Hoffman, J.D., Sabo, D., Bliss, J., and Hoy, W.K. (1994) 'Building a culture of trust'. *Journal of School Leadership*, 4 (5), 484–501.

Hoy, K.H., and Miskel, E.G. (2013) *Educational Administration: Theory, research, and practice.* 9th ed. New York: McGraw-Hill.

Mineo, D. (2014) 'The importance of trust in leadership'. *Research Management Review*, 20 (1), 1–6.

Pink, D.H. (2009) *Drive: The surprising truth about what motivates us.* New York, NY: Riverhead Books.

Rousseau, D.M., Sitkin, S.B., Burt, R., and Camerer, C. (1998) 'Not so different after all: A cross-discipline view of trust'. *Academy of Management Review*, 23 (3), 393–404.

Sergiovanni, T.J. (2007) *Rethinking Leadership: A collection of articles.* Thousand Oaks, CA: Corwin Press.

Travers, P.D., and Rebore, R.W. (2000) *Foundations of Education: Becoming a teacher.* Needham Heights, MA: Allyn and Bacon.

Tschannen-Moran, M. (2001) 'Collaboration and the need for trust'. *Journal of Educational Administration*, 39 (4), 308–31.

— (2009) 'Fostering teacher professionalism: The role of professional orientation and trust'. *Educational Administration Quarterly*, 45, 217–47.

Urban, W.J., and Wagoner, J.L. (2004) *American education: A history.* 3rd ed. New York: McGraw Hill.

Walsh, J., Kemerer, F., and Maniotis, L. (2014) *The Educator's Guide to Texas School Law.* 8th ed. Austin, TX: University of Texas Press.

Wong, K.K., and Nicotera, A. (2007) *Successful Schools and Educational Accountability: Concepts and skills to meet leadership challenges.* Boston, MA: Pearson Education, Inc.

Chapter 10

Themes, dreams, and final thoughts
Dean Fink and Norman McCulla

This book is a little different from most edited books in which authors have pretty much carte blanche to write what they want. The authors of the country chapters in this work agreed to use a standard questionnaire and interview protocol so we could make some comparisons across nations. Moreover, they wrote their chapters with the initiating chapters in mind, taking from them a series of windows through which to look at our topics of trust and distrust. In spite of or perhaps because of these constraints they have succeeded admirably in helping us to understand at a very deep level how the unique structures, geography, history, and politics of each system should give pause to those who would 'cherry pick' features from one system to replicate elsewhere. It just doesn't work. As Pasi Sahlberg, the well-known Finnish educator, has warned:

> ... politicians and policy makers should be careful when borrowing ideas from other countries, be they Singapore, Canada, or Finland. What has made an education system work well in one country won't necessarily work in another. Policy makers should also be aware of the myths about these systems and what made them successful.
>
> (Sahlberg, 2015a)

This is the first and most obvious theme that we can draw from our research. In this, the final chapter of our book, we attempt to describe and explain what we have learned from our research within and across our respective nations.

Context counts
While each country's educational system is unique, the titles to our chapters suggest that these countries share a common policy challenge of sorting through the various structures, ideologies, policies, and practices that swirl across the globe, each with its advocates promising profound and positive

changes. Consider the sub-titles for the book chapters, each chosen quite independently by the authors:

- Australia – Halfway to anywhere?
- Canada – At the tipping point
- Finland – Trust under pressure
- Lithuania – Faster than history, slower than a lifetime?
- Sweden – A 'postmodern cocktail'
- The United Kingdom (England) – Reform in a hurry
- The United States – And the pendulum swings

They all speak to a time of uncertainty and complexity when key decisions about the future directions of education are called for. They speak too of a time when school education is very much at a crossroads in their jurisdictions and when wise decisions are called for from politicians, system leaders, and principals alike. Underpinning these decisions are issues of trust: who or what should policy makers trust to move their educational systems forward? Who should policy implementers, such as principals and teachers, trust to move their schools forward? How might there be a better alignment between policy makers and policy implementers, one centred on mutual trust? It is attaining this alignment that has been the focus of our work.

The first two nations listed, Australia and Canada, originated as British colonies; they still belong to the British Commonwealth and both pay homage to Elizabeth II as Queen. Both nations confronted geographical challenges by designing federal systems and devolving education responsibilities to states (in Australia) or provinces (in Canada). In education policy, however, they appear more different than similar. New Public Management, or what we have called the production model of education, has made far greater inroads in Australia than in Canada. As Marks and McCulla have stated in Chapter 3 of this volume, 'Australian schools have become far more dynamic, corporate, goal-centred, results-driven, and competitive. However it could also be argued, as from the findings in this study, that these changes have come at the price of a decline in the professional confidence of, and public trust in, the teaching profession.' Their subtitle 'Halfway to anywhere' suggests that the current uncertainty within Australian educational circles is creating a professional nervousness about future directions concerning the balance of power between federal and state governments, the philosophical relationship between public and private education, and the influence of a private enterprise culture in education that is centred more on personal gain. In such a scenario education policy is determined essentially by market forces, rather than the pursuit of a common good. They report that there are, however, fledgling signs that things might be changing, suggesting the emergence of a greater trust and professional respect from governments and employing authorities, and a better balance between trust and verification.

Canada is different in two significant ways from Australia and indeed from most other countries: its federal government plays a very limited role in pre-university education, and Canadian teachers' unions remain very strong. The constitutional limitations on the Canadian federal government prevent it from imposing the kind of conformity in curriculum, student assessment, and teachers' and principals' qualifications and evaluations that one sees in Australia, England, and most of the United States. Moreover, the unions, working in the name of teacher professionalism, continually battle with provincial governments over working conditions. As the president of a union in Ontario stated, concerning a contemporary dispute with his province, '(we're looking for improvements) that reflect a tangible appreciation on the part of government and the school boards of the value and the significance of the work we do' (Williams, 2015). The strength of the unions has enabled Canadian teachers to be reasonably well paid, experience decent working conditions, and have a voice or at least some influence on most policy issues. Teaching is still a prized job in virtually all Canadian provinces, and attracts high quality graduates. Importantly, teacher supply is not an issue generally in Canada. The challenges to the profession posed by New Public Management are, however, only an election away in most provinces. Politicians of the political right would love to weaken the unions, bring in right-to-work legislation, and follow their American brethren by instituting most of the trappings of the production model – hence the title 'Canada: At the tipping point'. Their motives are more ideological and for the most part have little to do with educational improvement, since Canadian students do reasonably well on virtually every international measure of educational accomplishment. Canada would fit our definition of a high-trust, high-distrust system: a calculative and negotiated relationship centred on power relations. While teachers are generally trusted in Canadian society, there exists a reciprocal wariness between teachers and their unions on one side and policy makers and society in general on the other.

Like Canada, teaching in Finland is still considered a prestigious job and attracts high-quality applicants. Its unions are strong, and schools and teachers enjoy a considerable degree of professional autonomy. Of our seven countries in this study, Finland is the prototype of what we have called the professional model of education and our best example of a high-trust, low-distrust society. But as its chapter title, 'Finland: Trust under pressure', suggests, there are dark clouds hovering on the horizon. The worldwide recession that began in 2008 has hit Finland particularly hard. Its forest industries have suffered from a lack of demand on the world markets and its manufacturing, particularly its most renowned manufacturer Nokia, have experienced serious difficulties. Calls for marketization of the public sector and for greater emphasis on the private sector indicate that Finland will also experience both internal and external pressures to rein in its public services and put them on a privatized path (Crouch 2015). New Public Management is already a factor at the university level (Salo, 2014, pers. comm.). As Naomi Klein (2007) explains in *The Shock Doctrine,* severe economic shocks such as the one Finland has experienced are often followed by privatization, government deregulation, and deep cuts to social spending, ushering in all the trappings of the 'low-trust' audit society.

Finland's next-door neighbour Sweden led the world toward the marketization of state education but now finds itself at an educational crossroads. As Lars Svedberg's chapter outlines, Sweden presents a bewildering picture of a high-trust society that has blended a complex mixture of public and private education into what Svedberg calls 'a postmodern cocktail'. As he explains, 'The question of "who you can trust" is particularly topical now in Sweden, where the former citizen of the welfare state has been transformed gradually into a customer in an educational marketplace. The learner is increasingly conceptualized as a consumer and education as a consumer good' (Svedberg, Chapter 7, this volume). With comparatively limited standardized testing, and with finance and policy still under municipal control, it shares common features with its easterly neighbour Finland. But the introduction of 'independent schools', some run for profit, has produced competition for state schools. Now educating approximately 15 per cent of students, and funded (as state schools are) partly from the public purse, these schools' advent has profoundly changed the educational landscape, to the point that the Swedish government has appointed a commission to respond to an OECD policy review that challenged Sweden to 'urgently reform' its school system in light of its plummeting PISA achievement scores. The OECD review recommended raising the status and salaries of teachers, placing higher expectations on students, and improving the integration of immigrants, who on average score lower than native students. 'I used to look at Sweden as the model for education,' said Andreas Schleicher, director of OECD's education unit. 'But it was sort of in the early 2000s that the Swedish school system somehow seems to have lost its soul' (Ritter, 2015).

Most disturbing to many Swedes is the growing inequality in the educational experiences open to children. As the Minister of Education at the time of writing stated, 'Instead of breaking up social differences in the education system, we have a system that's creating a wider gap between the ones that have and the ones that have not' (Weale, 2015). The political left calls for the dismantling of the voucher system that supports the independent schools, while the political right advocates greater regulation of students and teachers and more oversight of both. It would appear that the cocktail is in for some major modifications of its ingredients. The high-trust, low-distrust system that older Swedes remember has moved in the direction of an underperforming low-trust, high-distrust society as teachers and government look to right the educational ship.

Few nations have experienced the profound economic, social, and political changes that Finland and Sweden's Baltic neighbour Lithuania has undergone in the past 25 years. Its capital, Vilnius, for example, has changed since the early 1990s from a shabby, rundown, dreary city with a decaying and crumbling historic centre into a vibrant, modern European metropolis with a refurbished 'old city', modern shopping centres and, at least on the surface, a vibrant economy (Khan, 2015). The replacement of the restraints and predictability of the low-trust Soviet system with the vicissitudes of the global marketplace has brought opportunity and improved lifestyles for some. But this transformation has not been without costs. Markets are the best way societies have found to distribute goods and services but they do not do so equitably, and as a result the gap between the rich and poor in Lithuania has widened considerably and the distrust between the state and the citizens is growing due to the former's market-oriented policies. The older and more vulnerable find themselves worse off in this brave new world, and many younger people are leaving to find opportunities elsewhere. As a result Lithuania is losing some of it best and brightest.

As Pranckūnienė and Ruškus explain in Chapter 6 of this volume, Lithuania's educational leaders sought to model their newly independent country after Finland, emulating the nation-building strategy adopted by the latter after its independence in 1917 by using education to stress the new nation's language, culture, and national identity. But Finland's independence was never buffeted by the vagaries of contemporary international capitalism. The three periods of contemporary Lithuanian education that the authors here identify reflect the compelling and often conflicting social forces faced by contemporary Lithuanian educators. From 1990–7, Lithuania aimed for humanization, democratization, and modernization; from 1998–2002 the drive was for continuity and accessibility of education and equal opportunities for all. Since then, however, these goals have lost some of their lustre in the pursuit of cost-effectiveness, quality defined in terms of test scores, and data-driven management. The authors in this volume capture the nature of changes in their country and other post-Soviet nations, borrowing for their title Donskis's observation that 'Lithuania and other Baltic states ... have developed "faster than history" – faster than history but slower than a lifetime. ... A human lifetime proves to witness the sweeping change of a society' (Donskis, 2005). While Lithuania's educators continue to develop an educational system that looks more like Finland's than Sweden, outside pressures suggest that the reverse may be happening.

A significant influence on Lithuanian educational policies, and arguably on many jurisdictions throughout the western world, has been England, and its transition over the course of twenty years from a rather decentralized, high-trust, professionally oriented educational system to one with all the trappings of a production model. While twenty years seems like a long time, Tom Whittingham's subtitle 'Reform in a hurry' captures the prevailing feeling among British educators over that period. If examined at any given point in the twenty years, the change process seems frenetic, unfocused, often contradictory, and confrontational. Looked at from the longer perspective, however, the transformation of the British system towards a production model looks focused and inexorable. Tomlinson captured the early stages of the transition by noting that a system which had, for the previous 35 years:

> ... been run through broad legislative objectives, convention
> and consensus had been replaced by one on contract and
> management. ... The aim was to make an irreversible change
> in the public education system to that already achieved in other
> aspects of economic policy, such as trade union legislation, the
> sale of council houses[1] and the privatization of nationalised
> industries.
>
> (Tomlinson, 1992: 48)

As Whittingham has explained in his chapter, successive Labour governments, the subsequent Coalition, and now the Conservative government (uninhibited by its former Liberal Democratic partner), have continued to build on the Thatcherite tradition. There is a remarkable agreement across the political spectrum that Britain's rather mediocre international performance can be resolved only through the introduction of focused and prescriptive low-trust policies that require systematic accountably measures and quality control, rather than by mobilizing, supporting, and freeing education professionals to improve British schools and their international standing. To ensure compliance with top-down policies, all parties seem to concur that teachers, school heads, and schools in general must be subjected to constant monitoring through accountability checks carried out by the much disliked, indeed feared, Ofsted quango. As an outside observer with considerable experience supporting, observing, and interacting with British heads and teachers and the British school system in general, Fink would suggest that the greatest disappointment for British professionals – and arguably New Labour's greatest educational mistake – was the perpetuation of Ofsted's 'reign of terror' (Brighouse, 1997: 106) and the placing of confidence in a confrontational first chief inspector. Chief inspectors have changed over time, and inspection requirements have shifted, often without too much warning to schools, but – as Tom Whittingham has so clearly indicated – the message from policy makers to the people they count on to implement policies remains: we don't trust you.

In turn, the teaching profession in England, through its unions and headteacher organizations, has taken a confrontational, high-distrust, and on occasion obstructionist approach to government over time. Unions, like the academic community, local governments, and school governors, have generally been excluded by central government from the process of making educational policy. In fact, changes in educational policy have tended to take the form of top-down regulations and circulars rather than serving as the outcome of robust parliamentary debate. As Bangs and his colleagues (2011) report, all parties have developed policy through 'kitchen cabinets' of unelected policy advisers drawn from private think-tanks and consulting firms, which in turn suggests distrust of those most knowledgeable about the state of education – educators and the academic community. This centralization of policy in Whitehall, as Whittingham has described, has resulted from the gradual but relentless erosion of the roles of local authorities in education policy development and practice. While some authorities were weak and ineffective, many authorities and their advisory staffs were powerful agents of positive change for British students (Fink, 2010). Perhaps more importantly from the trust perspective of heads and teachers, the people who shaped their professional lives, and who had for the most part supported them on a daily basis, were no longer a phone call away. The eponymous 'they' of most school jurisdictions became a remote, often invisible, and seemingly powerful, not-to-be-trusted 'they'.

It is unfortunate that the many outstanding examples of British policies and practices that have had the potential to effect significant change have foundered on the shoals of the ideology of New Public Management. Promising and creative innovations, such as the National College for School Leadership, the Beacon Schools Project, and the School Improvement

Partnerships among school heads, have morphed into something quite different from their original intentions or completely disappeared as successive governments threw out the 'old' to introduce their often untested 'new'.

While Ofsted may argue that standards have improved, and perhaps they have, there seem to be a lot of side effects from the way in which England's low-trust, high-distrust model of education produced these results. For example, the following brief sample of education stories in one British newspaper over the past year suggests all is not well with the British low-trust approach:

- 'Four in ten new teachers quit within a year' (Weale, 2015).
- 'Cheating found to be rife in British schools and universities' (Adams, 2015a).
- 'Lost generation of children deprived of school sports' (Watson and Lloyd, 2015).
- 'More than 400,000 schoolchildren being taught by unqualified teachers' (Wintour, 2014).
- 'Policies for improving schools had no effect' (Adams, 2015b).

There is little evidence that contemporary government policies that focus on free schools and academies, or the addition of regional 'tsars' to compensate for the loss of 'middle-level' local authorities, can resolve these issues, because they do not deal with the fundamental problem: a prevailing lack of trust among those that count in education. As well-known British educator Roy Blatchford argues:

> What is needed is mutual trust in education: between central government and teachers and between local and national politicians. The successful future of our schools is one in which governments meddle less, and trust more. And teachers demonstrate an altogether new professionalism.
>
> (Blatchford, 2014: n.p.)

As Whittingham has shown in his chapter on England, a persistent and insistent political argument for the transformation of education in that country from a professional to a production model is the United Kingdom's need to compete in an increasingly integrated global economy. If the logic of this argument held together, then using PISA results as a guide, Finland should have the most vibrant economy and the United States the most stagnant. In fact, the economic success of the seven nations we have studied is almost in inverse order to their success on PISA and most other international educational comparisons. For example, using recent data from the International Monetary Fund (IMF, 2013), the economic order is as shown in Table 10.1.

Table 10.1 Economic rank order of countries examined in this book

Country	2013 GDP (purchasing power parity), US dollars (billions)
United States	16,768.05
United Kingdom	2,320.44
Canada	1,518.41
Australia	1,052.60
Sweden	418.217
Finland	218.296
Lithuania	75.408

Source: IMF (2013)

This is not to suggest of course that education is unimportant to the economic success of a nation, but it is only one of many significant factors such as the size of a nation's population, its population density, its available natural resources, its geographic location, its history of entrepreneurialism, and the stability of its government, to mention just a few. To narrow in on economics as the sole purpose for education is to ignore the traditional purposes of education related to inquiry, equity, social justice, and the common social good. Moreover, the preoccupation with competition as an operating principle undermines the levels of trust necessary for a nation to pull together and cooperate to achieve broad national goals, including economic ones.

Such cohesion is perhaps most difficult to achieve in a nation as large, populous, diverse, and complex as the United States. It has always been a mystery why a nation with so many of the world's finest universities, a productive and dynamic educational research community, and a well-deserved reputation for achieving great things – such as landing a man on the moon – has produced a pre-university education system that seems to engender so much criticism and lack of public trust and, arguably, to produce lacklustre results (Ravitch, 2010, Berliner and Biddle, 1995; Tyack and Cuban, 1995). Perhaps part of the answer, as Craig Hammonds has described in his chapter, is the fact that there is not one American educational system but in fact 50 systems: one for each state in the union, and each a product of its own unique history, culture, and politics. Within each state is a wide variety of school districts, each with its own school board. Some states include huge school jurisdictions, such as New York and Chicago, that educate more children than many of the nations in our study, as well as many small towns and rural districts that might operate only three or four schools. Historically, the responsibility to educate American children belonged to these local school districts and their principals and teachers. As Hammonds points out, the American constitution leaves education almost by default to the states, with the federal government up until the mid-1950s having little involvement in education from kindergarten to Grade 12. Similarly, most states left education to the locally elected school boards and their professional staffs. Needless to say, there was great diversity across the nation in terms of standards, structures, and practices – some outstanding, others less so. For example, the former states of the Confederacy perpetuated the secondary status of Black students after the Civil War through a policy of 'separate but equal' schooling. Since neither Congress or successive Presidents had the power or indeed the will to address this abuse, it was left to the third branch of the American government, the courts – and particularly the Supreme Court, through its ruling in the Brown versus the Board of Education case in 1954 – to declare 'separate but equal' unconstitutional. The enforcement of this court's order and subsequent orders for schools to provide opportunities for students with special needs opened the door to the federal government's entry into the field of education. In 1965, as part of Lyndon Johnson's Great Society initiative, Congress approved the allocation of substantial amounts of money to the states to improve the quality of education for low-income and minority students through the Elementary and Secondary Schools Act. This act established the precedent for the federal government to use its considerable economic power to encourage often cash-strapped states to buy into federal programmes such as *No Child Left Behind* in the 1990s and *Race for the Top* during the Obama presidency. The federal government provides only about 9 per cent of the nation's educational funding, ranging between 5 per cent of the total spent in more affluent states like Massachusetts to 16 per cent for more impoverished states such as Louisiana (Louis and Van Velzen, 2012), but exerts inordinate influence on state-supported education.

The pendulum has indeed swung, as Hammonds has described, from a very decentralized and, some may well argue, chaotic professional-based education model to a system with all the trappings of New Public Management: markets, competition, accountability, vouchers, right-to-work legislation, and charter schools. It is the market that has come to define educational policy.

Having said this, we are reminded of the advice, attributed to Mark Twain, that 'All generalizations are false, including this one'. It is difficult to talk about an American education system because states still control education and the federal government must work through them, and because the states in turn still work through a myriad of school districts, some large and powerful and some small and relatively obscure.

One significant aspect among many that differentiates the United States from our other nations is its funding system. Per-pupil support in the United States ranges between US$10,000 and US$15,000 per pupil, depending on the state and its policies (Louis and Van Velzen, 2012). On average, states supply about 45 per cent of the funding for schools and local taxpayers the other 45 per cent. The tax bases in all states and communities vary widely in their ability to support schools (Johnson, 2015). Even within the same city, students in the more affluent parts of town are funded at a much higher level than students in the poorer areas. This inequity in most American states is the single most important reason that American schools languish at or below the median on most international measures of student proficiency (Darling-Hammond, 2010; Ravitch, 2010).

There are some signs that the system that has swung so far in a neo-liberal direction that it may be righting itself to create a better balance between trust and verification. There are, for example, important and strident voices calling for the elimination or at least the curbing of the power of the federal Department of Education (Bruni, 2015), a significant reaction against the Common Core (Kirp, 2014), and a growing backlash against standardized testing (Taylor and Rich, 2015). Supporters of public education such as the Network for Public Education are pressuring Congress to bring some 'sanity' to the system and particularly to the use of high-stakes tests. In spite of abundant evidence that a system built around school choice, vouchers, charter schools, and accountability testing benefits some but excludes others, there are powerful and well-financed forces bent on maintaining the status quo or pushing what exists even further. Right-leaning foundations with billions of discretionary funds continue to pour billions into programmes that undermine free, open public education. In addition, powerful private corporations that stand to benefit from greater privatization of education push the production agenda. For example, technology companies, such as 'the Learning Accelerator', which champions the idea of blended learning, find a ready audience among policy makers, who assume that such systems offer greater learning with fewer teachers (Ravitch, 2015) – not forgetting the fact that computers don't have unions. Similarly, large publishing companies make huge profits from testing: they use their financial and political clout to oppose any reduction of testing, regardless of its effect on children, and consistently advocate for new standards which mean more tests and more profits. All of these forces have found political voices in both political parties and contribute generously to supportive politicians' electoral campaigns. Even a cursory examination of the various competing forces and cross-currents in American education supports Hammonds's statement that the 'educational systems in the United States are complex', but as our data shows and Hammonds explains, principals and teachers are either lukewarm or opposed to many of the production-type directions. Without the active engagement and trust of the policy implementers it is hard to see how improvement in America's international standing will occur. It is an observation that is well grounded in the now rather voluminous literature on educational change.

It is absolutely clear from our case studies just how integral national contexts have been to shaping the education cultures in each nation as we know them today. It is a reminder that you cannot plan adequately for the future if you have no real understanding of the past, a point as applicable to individual schools as it is to school systems. On the other hand, it is also clear from the case studies how globalization and the espoused need to be 'economically competitive' are creating trends that are transcending national boundaries and leading to a degree of standardization as a result. It seems ironic that policies and mechanisms designed on the one hand to promote free markets, when combined with other policies designed for surveillance of teachers and their work, including international testing regimes, appear to be creating a bland standardization in teaching, a lack of trust within the teaching profession and between the profession and the society it serves, a myriad of other education issues reported by the media, including that of teacher retention, and overall results that are declining. It is also ironic, as we have noted, that school systems that ostensibly encourage choice and competition do not resource schools to compete on something that might even begin to resemble a more level playing field. The more you have and earn as a parent, the greater choice you have in the schools your children might attend.

Leadership in the crosshairs

The previous discussion attempted to categorize our seven nations, using the four trust/distrust quadrants introduced in our introductory chapters. Obviously, these categorizations are fluid and trends that already exist could radically reshape each nation's trust/distrust profile. Finland, for example, is trending towards a more calculative relationship between policy makers and implementers because of changing economic circumstances, and may well become a high-trust/high-distrust nation. Conversely, growing opposition to the widespread privatization agenda in the United States could alter its low-trust/high-distrust status to a more calculative stance. As the trust climate in each nation shifts, principals in schools must negotiate the vicissitudes of changing policies to deliver quality education for their students.[2] At the school level, they must rationalize the fallout from the centralizing forces of big government, in areas such as curriculum and testing, and, increasingly, big unions, which fight to maintain some degree of professional autonomy for teachers, while addressing decentralizing forces such as the delegation of non-educational decision-making in the name of school autonomy.

Principals as gatekeepers

What has become apparent in our study across nations is that principals have increasingly found themselves in the role of 'gatekeeper'. Our survey asked for an ideal and real response to the item 'School leaders must act as gatekeepers to protect teachers and children from the negative effects of some government and/or district policies', with responses given on a five-point Likert scale that ranged from strongly agree (5) to strongly disagree (1). The results follow.

Table 10.2 Principals' agreement scores by country for questionnaire item 15: 'School leaders must act as gate keepers to protect teachers and children from the negative effects of some government and/or district policies'

Nation	Ideal	Real	Difference
Australia	3.90	3.97	0.07
Canada	3.52	3.59	0.07
Finland	3.3	3.4	0.01
Lithuania	4.05	3.29	- 0.76
Sweden	3.00	3.39	0.39
United Kingdom (England)	3.13	4.27	1.14
United States	3.75	3.64	- 0.11

The ideal column reflects the historic gatekeeping role of principals and the real situation describes conditions obtaining at the time of the survey in 2014. In three of the nations (Finland, Canada, Australia) there is little difference between the perceived ideal and real situations, but in Lithuania and England there are significant disparities. Lithuanian principals played a significant gatekeeping role during the Soviet era but would appear to do so less at present, in the context of shifting policies described in Chapter 6. The UK (specifically, English) case, however, shows how the privatization/production agenda has turned principals (heads) into defenders of what they see as quality education for children. It would appear that headship in England has become a 'subversive activity'. The modest difference observable in Sweden may be the result of the 'cocktail' that Svedberg describes in his chapter on Sweden. Interestingly, and contrary to what one might predict, American principals see less need for gatekeeping now than in the past. Perhaps this is an indicator of the optimism Hammonds described in Chapter 9 as the educational pendulum swings back to a more professional approach to education in the US. Alternatively, it may mean that principals have become totally compliant and have abdicated their responsibility to provide leadership in educational matters: 'If you do the thinking, I am no longer responsible'.

Principals and government policies

Principals' responses to a second item, 'Government policies support quality public education for all regardless of family income', produce (with reference to the ideal scenario) a rank order that correlates very closely to the PISA rankings described elsewhere.

Table 10.3 Principals' agreement scores and ordinal rank by country for questionnaire item 1, 'Government policies support quality public education for all regardless of family income'

	Ideal (rank)	Real (rank)	Difference (rank)
Australia	3.8 (5)	2.88 (4)	0.98 (5)
Canada	3.87 (2)	3.19 (2)	0.68 (2)
Finland	4.37 (1)	4.2 (1)	0.6 (1)
Lithuania	3.86 (4)	3.14 (3)	0.72 (3)
Sweden	4.34 (2)	3.03 (4)	1.31 (7)
United Kingdom (England)	3.31 (7)	2.20 (6)	1.11 (6)
United States	3.52 (6)	2.61 (5)	0.91 (4)

We would suggest that this data reflects the confidence of Finnish and Canadian principals, the hopes of Lithuanian principals, the increasing disillusionment of Australian and Swedish principals, the discouragement of British principals, and arguably the general acceptance of the status quo by American principals.

Principals and institutional trust

To determine principals' institutional trust, which we defined elsewhere as 'the degree to which an organization's various constituencies continue to have confidence in its competence, integrity, and sustainability', we calculated the results for each country using the following six items from the trust questionnaire as indicators:

- Government policies support quality public education for all regardless of family income (Item 1).
- The educational system supports its school leaders in ways that make them more effective (Item 3).
- The educational system backs its teachers when their professionalism is questioned by the press and other media sources (Item 4).
- Quality leadership is one of the educational system's highest priorities (Item 12).
- School leaders feel valued by senior levels of government (Item 13).
- Leadership development has strong support from higher levels of government (the province, state etc.) (Item 14).

The aggregated results (5 strongly agree, 1 strongly disagree) are shown in Table 10.4. In many ways they parallel the themes of our country chapters: the confidence, perhaps even smugness, of Finnish principals, the hopes for better days among their Lithuanian and American colleagues, the uncertainty of Australian and Canadian principals as production values and practices permeate their respective countries, and the continuing distrust of Swedish and particularly British principals (heads) in their governments' policies.

Table 10.4 Principals' mean agreement with all institutional trust questionnaire items by country

Country	Mean agreement with institutional trust items
Finland	3.6
Lithuania	2.93
United States	2.91
Australia	2.79
Canada	2.77
Sweden	2.42
United Kingdom (England)	1.85

Principals and unions

Principals must also deal with teacher organizations, which in some countries have grown more militant as the values of the production model have become more established and as 'right-to-work' legislation, workplace agreements, and similar means to curb the power of unions become more popular among right-leaning politicians. This is especially so in countries such as Canada where teachers and principals are represented by separate associations.

While a highly debated concept, especially in the United States (Farley, 2010; Carini, 2002), our data suggests that strong unions may have contributed to better student results by providing professional push-back against the forces of privatization and New Public Management, especially when principals act in concert with teachers. Principals and local school districts, however, are more often than not caught in the conflict between two behemoths, big government and big unions. It is interesting therefore to consider how principals responded to our survey item on trust in unions.

Those principals who were not part of the teachers' bargaining unit in Canada, such as in Ontario and British Columbia (see Chapter 4), were very negative on the item 'Unions are an agency for school improvement in school systems and schools'. Of our seven nations, on the five point scale, Canada scored lowest at 2.41 when asked to describe the 'real' situation. This low score probably reflects job (industrial) actions at the time of the survey's administration in both large provinces, as well as the legislated exclusion of principals from the teachers' unions by production-leaning governments that believed that education should be run like a business and that principals, as managers, must be separated from their workers, the teachers.

These political decisions removed the moderating effect on unions of principals, who generally see the larger picture. As a result, over the last 20 years, unions – particularly in British Columbia and Ontario – have become more strident and militant. Principals are now in the uncomfortable and often contradictory position of representing their school districts' and provincial policies while trying to bring about school improvement with a staff that follows the lead of their unions. Building collaborative cultures is difficult enough (Stoll and Fink, 1996) for principals without the added burden of negotiating these political waters. Once again, education politics and policies that are designed to drive a wedge between principals and their staff on industrial matters cannot be seen to be conducive to developing high-trust relationships at the individual school level. It is hard to run with the hares when you are also required to hunt with the hounds.

Except for in Canada, there is no discernable pattern concerning principals' support for and trust in teachers' unions or their degree of influence on government policies. Finland, where principals are included in the teachers' bargaining unit, returned the highest agreement score on our five-point scale at 3.1. Australian principals, who are part of teachers' unions in each state and nationally, scored 2.68, and do play a high-profile role in influencing government policies. Sweden scored 2.73 on our five-point scale. Its secondary principals, who appear to be quite influential as advisors to government, operate outside the teachers' union, whereas most of their elementary colleagues are within the teachers' union. The two lowest-achieving nations on PISA in our sample, the United Kingdom and the United States, scored 2.92 on this item. The United Kingdom's two major principals' organizations and three largest teachers' unions appear to have little impact on policy. The United States, which has a mixture of union and non-union states and separate principals' organizations in most states, has had only modest success at holding back the forces of privatization.

In Lithuania, at 2.59 on our measures, the four teachers' unions (which include some principals) and an additional, rather ineffective principals' association tend to weaken their influence on policy by competing among themselves.[3] Where there exist multiple unions and principals' associations, such as in Lithuania and the United Kingdom, governments often overcome opposition by playing one organization off against another. These large-scale dramas often add to the political challenges facing principals in schools. Our study has suggested that, with the directions and destiny of the teaching profession controlled by the political process in each of the jurisdictions, and with principals called upon increasingly to be policy advocates and implementers, not designers, or at best recognized as having a limited voice among many in the policy-making process, it has been teacher unions more than any other group that have had the power to act as a voice on behalf of the teaching profession. We also note in a number of the countries studied how easy it is for the political process and the media to dismiss this voice as 'self-serving' when it does not fit easily with the policy agenda of the day.

Principals' autonomy

A consistent agenda item for New Public Management is to delegate managerial tasks to schools that were in the past handled more centrally by middle-level governing bodies such as school districts, while paradoxically centralizing educational policies at the same time. Andy Hargreaves (2015) discriminates between 'school autonomy', whereby schools and particularly the principal are allowed to deal with a wide variety of managerial, financial, and personnel issues, and 'professional autonomy', which encourages professional leaders and teachers to make decisions in the best interests of students. Governments, especially those that promote charter schools, free schools, or academies that do not conform to traditional hiring practices, support 'school autonomy' on the premise that student achievement can improve while costs are cut if principals and heads are allowed to hire young and often inexperienced teachers.

New Public Management operates on the principle that principals and schools will welcome such school autonomy. To test this premise we included the following two items in our survey:

- Schools need complete autonomy to pursue a school improvement agenda (Item 2).
- School leaders need to be in charge of all aspects of the school's operation (maintenance, construction, transportation etc.) to ensure effective teaching and learning in schools (Item 9).

In all seven countries, the aggregated scores showed that the ideal and real were almost the same. For example, on the five-point scale for England, where principals have considerable autonomy on non-educational items, the ideal was 3.05 and the real was 2.99. In Canada, where middle level agencies tend to deal with many of the items listed in item 9, its scores were ideal 2.72 and real 2.74. This congruency suggests that principals in countries such as Canada are satisfied with the status quo and don't want to be delegated additional managerial tasks. It also might suggest that principals in some countries such as Sweden, the UK, and US, which have bought into free schools, academies, and charter school models that lack constraints on who they can hire to teach, have become complicit in schemes to de-professionalize teaching (Hargreaves, 2015). Trends in this area suggest that there may be a significant difference between complete school autonomy and structures within which school principals have greater authority to make decisions in the best interests of their students. Attaining the appropriate balance between trust and verification once again appears to be the key.

Principals and relational trust

Social capital, as described in Chapter 1, involves building external and internal organizational relationships. Perhaps the most important relationships principals build are inside their own buildings. Elsewhere we borrowed Bryk and Schneider's (1996) definition of relational trust as a form of trust that is 'formed through the mutual understandings that arise out of the sustained associations among individuals and institutions' (Bryk and Schneider, 1996: 6). There were 16 items in our survey for principals that related to relational trust,[4] and 12 relation trust items in our survey for teachers.[5] The aggregated results are shown in Table 10.5.

Table 10.5 Aggregated agreement scores by country for relational trust questionnaire items among principals (scores among teachers in brackets)

Country	Ideal (teacher ideal)	Real (teacher ideal)	Difference (teacher difference)
Australia	4.16 (3.9)	4.0 (3.58)	0.16 (0.32)
Canada	4.08 (3.99)	3.99 (3.40)	0.09 (0.59)
England	4.04 (4.24)	3.34 (3.9)	0.7 (0.34)
Finland	4.23 (4.5)	3.76 (3.6)	0.47 (0.9)
Lithuania	3.93 (3.72)	3.68 (3.76)	0.24 (- 0.04)
Sweden	4.10 (3.94)	3.80 (3.29)	0.30 (0.65)
USA	4.06 (3.93)	3.84 (3.6)	0.22 (0.33)

What is interesting about these figures is how close the 'ideal' is to the 'real' for each country, and the degree to which principals' views agree with teachers' perspectives. The similarity of each nation's scores to each other is also notable. With the exception of the disparity between the ideal and real scores given by English headteachers, and discounting the idealism of Finland, it would appear that relational trust is a positive feature in almost every nation. It seems highly important to note that this finding is at odds with our investigations of levels of trust between schools and their jurisdictional institutions, which appear to be in decline or at a 'tipping point' that may push school cultures towards a production model and erode principals' ability to act as gatekeepers on behalf of students and teachers. Principals are indeed in the crosshairs of multiple external forces that promote production values and internal forces that try to maintain teachers' professionalism and resilience. Our data suggests that they have at least maintained relational trust within schools.

Teachers: Professionals or puppets?

In each of the countries we have studied we have seen the interplay of two quite different educational models. Teachers try to maintain their professional autonomy on behalf of what they see as their students interests (and perhaps their own), in the face of competing managerial policies that tend to undermine teachers' professionalism and autonomy in the name of quality, consistency, and economic contributions. While teachers and principals would appear to get along, based on our aggregated data, a more in-depth view of the survey items suggests that there are a number of sticking points that have the potential to create unrest within schools. Three in particular can be observed in relation to the following items from the teacher survey:

- School leaders maintain trust by addressing poor teacher practice promptly and effectively (Item 16).
- School leaders admit mistakes openly and promptly (Item 20).
- School leaders at all levels share decision-making with staff members (Item 26).

Table 10.6 presents a comparison of the ideal (what teachers think the item should be) and the real (what they say exists at present) scores given by teachers from each country to each of these three questionnaire items, all of which pertain to issues with the potential to undermine relational trust. The real-situation score is given in brackets.

Table 10.6 Agreement scores by country for questionnaire items of concern in teachers' relationships with principals

Country	Real-situation scores (ideal-situation scores)		
	Item 16	Item 20	Item 26
Australia	3.80 (2.99)	3.4 (2.22)	3.7 (2.95)
Canada	3.83 (2.62)	2.94 (2.23)	3.72 (3.21)
Finland	4.0 (3.2)	3.0 (2.6)	4.1 (3.6)
Lithuania	3.61 (3.46)	3.16 (2.77)	3.86 (3.6)
Sweden	4.04 (3.62)	4.20 (4.11)	4.35 (4.21)
United Kingdom	4.21 (3.38)	4.16 (2.59)	4.06 (3.39)
United States	3.86 (2.83)	3.07 (2.65)	3.53 (3.22)

Teacher performance (Item 16)

On the positive side, it is interesting that teachers are concerned that principals do not address poor teacher performance as well as they would like.[6] The 'new professionalism' that Roy Blatchford has called for requires systematic and rigorous approaches to evaluating teacher performance in ways that support the improvement of all teachers but also purge school systems of poor teachers. Unfortunately, as our data suggests, unions and other teacher organizations have made dismissals virtually impossible.[7] This failure to address poor performance is one of the main criticisms made by business-oriented observers. In response, and as part of the production model, there is a burgeoning global industry developing schemes to evaluate teachers' performance (Harris, 2015; Rich, 2014). Some are simple to the point of being simplistic, such as those that rate teachers based on students' test scores; others are quite elaborate and involve multiple stakeholders such as students and parents. Teachers across our sample were cautiously open to student involvement in their evaluation. The average score on the item 'Students' views on teachers' performance is part of teachers' performance review' was 3.2 out of 5. Whatever the system, teachers need to trust its fairness, rigour, and attention to students' learning in the broadest sense. Principals, in turn, were even more positive about teachers' involvement in their evaluation. Principals gave a 3.8 agreement score to the item 'Teachers' views on school leaders' performance is part of leaders' performance review'.

Transparency (Item 20)
School or system leaders who deny, ignore, or spin their own failures but are quite prepared to confess the sins of those beneath them in the hierarchy undermine trust. Hargreaves (2015) contends that transparency is the *result* of trust, not a cause, and the discrepancy identified in item 20 has the potential to damage relational trust.

Shared decision-making (Item 26)
Finally, in spite of all the literature advocating shared decision-making, our data suggests that many teachers are suspicious or downright cynical about this phenomenon. It often means dumping down jobs that senior leaders don't want to do. There also appears to be a significant divergence between principals' views of shared decision-making and those of teachers. From a leader's point of view, there are many areas in which he or she is responsible and vulnerable that are not amenable to shared decision-making – teacher tenure is an obvious one. It is often useful for staff to engage in dialogue on which decisions belong to the principal and which to the staff, on who initiates decisions, who has input into decisions, who must carry them out, and who makes the final decision. This is an example of the kind of transparency and straight-talk that builds trust (Fink, 2015).

Teacher–teacher relationships
To examine the relational culture among teachers we identified six items from our survey that related directly to teacher–teacher relationships in schools.[8] In every country the aggregated totals for both real and ideal scenarios exceeded 4.0, which would indicate that the relational bonds within teaching have remained relatively strong as the profession has negotiated wave after wave of governmental policy imperatives,

bureaucratic restructuring, unsympathetic media, and the challenges of the education marketplace. In the jurisdictions we have studied, the professional resilience often called for from teachers has, it seems, been exemplified by the profession itself. That said, we have noted the common thread to greater surveillance and compliance demands concerning teachers' work in what might be termed an 'audit culture' within a production model. Where this culture extends to onerous reporting demands and standardization of teaching, and where it takes substantial time and distracts from actually teaching students creatively and with purpose, teachers object and low-trust environments result.

Leadership practices that engender teachers' trust

From the existing literature on trust we identified the following leadership attitudes, competencies, and practices that engender trust within a school and included them in our survey.

- School improvement depends on school leaders' ability to build trusting relationships with all staff members (Item 6).
- Teachers trust of their leaders is conditional on the leader's competence (Item 7).
- School leaders need to know and show concern for staff members' personal circumstances (Item 8).
- School leaders must act as a gatekeeper to buffer or protect teachers and children from the negative effects of some government and/or district policies (Item 12).
- School leaders maintain trust by addressing poor teacher practice promptly and effectively (Item 14).
- School leaders are knowledgeable about effective teaching practices and contemporary learning theories (Item 15).
- Teachers' willingness to support each other's teaching is crucial to school improvement (Item 16).
- School leaders act with integrity; they 'walk their talk' (Item 23).
- School leaders address teachers' feelings of vulnerability (Item 24).
- School leaders share decision-making with staff members (Item 26).
- Trustworthy leaders at all levels say what they mean and mean what they say (Item 27).

The aggregated survey results for these dimensions of trustworthy leadership are presented in Table 10.7.

Table 10.7 Aggregate agreement scores by country for questionnaire items concerning leadership practices that engender teachers' trust

Nation	Ideal	Real	Difference
Australia	3.96	3.55	0.41
Canada	3.87	3.34	0.53
Finland	4.04	3.57	0.47
Lithuania	4.08	3.61	0.47
Sweden	4.25	3.37	0.88
UK (England)	4.03	3.74	0.29
USA	3.84	3.53	0.31

What is remarkable on this dimension is the similarity of results from country to country. The only discrepancy from ideal to real of any significance is Sweden; its teachers' higher expectations of leadership (ideal) make their scores somewhat out of line. Since there was such agreement, we next looked at each item across our seven countries and rank-ordered them in terms of how teachers rated their importance, calculating differences between the ideal and real (see Table 10.8).

Table 10.8 Teachers' agreement scores for individual leadership practice questionnaire items in real and ideal scenarios

Item	Ideal (Rank)	Real (Rank)	Difference
6. Building trusting relationships	4.38 (2)	3.88 (2)	0.5
7. Leader's general competence	4.43 (1)	4.14 (1)	0.29
8. Personal concern	3.9 (5)	3.56 (5)	0.34
12. Gatekeeper	4.01 (4)	3.6 (3)	0.41
14. Addressing poor practice	3.78 (7)	2.98 (8)	0.8
15. Educationally knowledgeable	3.82 (9)	3.53 (6)	0.29
23. Integrity	3.89 (6)	2.92 (9)	0.97
24. Addressing vulnerabilities	3.45 (10)	2.82 (10)	0.63
26. Shared decision-making	3.75 (8)	3.48 (7)	0.27
27. Transparency	4.2 (3)	3.56 (4)	0.46

This data suggests that leaders who build relational trust in schools will be those who are competent in their role; they build trusting relationships that are open, honest, and transparent. They are effective gatekeepers, and show concern for staff members' personal lives. From teachers' perspectives, the greatest failings of existing leaders is the inconsistency between their words and deeds, their inability to address (or lack of concern with) the vulnerabilities teachers may feel or experience, their failure to act on poor educational and teaching practices, their lack of open, honest communications, and a general inability to earn teachers' trust.

Day and Gu (2010) have pointed to the power of education policy in defining the limits of teacher professionalism and either enabling or inhibiting professional identity and resilience. Our study has revealed just how important policy frameworks are to trust relationships with classroom teachers, how important school leaders are in developing these relationships, and indeed how important the self-trust of leaders and their own capacity to lead with moral purpose and vision are to effective schools. Encouraging the things of which you approve and discouraging the things of which you disapprove is how school leaders exert their own authority and control over external and internal school environments. It explains in part why some change processes succeed and others fail at the school level.

Verification

The casual reader of this book may have missed the word 'and' in our title *Trust <u>and</u> Verify: The real keys to school improvement*. Verification is an important part of school improvement as a counterbalance to trust, thus the 'and'. Michael Power, in his book *The Audit Society*, explains that verification is a normal part of daily living. It is often unconscious, such as checking to see that the front door is locked, your teenager is in from her date, and the car has enough gas (petrol) to get you to work and so on. You probably overtly check your bank's statement of your accounts, the receipt from the grocery store cashier, and your child's school report card. In the process, you are holding your, bank, grocery store, and child and school to account – a process of logical, sensible, and necessary accounting. 'Accounting and account giving are part of what it is to be a rational individual' (Douglas, 1992: 132). We check explicitly in circumstances of doubt, mistrust, danger, or conflict. Do we demand an audit, see the grocery store manager, or request an interview with the principal? If dissatisfied, do we hire a lawyer, an accountant, or go to the press? 'Methods of checking and verification are diverse, sometimes perverse, sometimes burdensome and always costly', as Power (1999: 1) observes. Just as it is hard to imagine a society in which everyone is always trusted, it is equally difficult to imagine a society in which people always check everything. 'Trust releases us from checking' (ibid.). Our personal and societal dilemma is where to draw the line.

What we need to decide as individuals, organizations and societies is how to combine checking and trusting. What kinds of activities should be checked? How much explicit checking is enough? How does checking affect those who are checked and when does the demand for monitoring become pathological? Can the benefits of checking be demonstrated?

(Power, 1999: 2)

As Power explains, checking up on each other is more than a question of technical expertise: it is also a cultural issue, which takes us back to the observation that initiated this book. Some countries appear more trusting than others and therefore accept different forms of educational checking. 'Much depends on what the community or society demands and this in turn is often a function of what it is prepared to trust and the types of risk to which it feels vulnerable' (Power, 1999: 3).

The interplay between the light-touch accountability that is inherent in the professional model of education and the heavy touch that motivates and drives the production model are woven throughout our seven country chapters. For example, Finland uses a very light touch and trusts its teachers' and principals' professionalism to provide high-quality education for its young people. Others nations trust such accountability systems as standardized testing and inspections to drive educational improvement.

The question we asked in the introductory chapters remains: where is the 'sweet spot' between trust and verification, because both are necessary and useful? Our data suggests that teachers and principals are cautiously open to and supportive of reasonable accountability measures and recognize that checking on teachers, principals, and schools' performances is necessary in publicly supported school systems. Three of our survey items attempted to probe teachers' and principals' attitudes on verification-related issues:

- School leaders maintain trust by addressing poor teacher practices promptly and effectively (Item 14 on the principals' survey, Item 16 on the teachers' survey).[9]
- Students' views on teachers' performance is part of teachers' performance review (Item 18 on the principals' survey)/Teachers views on school leaders' performance is part of leaders' performance review (Item 19 on the teachers' survey).
- The public and policy makers deserve independent information on the successes and failures of each school (Item 28 on the principals' survey).

Table 10.9 compares principals' and teachers' responses on these three items.

Table 10.9 Principals' and teachers' agreement scores for verification-related questionnaire items

Item	Teachers	Principals (Heads)
14 (16)	3.73 (3.1)[10]	4.17 (3.88)
18 (19)	3.25 (2.93)	3.25 (2.93)
28	3.6 (3.3)	3.75 (3.5)

The results here suggest that principals and teachers are open to innovative approaches to verification and recognize the public's need to know (Item 28). As mentioned previously, both principals and teachers are somewhat supportive of more rigorous evaluation of poor performers. Teachers are suspicious of student involvement in their evaluation whereas principals appear quite positive about teachers' engagement in their performance review. Student evaluations can spot the mediocre or poor teacher very effectively. Teacher contributions to principal performance reviews suggest that a version of a 360-degree evaluation system such as those used in business has the potential to meet verification needs while supporting principals' professional growth. In Canada, the US, and the UK, our data on these items suggests that teachers seem very wary of student involvement in their evaluation, while in the UK and US principals seem quite concerned about having teachers evaluate their performance. Underlying the apparent wariness is a lack of trust in how data will be used. Pasi Sahlberg says, 'Don't be fooled by data: PISA is a good servant and a bad master' (Sahlberg, 2015b). Replace PISA in this sentence with other large-scale verification schemes, such as the mass standardized test systems NAPLAN (Australia), EQAO (Ontario), and GCSEs (England), and the same caveat applies: principals and teachers have every right to be suspicious and distrustful.

Conclusion

Perhaps two things stand out more than any others from this study. The first is just how pivotal the role of the principal is in developing high-trust relations in schools, and in developing the relationship between the school and the employing authority and jurisdiction it serves. The second thing is the significance of the overall levels of trust that exist between the political system and the broader society with the teaching profession. Levels of trust between a teaching staff and their principal in individual schools also reflect this in part, and in so doing influence each teacher's sense of professionalism.

Each of the case studies outlined in this research has clearly shown the richness of the socio-cultural and historical backgrounds that have made each of the jurisdictions what it is today. There is an immense challenge to our political leaders here, which can be reduced to a simple question: in seeking to develop high-performing schools that promote equity and the development of all young people to their maximum potential, do they favour a high-trust professional model or a low-trust production model of education? The evidence in this study suggests that they have increasingly favoured the latter, with some rare exceptions such as Finland where looser rather than tighter controls over the profession remain the norm – albeit, as our case study has shown, not without threat. If production models are to be favoured, we cannot help but note the general concern about declining test scores in those jurisdictions where it is more prevalent, and the range of subsidiary issues impacting upon production-model schools that are constantly reported in the media.

A key message from the data is that there are significant numbers of principals and teachers out there in each national jurisdiction who are attempting to build high-trust relationships in their schools in circumstances where the external environment is at best not conducive and at worst, antithetical – even hostile – to their doing so, and in some cases is becoming more so. There is a gap in these principals' minds between the ideal scenario and what they are experiencing day by day in schools.

Where there is devolution in matters of curriculum, pedagogy, assessment, school management, teacher professional development, and the like, and where there are looser rather than tighter controls in place to verify and assure quality, levels of trust between the school and its community (indeed, across the society) do tend to be higher. Unquestionably, it is both context and place that are the key determinants of the extent of this trust, while the individual principal is the major variable in determining how it is enacted.

Of course, there are good and in some situations wonderful things happening in individual schools. Often one suspects that such schools are thriving despite 'the system'. These successes are usually the result of the principal's values and moral purpose in being there in the first place, his or her capacity to enact a gatekeeper's role and ability to build strong learning cultures for students and teachers alike. Such observations may well be the starting points for true education reform for education policy makers who have the courage to move beyond the need to standardize, surveil, and control in favour of enabling and supporting good teaching and leadership practice. An education marketplace purportedly offering real choice, competition, and opportunities to fully develop all young people regardless of the school they attend needs its frameworks within which to plan and to verify performance, but not in ways that build distrust, or demoralize and distance teachers from their chosen vocation.

Notes

[1] 'Council housing' refers to public housing for people on low incomes.

[2] We use the term 'principal' throughout to describe the person within a school who is ultimately responsible for its policies and practices. This covers, inter alia, headteachers in England and Directors in some former Soviet settings.

[3] Eglė Pranckūnienė, personal communication.

[4] The following items from our principals' survey (see Appendix 1a) relate to relational trust: 7, 8, 11, 15–18, 20–7, 29.

[5] The following items from our teachers' survey (see Appendix 1b) relate to relational trust: 6, 7, 8, 12, 14, 15, 20, 21, 23, 24, 26, 27, 29.

[6] Conversely, principals were much more positive about their dealings with poor performance.

[7] Item 5 in our principals' survey, plus many interviews with teachers and principals, supports this comment.

[8] Items 6, 16, 17, 21, 25, and 29 (see Appendix 1b).

[9] Teachers' items are numbered in the survey 14, 18, 28; corresponding principals' items are numbered 14, 17, 28.

[10] Note that the 'real situation' score is given in brackets. Ideal is 3.73 on the five-point scale (real is 3.1).

References

Adams, R. (2015a) 'Cheating found to be rife in British schools and universities'. *The Guardian*, 15 June. Online. www.theguardian.com/education/2015/jun/15/cheating-rife-in-uk-education-system-dispatches-investigation-shows (accessed 23 July 2015).

— (2015b) 'Policies for improving schools had "no effect", finds parliamentary inquiry'. *The Guardian*, 25 January. Online. www.theguardian.com/education/2015/jan/25/government-policies-improving-uk-schools-had-no-effect-parliamentary-inquiry (accessed 23 July 2015).

Bangs, J., Macbeath, J., and Galton, M. (2011) *Reinventing Schools, Reforming Teaching: From political visions to classroom reality*. London: Routledge.

Berliner, D. and Biddle B. (1995) *The Manufactured Crisis: Myths, frauds and the attack on America's school system*. New York: Addison-Wesley.

Blatchford, R. (2014) 'What is the legacy of the Education Act, 70 years on?' *The Guardian*, 22 April. Online. www.theguardian.com/education/2014/apr/22/1944-education-act-butler-policy-today (accessed 18 July 2015).

Brighouse, T. (1997) 'Leading and managing primary schools: The changing world of the education authority'. In Cullingford, C. (ed.) *The Politics of Primary Education*. Buckingham: Open University Press.

Bruni, F. (2015) 'The education assassins'. *New York Times*, 31 May. Online. www.nytimes.com/2015/05/31/opinion/sunday/frank-bruni-department-of-education-assassins.html?_r=0 (accessed 2 August 2015).

Bryk, A.S., and Schneider, B. (1996) 'Social trust: A moral resource for school improvement'. Online. https://ccsr.uchicago.edu/sites/default/files/publications/socialtrust_amoralresourceforschoolimprovement.pdf (accessed 8 August 2015).

Carini, R. (2002) 'Teacher unions and student achievement'. In Molnar, A. *School Reform Proposals: The research evidence*. Greenwich, CT: Information Age Publishing, 197–216.

Crouch, D. (2015) 'Finland after the boom: "Not as bad as Greece, yet, but it's only matter of time"'. *The Guardian*, 15 April. Online. www.theguardian.com/world/2015/apr/15/finland-boom-election-recession-oulu-miracle-timber-nokia (accessed 6 July 2015).

Darling-Hammond, L. (2010) *The Flat World and Education: How America's commitment to equity will determine our future.* New York: Teachers College Press.

Day, C., and Gu, Q. (2010) *The New Lives of Teachers.* New York: Routledge.

Donskis, L. (2005) 'The unbearable lightness of change'. In Samalavičius, A. (ed.) *Forms of Freedom: Lithuanian culture and Europe after 1990.* Vilnius: Kultūros barai.

Douglas, M. (1992) *Risk and Blame: Essays in cultural theory.* London: Routledge.

Farley, R. (2010) 'Randi Weingarten says students in strong union states perform better academically'. *Tampa Bay Times: PolitiFact.com,* 2 September. Online. www.politifact.com/truth-o-meter/statements/2010/sep/02/randi-weingarten/randi-weingarten-says-students-strong-union-states/ (accessed 2 August 2015).

Fink, D. (2010) *The Succession Challenge: Building and sustaining leadership capacity though succession management.* London: Sage.

— (2015) 'Trusting our schools: The "soft" side of decision making'. In Chitpin, S., and Evers, C. (eds) *Decision Making in Educational Leadership: Principles, policies and practice.* New York: Routledge, 148–62.

Hargreaves, A. (2015) 'Autonomy and transparency: Two good ideas gone bad'. In Evers, J., and Kneyber, R. (eds) *Flip the System: Changing education from the ground up.* London: Routledge.

Harris, E.A. (2015) '20% of New York State students opted out of standardized tests this year'. *New York Times*, 13 August. Online. www.nytimes.com/2015/08/13/nyregion/new-york-state-students-standardized-tests.html (accessed 13 August 2015).

IMF (2013) 'Report for selected countries and subjects'. Online. http://tinyurl.com/guu3crv (accessed 4 February 2016).

Johnson, K. (2015) 'Washington State faces $100,000-a-day fine until schools plan is reached'. *New York Times*, 14 August. Online. www.nytimes.com/2015/08/14/us/washington-state-faces-dollar100000-a-day-fine-until-schools-plan-is-reached.html (accessed 14 August 2015).

Khan, S. (2015) '36 Hours in Vilnius, Lithuania'. *New York Times*, 12 July. Online. www.nytimes.com/2015/07/12/travel/what-to-do-in-36-hours-in-vilnius-lithuania.html (accessed 12 July 2015).

Kirp, D.L. (2014) 'Rage against the common core', *New York Times*, 28 December. Online. www.nytimes.com/2014/12/28/opinion/sunday/rage-against-the-common-core.html? (accessed 2 August 2015).

Klein, N. (2007) *The Shock Doctrine: The rise of disaster capitalism.* Toronto: Alfred A. Knopf.

Louis, K.S., and van Velzen, B. (2012) *Educational Policy in an International Context: Political culture and its effects.* New York: Palgrave Macmillan.

Powers, M. (1999) *The Audit Society: Rituals of verification.* Oxford: Oxford University Press.

Ravitch, D. (2010) *The Death and Life of the Great American School System: How testing and choices are undermining education.* New York: Basic Books.

— (2015) 'Carole Marshall: "The big lie behind Rhode Island's strategic plan for education"'. *Diane Ravitch Blog*. Online. http://dianeravitch.net/2015/07/28/carole-marshall-the-big-lie-behind-rhode-islands-strategic-plan-for-education/ (accessed 2 August 2015).

Rich, M. (2014) 'In Washington State, Political Stand Puts Schools in a Bind', *New York Times*, 4 October. Online. www.nytimes.com/2014/10/05/us/in-washington-state-political-stand-puts-schools-in-a-bind.html (accessed 13 August 2015).

Ritter, K. (2015) 'Sweden's failing schools a growing embarrassment for Scandinavian welfare state'. *The Toronto Star,* 4 May. Online. www.thestar.com/news/world/2015/05/04/swedens-failing-schools-a-growing-embarrassment-for-scandinavian-welfare-state.html (accessed 7 July 2015).

Sahlberg, P. (2015a) 'Britain should be wary of borrowing education ideas from abroad'. *The Guardian*, 27 April. Online. www.theguardian.com/politics/2015/apr/27/britain-borrowing-education-ideas-finland (accessed 2 July 2015).

— (@Pasi_Sahlberg) (2015b) 'Don't be fooled by data #1: PISA is good servant but bad master. #ICP2015LED'. Online. https://twitter.com/pasi_sahlberg/status/628518128855711744 (accessed 17 August 2015).

Stoll, L., and Fink, D. (1996) *Changing Our Schools: Linking school effectiveness and school improvement*. Milton Keynes: Open University Press.

Taylor, K., and Rich, M. (2015) 'Teachers unions fight standardized testing, and find diverse allies'. *New York Times*, 20 April. Online. www.nytimes.com/2015/04/21/education/teachers-unions-reasserting-themselves-with-push-against-standardized-testing.html (accessed 2 August 2015).

Tomlinson, J. (1992) 'Retrospect on Ruskin: Prospect on the nineties'. In Williams, M., Dougherty, R., and Banks, F. (eds) *Continuing the Education Debate*. London: Cassel, 43–53.

Tyack D. and Cuban, L. (1995) *Tinkering Toward Utopia: A century of public school reform*. Cambridge, MA: Harvard University Press.

Watson, M.C., and Lloyd, J. (2015) 'Lost generation of children deprived of school sports'. *The Guardian,* 10 July. www.theguardian.com/education/2015/jul/10/lost-generation-of-children-deprived-of-school-sports (accessed 23 July 2015).

Weale, S. (2015) '"It's a political failure": how Sweden's celebrated schools system fell into crisis'. *The Guardian*, 10 June. Online. www.theguardian.com/world/2015/jun/10/sweden-schools-crisis-political-failure-education (accessed 7 July 2015).

Williams, R. (2015) 'Halton Public Schools teachers could be on strike by the end of April'. *Milton Canadian Champion,* 16 March. Online. www.insidehalton.com/news-story/5479756-updated-halton-s-public-high-school-teachers-could-be-on-strike-by-the-end-of-april/ (accessed 20 March 2015).

Wintour, R. (2014) 'More than 400,000 schoolchildren being taught by unqualified teachers'. *The Guardian*, 29 December. Online. www.theguardian.com/education/2014/dec/29/more-than-400000-schoolchildren-taught-unqualified-teachers-tristram-hunt-gove (accessed 25 July 2015).

Instrument for school leaders (principals, heads, and assistant principals)

These appendices present the full texts of the two questionnaires referred to throughout the text: Appendix 1a presents the questionnaire given to leaders, and Appendix 1b the questionnaire given to teachers. The basic texts were adapted for each country and translated for Finns, Swedes, and Lithuanians. The sections that elicited demographic information in both instruments were adjusted to account for different organizational structures and nomenclature. We have listed the categories here:

- Present position
- Location (state, province, etc.)
- Type of school
- Birth year
- Gender
- Total years of experience (education-related)
- Total years as school leader
- Total number of years as leader in present school

Instructions to participants
Completion of the survey should take no more than 15 minutes. Please read each statement and circle the appropriate response on the left to express how important you think the item is in building trust in education. For the same item, circle the appropriate response on the right to register how closely you feel the item describes your situation in your school and local authority at the moment.

The five-point scale for both ideal and real was as follows for both instruments:

1. Strongly disagree
2. Disagree
3. Uncertain
4. Agree
5. Strongly agree

Leaders' items

1. Government policies support quality public education for all, regardless of family income.
2. Schools need complete autonomy to pursue a school improvement agenda.
3. The school board supports its school leaders in ways that make them more effective.
4. The school board backs its teachers when their professionalism is questioned by the press and other media sources.
5. Unions are an agency for school improvement in school systems and schools.
6. Unions protect all teachers regardless of their competence.
7. School improvement depends on school leaders' ability to build trusting relationships with all staff members.
8. School leaders' trust of teachers should be conditional on their teaching performance and results.
9. School leaders need to be in charge of all aspects of the school's operation (maintenance, construction, transportation, etc.) to ensure effective teaching and learning in schools.
10. School leaders feel valued by senior levels of government.
11. Leaders at all levels need to know and show concern for staff members' personal circumstances.
12. Quality leadership is one of the provincial educational system's highest priorities.
13. The provincial educational system is prepared to pay for quality leadership.
14. Leadership development has strong support from higher levels of government.
15. School leaders must act as gatekeepers to buffer or protect teachers and children from the negative effects of some government and/or district policies.
16. School leaders maintain trust by addressing poor teacher practice promptly and effectively.
17. School leaders are knowledgeable about effective teaching practices and contemporary learning theories.
18. School leaders place the welfare of their students above all other stakeholders (government, teachers, unions, and even parents).
19. Teachers' views on school leaders' performance is part of leaders' performance review.
20. Board and school leaders admit mistakes openly and promptly.

21. Schools operate most effectively on behalf of children within a culture of trust.
22. School leaders act with confidence and authority in their dealings with students and parents.
23. School leaders act with integrity: they 'walk their talk'.
24. Teachers can be candid with their school leaders.
25. Teachers rally behind their school leaders in difficult situations.
26. School leaders at all levels share decision-making with staff members.
27. Trustworthy leaders at all levels say what they mean and mean what they say.
28. The public and policy makers deserve independent information on the successes and failures of each school.
29. Working in a 'high-trust' environment makes a teacher a more effective professional in promoting student learning.
30. It is best to trust the leadership of those in charge by going along with what they want.

Instrument for teachers

Demographic information

- Type of school you teach in
- Birth date (year)
- Gender
- Total years' experience as a teacher
- Years in present school district

Teachers' items

1. Government policies support quality public education for all, regardless of family income.
2. Schools need complete autonomy to pursue a school improvement agenda.
3. The educational system backs its teachers when their professionalism is questioned by the press and other media sources.
4. Teacher unions are an agency for school improvement in school systems and schools.
5. Teacher unions protect all teachers regardless of their competence.
6. School improvement depends on school leaders' ability to build trusting relationships with all staff members.
7. Teachers trust of their leaders is conditional on the leader's competence.
8. School leaders need to know and show concern for staff members' personal circumstances.
9. Quality teaching is one of the educational system's highest priorities.
10. The educational system is prepared to pay for quality teaching.
11. Developing teachers' professional capacity has strong support from higher levels of government.
12. School leaders must act as a gatekeeper or buffer to protect teachers and children from the negative effects of some government and/or district policies.
13. Teachers have the time and space to work collaboratively.
14. School leaders maintain trust by addressing poor teacher practice promptly and effectively.

15. School leaders are knowledgeable about effective teaching practices and contemporary learning theories.
16. Teachers' willingness to support each other's teaching is crucial to school improvement.
17. School improvement requires mutual trust between teachers and parents.
18. Students' views on teachers' performance is part of teachers' performance review.
19. District and school leaders admit mistakes openly and promptly.
20. Schools operate most effectively on behalf of children within a culture of trust.
21. Teachers' assessment includes more than just test scores.
22. School leaders act with integrity; they 'walk their talk'.
23. School leaders address teachers' feelings of vulnerability.
24. In difficult situations teachers support their school leaders.
25. School leaders share decision-making with staff members.
26. Trustworthy leaders at all levels say what they mean and mean what they say.
27. The public and policy makers deserve independent information on the successes and failures of each school.
28. Working in a 'high-trust' environment makes a teacher a more effective professional in promoting student learning.
29. It is best to trust the leadership of those in charge by going along with what they want.

Live examples

Examples of the live survey as administered to Australian educators can be found at www.surveymonkey.com/s/Trust_Aus_Leaders (Australian leaders' survey) and www.surveymonkey.com/s/TRUST_AUS_Teachers (Australian teachers' survey).

Index

Index

legitimacy 164, 169
Levin, Benjamin 88, 174
Lewicki, Roy 14–15, 28, 31
lifelong learning 137–8
'light touch' regulation 41–2, 229
Lin, N. 14
Lincoln, Abraham 37–40
Lindsay, Norman 70
Lingis, Alphonso 139–40
Lithuania 4–6, 131–51, 209–10, 217–21; history of 131–2, 209; level of trust in society 140–1; National Leadership Forum 151; societal change in 149–50
Liusvaaras, L. 110
local education authorities (LEAs) 174–6, 211
localization of decision-making 55, 70–1, 174
Lord Byron High School 24–6, 35–6, 40
Lortie, D.C. 126
Louis, Karen Seashore 1
Lukšienė, Meilė 134, 150

McAllister, D.J. 41
McCulla, Norman xii, 206 (co-author of Chapters 3 and 10)
McKinsey & Co. 176, 183
'management by objectives' 154–5
Mandela, Nelson 16
market fundamentalism 19
marketization in education 51, 137, 151, 167, 208
Marks, Warren xii, 206 (co-author of Chapter 3)
Mead, Margaret 25
Mehta, J. 77, 82–3
Melbourne Declaration (2008) 54
Meyer, J.W. 168
Milne, Seumas 176
Mineo, D. 191
mission, educational 95, 145
mistakes; admitting to 112–13, 160–1, 164, 224; learning from 26
moral purpose in education 70–1, 231
Morgan, Nicky 174
Morris, Estelle 183–4
Moss Kanter, Rosabeth 96
motivation of educators 195, 197
My School website (Australia) 57

'naming and shaming' of schools 42, 77, 163, 172–3
A Nation at Risk report (US, 1983) 187–8
National College for School Leadership 211–12
neo-conservatives 19
neo-liberalism 16–19, 51, 54, 80; in Lithuania 133, 136–7, 141, 149, 151
Network for Public Education 215
New Brunswick 74–5, 78–81, 97–8

'new professionalism' (Blatchford) 224
'new public management' (NPM) 18, 137, 149, 154, 167, 206–8, 211, 214, 220–2
New South Wales 46–7
No Child Left Behind (NCLB) Act (US, 2001) 188, 192, 202, 214
Nokia (company) 208
Norkus, Z. 132
Norris, N. 107

Obama, Barack 34, 188–9, 214
Office for Standards in Education (Ofsted) 41–2, 171–6, 181–4, 211–12
Office of Qualifications and Examinations Regulation (Ofqual) 181
O'Neill, Onora 184
Ontario 24, 40, 77–81, 97–8, 220
openness 62, 85, 145
organic trust 34
Organization for Economic Co-operation and Development (OECD) 19, 131, 173, 208
organizational culture 145, 166
overconfidence 36, 69
oxytocin 2

parental choice of school 50, 70, 216
parental involvement in education 114, 127, 176
pay, performance-related 20, 34, 57, 71, 144, 174
pedagogical knowledge of school leaders 61, 85, 201
peer pressure 13
'pendulum swings' in education policy 189, 214, 218
performance reviews; for school leaders 68, 225; for teachers 225, 229–30
Peters, Tom 17
Pink, Daniel 195
Pinochet, Augusto 16
PISA see Programme for International Student Assessment
Piscu village school 12–16
policy for education 49, 51, 88, 106–9, 218, 228; unrelated to practice 150
policy making; drivers of 5; educators' involvement in 88, 179, 211, 221; and the implementation of policy 1, 83, 180–1, 184, 192–3; 'ladder' of 201; levels of 3–4; problems of 33
Powers, Michael 40, 42, 167, 169, 228–9
Pranckūnienė, Eglė xii–xiii, 134, 209 (co-author of Chapter 6)
principals see school principals
private education 76–7, 82
privatization 82, 208, 217, 220–1
problem seekers 96
'production' model of education 16–21, 40, 43, 174, 189, 206–7, 210, 212, 215, 219–20, 223, 226, 229, 231; in Canada 77, 80, 82, 97–8

242

Index